Education Reform in China

Over the past decade there has been radical reform at all levels of China's education system as it attempts to meet changing economic and social needs and aspirations. Changes have been made to pedagogy and teacher professional learning and also to the curriculum – both at school level, from kindergarten to year 12, and at higher education level. This book focuses on reform at the early childhood, primary and secondary levels, and education more broadly, and is the companion book to *China's Higher Education Reform and Internationalisation*, which covers reform at the higher education level.

Education Reform in China outlines the systematic transformation that has occurred in school curriculum goals, structure and content, teaching and learning approaches, and assessment and administrative structures, including the increasing devolvement of control from the centre to provincial, district and school levels. As well as illustrating the changes that are occurring within classrooms, it demonstrates the continuity of cultural and educational ideas and values in the midst of these changes, showing that reform does not just involve the adoption of foreign ideas, but builds on and even resurrects traditional Chinese educational values. Importantly, it considers how exchanges of people and ideas can contribute to new ways of working between Western and Chinese educational systems.

Janette Ryan is Director of the UK Higher Education Academy's Teaching International Students project and a Research Associate at the China Centre, University of Oxford, UK. Her publications include *China's Higher Education Reform and Internationalisation* (also published by Routledge).

Routledge Contemporary China Series

1 Nationalism, Democracy and National
Integration in China
Leong Liew and Wang Shaoguang

2 Hong Kong's Tortuous
Democratization
A comparative analysis
Ming Sing

3 China's Business Reforms
Institutional challenges in a
globalised economy
*Edited by Russell Smyth and
Cherrie Zhu*

4 Challenges for China's Development
An enterprise perspective
*Edited by David H. Brown and
Alasdair MacBean*

5 New Crime in China
Public order and human rights
Ron Keith and Zhiqiu Lin

6 Non-Governmental Organizations
in Contemporary China
Paving the way to civil society?
Qiusha Ma

7 Globalization and the Chinese City
Fulong Wu

8 The Politics of China's Accession
to the World Trade Organization
The dragon goes global
Hui Feng

9 Narrating China
Jia Pingwa and his fictional world
Yiyan Wang

10 Sex, Science and Morality in
China
Joanne McMillan

11 Politics in China Since 1949
Legitimizing authoritarian rule
Robert Weatherley

12 International Human Resource
Management in Chinese Multinationals
Jie Shen and Vincent Edwards

13 Unemployment in China
Economy, human resources and
labour markets
*Edited by Grace Lee and Malcolm
Warner*

14 China and Africa
Engagement and compromise
Ian Taylor

15 Gender and Education in China
Gender discourses and women's
schooling in the early twentieth
century
Paul J. Bailey

16 SARS
Reception and interpretation in three
chinese cities
*Edited by Deborah Davis and
Helen Siu*

17 Human Security and the
Chinese State
Historical transformations and the
modern quest for sovereignty
Robert E. Bedeski

18 **Gender and Work in Urban China**
Women workers of the unlucky generation
Liu Jieyu

19 **China's State Enterprise Reform**
From Marx to the market
John Hassard, Jackie Sheehan, Meixiang Zhou, Jane Terpstra-Tong and Jonathan Morris

20 **Cultural Heritage Management in China**
Preserving the cities of the Pearl River Delta
Edited by Hilary du Cros and Yok-shiu F. Lee

21 **Paying for Progress**
Public finance, human welfare and inequality in China
Edited by Vivienne Shue and Christine Wong

22 **China's Foreign Trade Policy**
The new constituencies
Edited by Ka Zeng

23 **Hong Kong, China**
Learning to belong to a nation
Gordon Mathews, Tai-lok Lui, and Eric Kit-wai Ma

24 **China Turns to Multilateralism**
Foreign policy and regional security
Edited by Guoguang Wu and Helen Lansdowne

25 **Tourism and Tibetan Culture in Transition**
A place called Shangrila
Åshild Kolås

26 **China's Emerging Cities**
The making of new urbanism
Edited by Fulong Wu

27 **China-US Relations Transformed**
Perceptions and strategic interactions
Edited by Suisheng Zhao

28 **The Chinese Party-State in the 21st Century**
Adaptation and the reinvention of legitimacy
Edited by André Laliberté and Marc Lanteigne

29 **Political Change in Macao**
Sonny Shiu-Hing Lo

30 **China's Energy Geopolitics**
The Shanghai Co-operation Organization and Central Asia
Thrassy N. Marketos

31 **Regime Legitimacy in Contemporary China**
Institutional change and stability
Edited by Thomas Heberer and Gunter Schubert

32 **U.S.-China Relations**
China policy on Capitol Hill
Tao Xie

33 **Chinese Kinship**
Contemporary anthropological perspectives
Edited by Susanne Brandtstädter and Gonçalo D. Santos

34 **Politics and Government in Hong Kong**
Crisis under Chinese sovereignty
Edited by Ming Sing

35 **Rethinking Chinese Popular Culture**
Cannibalizations of the canon
Edited by Carlos Rojas and Eileen Cheng-yin Chow

36 **Institutional Balancing in the Asia Pacific**
Economic interdependence and China's rise
Kai He

37 **Rent Seeking in China**
Edited by Tak-Wing Ngo and Yongping Wu

38 China, Xinjiang and Central Asia
History, transition and crossborder
interaction into the 21st century
*Edited by Colin Mackerras and
Michael Clarke*

**39 Intellectual Property Rights in
China**
Politics of piracy, trade and protection
Gordon Cheung

40 Developing China
Land, politics and social conditions
George C. S. Lin

**41 State and Society Responses to
Social Welfare Needs in China**
Serving the people
*Edited by Jonathan Schwartz and
Shawn Shieh*

**42 Gay and Lesbian Subculture in
Urban China**
Loretta Wing Wah Ho

**43 The Politics of Heritage Tourism
in China**
A view from Lijiang
Xiaobo Su and Peggy Teo

44 Suicide and Justice
A Chinese perspective
Wu Fei

**45 Management Training and
Development in China**
Educating managers in a globalized
economy
*Edited by Malcolm Warner and
Keith Goodall*

**46 Patron-Client Politics and Elections
in Hong Kong**
Bruce Kam-kwan Kwong

**47 Chinese Family Business and the
Equal Inheritance System**
Unravelling the myth
Victor Zheng

**48 Reconciling State, Market and
Civil Society in China**
The long march towards prosperity
Paolo Urio

49 Innovation in China
The Chinese software industry
Shang-Ling Jui

**50 Mobility, Migration and the
Chinese Scientific Research System**
Koen Jonkers

51 Chinese Film Stars
*Edited by Mary Farquhar and
Yingjin Zhang*

52 Chinese Male Homosexualities
Memba, Tongzhi and Golden Boy
Travis S. K. Kong

**53 Industrialisation and Rural
Livelihoods in China**
Agricultural processing in Sichuan
Susanne Lingohr-Wolf

**54 Law, Policy and Practice on
China's Periphery**
Selective adaptation and institutional
capacity
Pitman B. Potter

55 China-Africa Development Relations
Edited by Christopher M. Dent

**56 Neoliberalism and Culture in China
and Hong Kong**
The countdown of time
Hai Ren

**57 China's Higher Education Reform
and Internationalisation**
Edited by Janette Ryan

58 Law, Wealth and Power in China
Commercial law reforms in context
Edited by John Garrick

59 Religion in Contemporary China
Revitalization and innovation
Edited by Adam Yuet Chau

60 Consumer-Citizens of China
The role of foreign brands in the
imagined future China
Kelly Tian and Lily Dong

**61 The Chinese Communist Party and
China's Capitalist Revolution**
The political impact of the market
Lance L. P. Gore

62 China's Homeless Generation
Voices from the veterans of the Chinese
civil war, 1940s–1990s
Joshua Fan

**63 In Search of China's Development
Model**
Beyond the Beijing consensus
*Edited by S. Philip Hsu, Suisheng Zhao
and Yu-Shan Wu*

**64 Xinjiang and China's Rise in Central
Asia, 1949–2009**
A history
Michael E. Clarke

65 Trade Unions in China
The challenge of labour unrest
Tim Pringle

66 China's Changing Workplace
Dynamism, diversity and disparity
*Edited by Peter Sheldon, Sunghoon Kim,
Yiqiong Li and Malcolm Warner*

67 Leisure and Power in Urban China
Everyday life in a medium-sized
Chinese city
Unn Målfrid H. Rolandsen

68 China, Oil and Global Politics
*Philip Andrews-Speed and Roland
Dannreuther*

69 Education Reform in China
Changing concepts, contexts and
practices
Edited by Janette Ryan

Education Reform in China

Changing concepts, contexts and practices

Edited by Janette Ryan

Routledge
Taylor & Francis Group

LONDON AND NEW YORK

First published 2011
by Routledge
2 Park Square, Milton Park, Abingdon, Oxon OX14 4RN

Simultaneously published in the USA and Canada
by Routledge
711 Third Avenue, New York, NY 10017

Routledge is an imprint of the Taylor & Francis Group, an informa business

British Library Cataloguing in Publication Data
A catalogue record for this book is available from the British Library

Library of Congress Cataloging in Publication Data
Education reform in China / edited by Janette Ryan.
    p. cm. – (Routledge contemporary china series)
  Includes bibliographical references and index.
  1. Education–China.   2. Educational change–China.
3. Education and globalization–China.   I. Ryan, Janette.
  LA1133.E38 2011
  370.951–dc22

                                              2010047833

ISBN: 978-0-415-58223-0 (hbk)
ISBN: 978-0-203-81602-8 (ebk)

Typeset in 10/12pt Times New Roman
by Graphicraft Limited, Hong Kong

Printed and bound in Great Britain by
CPI Antony Rowe, Chippenham, Wiltshire

Contents

List of Contributors	xi
Acknowledgements	xiv
Introduction	1
JANETTE RYAN	

PART I
Curriculum policy and practice — 19

1 **Reflection in action: ongoing K-12 curriculum reform in China** — 21
JIAN LIU AND CHANGYUN KANG

2 **Constructing a cross-cultural teacher professional learning community in the context of China's basic education curriculum** — 41
CHANGYUN KANG, GAALEN ERICKSON, JANETTE RYAN AND
IAN MITCHELL

3 **Collaborative narration: our story in a cross-cultural professional learning community** — 61
CHANGYUN KANG, KEQIN LIU AND YUPING LI

PART II
Educational quality and access — 73

4 **Methods to evaluate educational quality and improvement in China** — 75
SALLY M. THOMAS AND WEN-JUNG PENG

5 **Education in the Tibetan Autonomous Region: policies and practices in rural and nomadic communities** — 92
GERARD A. POSTIGLIONE, BEN JIAO AND MELVYN C. GOLDSTEIN

PART III
Educational values and beliefs   111

6   **The changing landscapes of a journey: educational metaphors
    in China**   113
    LIXIAN JIN AND MARTIN CORTAZZI

7   **English language teachers as moral guides in Vietnam and
    China: maintaining and re-traditionalising morality**   132
    PHAN LE HA, PAUL MCPHERRON AND PHAN VAN QUE

PART IV
Reform and internationalisation in the disciplines   159

8   **Ten years of curriculum reform in China: a soft knowledge
    perspective**   161
    WEE TIONG SEAH

9   **Multidimensional citizenship education and an internationalised
    curriculum in a time of reform: is this the future trajectory for
    schools in China and Australia in the twenty-first century?**   185
    LIBBY TUDBALL

PART V
Mutual learning and adaptation   205

10 **Mutual learning and adaptation between China and the
    West through learning each other's language**   207
    JIEWEN ZHONG

11 **Bridging the East and West dichotomy: harmonising
    Eastern learning with Western knowledge**   224
    SHIJING XU

    Index   243

Contributors

Professor Martin Cortazzi is Visiting Professor in the Centre of Applied Linguistics at Warwick University. He has published extensively and his research interests include raising cultural awareness in English teaching and examining students' metaphors and narratives to explore issues in intercultural experience, identity, and cultures of learning.

Professor Gaalen Erickson is a Professor in the Department of Curriculum and Pedagogy at the University of British Columbia. He has had a long standing research interest in teacher professional development, practitioner inquiry and professional knowledge and is involved in a three country project on education reform in China.

Dr Melvyn C. Goldstein is a socio-cultural anthropologist at Western Case University specialising in Tibetan society. He conducts research on topics including nomadic pastoralism, the impact of economic reforms on rural Tibet, family planning and fertility, the revival of Buddhism, modern Tibetan history, and socio-economic change.

Dr Ben Jiao is Professor and Deputy Director of the Institute of Contemporary Tibet Studies at the Tibet Academy of Social Science. He is an expert on Tibetan family structure and educational developments in rural and nomadic areas. He is a consultant for many development agencies and NGOs on economic and social development.

Dr Lixian Jin is Reader in Linguistics and Intercultural Learning at De Montfort University, UK. With Professor Cortazzi, she has conducted research into Chinese and other learners of English for more than fifteen years. Their more than 100 publications, widely recognised in the West and East Asia, include *Researching Chinese learners* (2011).

Dr Changyun Kang was a key organiser of China's curriculum reform in the initial and middle periods until 2005. He was then a Visiting Professor at the University of British Columbia and is currently Professor and Special Advisor on International Initiatives to the President of Beijing Normal University, Zhuhai. He also holds the part-time position of Co-Director of the China Education Centre in the Faculty of Education and Social Work at the University of Sydney in Australia. His research bridges Western educational research with Chinese traditional wisdom and current school practices.

Mr Yuping Li is Associate Director of the Teaching and Learning Office in the Dongsheng Bureau of Education, Erdos City, Inner Mongolia. He has many years experience as a primary school teacher and principal and currently works as a consultant and adviser on curriculum and pedagogical reform in Inner Mongolia and Beijing.

Professor Jian Liu is assistant director of the National Centre for School Curriculum and Textbook Development at the Ministry of Education in China and also Head of Department of Curriculum Development of this Centre, Principal Researcher of the National Primary. He researches curriculum and pedagogy, K-12 Mathematics Education and teachers' professional development.

Ms Keqin Liu is Principal of Beijing Zhongguansun Number 4 Primary School, Secretary of the Chinese Association of Primary School Principals and a member of China's National 1–6 Mathematics Curriculum Standard Group. She is also a part-time Professor of Education at Beijing Normal University.

Dr Paul McPherron is a Lecturer in English for Foreign Students at Stanford University. His PhD from the University of California examined English language teaching reforms at a university in southern China. His research interests include globalisation and ELT and cultures of education in the English classroom.

Dr Ian Mitchell is a Senior Lecturer in the Faculty of Education at Monash University and co-founder and convenor of the teacher research network Project for Enhancing Effective Learning (PEEL). His research focuses on teacher change and professional learning and he is involved in a three country project on education reform in China.

Dr Wen-Jung Peng is a researcher at the Graduate School of Education, University of Bristol. Her research activities are currently located in various aspects of school effectiveness in different cultural contexts. Her other research interests include PE motivation, service science in management and educational research methods.

Dr Phan Le Ha is a Lecturer in the Faculty of Education at Monash University and holds honorary positions at universities in Vietnam. Her research interests include postcolonial Englishes and international education. Her book *Teaching English as an international language: Identity, resistance and negotiation* was published in 2008.

Professor Phan Van Que is Vice President of Hanoi Open University and also Dean of Faculty of English and Modern Languages. His research interests include language and culture, English language teaching, world Englishes and educational technology. He is very interested in Chinese studies, especially China's education, history and culture.

Professor Gerard A. Postiglione is Professor and Director of the Wah Ching Centre of Research on Education in China at the University of Hong Kong. His recent books include *Education and Social Change in China* (2006), *Going to School in East Asia* (2007) and *Border Crossing in East Asian Higher Education* (2009).

Dr Janette Ryan is Director of the UK Higher Education Academy *Teaching International Students* Project and a Research Associate at the China Centre at the University of Oxford, Visiting Professor at the Centre for Academic Practice and Research in Internationalisation at Leeds Metropolitan University and an Adjunct Lecturer in the Faculty of Education at Monash University. Her research interests include Western and Confucian scholarship and learning and cross-cultural teaching.

Dr Wee Tiong Seah is a Senior Lecturer in Education at Monash University. His research interests include the harnessing of socio-cultural factors in optimising mathematics pedagogy. His recent publications include two co-edited books, eight book chapters, three refereed journal articles, and numerous refereed conference papers.

Professor Sally M. Thomas is Professor of Education at the Graduate School of Education, University of Bristol. Her research interests include educational quality, effectiveness and improvement, school evaluation and self evaluation, professional learning communities, and education in developing countries.

Dr Libby Tudball is a Senior Lecturer in Education at Monash University. Her research interests include the internationalisation of education, studies of Asia, values and citizenship education and teacher professional learning and education. She organised an international conference on internationalisation in Malaysia in 2009.

Dr Shijing Xu is an Affiliated Research Associate at the National Research Center for Foreign Language Education, Beijing Foreign Studies University, China, and Assistant Professor, Faculty of Education, University of Windsor, Canada. Her current research is on the reciprocal adaptation and learning of newcomers in Canada. Her current research is on reciprocal learning between the East and the West.

Ms Jiewen Zhong has a Masters in Applied Linguistics from the University of Oxford. Her research interests include second language acquisition, psycholinguistics and bilingual education. She is actively involved in the Oxford Chinese Students and Scholars Association and the Oxford-Cambridge Education Forum.

Acknowledgements

I would like to acknowledge the funding provided by the Contemporary China Studies Programme at the University of Oxford which, along with further support received from Monash University, made it possible to convene the conference on 'Education Reform in China' at Keble College (University of Oxford) in March 2009 which provided the impetus for this book.

Introduction

Reform of education in China

Over the past decade, China has engaged in major and radical reform of all levels of its education system. This book examines various initiatives involved in the reform programme and the impacts of these changes, as well as the continuity of Chinese cultural and educational ideas and values in the midst of these changes. It charts China's K-12 (kindergarten to Year 12) reform across early childhood, primary and secondary education, and examines other aspects of Chinese education and educational cultures more broadly. It does so from a number of different perspectives, examining individual, social, cultural and historical factors and drawing on personal accounts as well as empirical studies by those most closely involved in the reform as well as international scholars charting these changes.

The rapid and extensive reform of all levels of China's education system stems from changing national and international economic and social needs and aspirations. This reform and change is occurring at both the primary and secondary levels and at the higher education level as well as more broadly within areas of education. This volume, a companion to *China's higher education reform and internationalisation* (Routledge 2011), focuses on reform of school education and education more broadly.

China has the world's largest education system and has undergone various periods of education reform over its long history. The current curriculum reform programme launched a decade ago, the eighth major reform of the modern period, is widely considered to be the most radical and ambitious educational reform initiative to date. Systematic transformation of school curriculum goals, structure and content, teaching and learning approaches, and assessment and administrative structures has occurred, and control has increasingly been devolved from the centre to provincial, district and school levels.

Unsurprisingly, these changes have posed major challenges for the many stakeholders involved. How well is China meeting these challenges; what do these changes look like; and what are the implications for quality, equity and capacity-building? These issues and their longer-term impacts are relevant for those working with Chinese scholars and students both in and outside China, and for those interested in education in China. The increased transnational flow of academics and students between education systems in China and the Western world (as well as developing countries) should provide new ways of knowing, making meaning and interacting. In order for genuine dialogue to occur between these systems, however, there needs to be a well informed debate that is based upon contemporary Chinese realities. This includes the immediate and longer term impacts of reform on Chinese students and the new generation of international students and Chinese scholars with whom Western schools and universities, and indeed other social and economic institutions, increasingly work.

Despite this radical and fundamental education reform, very little is known about this outside of China. Although much has been published in the fields of Chinese economics and politics, there are few works available that provide an overview of current developments in education in China. This book aims to fill this gap. It is an international, multidisciplinary, cross-cultural collaboration, drawing on work in China, Hong Kong, Vietnam, the UK, the US, Canada and Australia. It draws on a range of theoretical positions as well as diverse methodologies and includes empirical studies, using both qualitative and quantitative methodologies, as well as personal narrative accounts.

This book considers important questions such as:

- Has the rhetoric of the official curriculum reform policy of 'changing the teaching and learning focus from "basic knowledge and skills" to the "capacity of students to engage in critical thinking, problem solving and creativity"' been met?
- What does this reform look like in different educational contexts?
- How equitable is this increased educational provision? How are capacity and equity concerns influenced by the continuing competitiveness for places?
- What are the roles of traditional and contemporary 'Confucian' cultures of learning?
- What are the implications for those working with students and scholars from China?
- Is there a mobility of ideas across (and among) educational systems and cultures?
- Can we move towards new ways of knowing that take advantage of the interflow of Western and Chinese cultures of learning?

Education has in very recent times been officially recognised as one of China's most pressing national priorities by both the current President Hu Jintao and Premier Wen Jiabao, and its role in securing and maintaining China's economic position has been highlighted. At a meeting of the Standing Committee of the State Council on education reform and development on

15 May 2010 chaired by Premier Wen, the Committee stated that education was a national priority and called for an improvement in its quality, an increase in investment in education, a reduction in the differences between cities and rural areas and, interestingly, a reduction in the 'burden' of schooling for children (Standing Committee of the State Council 2010 http://www.prcgov.org/ 2010-05/12/content_9840333.htm). At this time, the government released the second draft of its 10 year blueprint for education for public discussion (http://www.moe.edu.cn/edoas/website18/zhuanti/2010zqyj/zqyjg.htm).

It is therefore timely that the broad-ranging and deep changes and contemporary state of education in China are better known and understood internationally. China's 'soft' power and influence have been steadily rising in recent years, especially in the wake of the global financial crisis of the late 2000s, and its economy is of increasing importance to countries in its own region as well as many Western countries such as Australia and large parts of the world where Chinese influence is growing such as Africa. These developments point to the need to better understand China's current realities and future trajectory in a world likely to be dominated by China, when, according to Martin Jacques in *When China rules the world: The rise of the middle kingdom and the end of the Western world* (2009), the US and Western countries will no longer dominate world affairs.

China's curriculum reform: challenges and opportunities for two-way learning and adaptation

The current education reforms in China have led to far-reaching changes in the operation of schools, the work of teachers and students, teacher research and professional development, student learning and assessment of learning, teacher preparation programmes and examination policies and processes. The areas covered by the reform are all-encompassing and include curriculum aims, design, content, structure, assessment and administration. At the start of the reform programme, teachers reported being bored with the conventional drill practice in classrooms and students were exhausted by the demands of a system that was overly focused on examination marks and memorisation of information that was far removed from students' own experiences and life worlds. The overall intention of the reform programme is to encourage and enable a move away from a transmission approach to teaching and learning and towards the encouragement of students' independence, creativity, problem solving skills and collaborative learning and to make their learning more aligned to their real life experiences and interests and to the needs of the nation for skills relevant to a more globalised world.

Unsurprisingly, these changes have led to challenges and tensions for the many stakeholders involved, especially teachers and students working within the new policies and practices. They have led to major challenges 'on the ground' in terms of how to introduce reform into the educational system in ways that respect and retain the best aspects of traditional teaching and learning practices while simultaneously learning from the best educational practices and curriculum reform in other countries. The reforms are overlaid on conventional teaching and learning practices in ways that sometimes make for 'hybrid' models that draw from Western models but have 'Chinese characteristics', or at other times in ways that can cause tensions and challenges, especially in relation to 'student-centred' versus 'teacher-centred' classrooms and the roles and relationships between teachers and students. Many of the reforms involve seemingly intractable problems such as how to align the new curriculum programme with a system of evaluation in the context of high-stakes assessment and fierce competition for university places. As many of the contributors to this volume demonstrate, despite outward reform of pedagogy and curriculum, many traditional and deep seated cultural practices and attitudes endure. The need to avoid sacrificing or eclipsing traditional national and local practices and wisdom is a challenge in any major national curriculum reform. Reform needs to take into account continuing cultural values and local contexts to avoid the pitfalls of 'top down' or externally imposed curriculum change. Despite criticisms and tensions, however, the overall picture a decade on from the instigation of the curriculum reform policy is an impressive though 'patchy' one. Continuing tensions point to the need for further debate and consultation and changes to teacher education and professional development as well as improvements in educational resources and support.

To date, the movement between Western and Chinese knowledge systems has mostly been unidirectional, from the West to China, with large numbers of Chinese students and scholars travelling abroad to learn from other countries, especially in the West, but given the rise of China and increasing recognition of its importance to the future of the rest of the world, there is an urgent need to also learn from China. As Wee Tiong Seah points out in his chapter in this book, the appeal of America's 'soft' power is diminishing in China due to the realisation of China's growing economic and political position in the world and changing power relations globally. At the same time, there is a recognition in China that it has finally firmly moved beyond the 'century of humiliation' at the hands of foreign powers and there is a new-found nationalism (as could be seen for example from the Beijing Olympics in 2008) and renewed pride in China's history of scholarly excellence, high student achievement and economic strength. As Seah points out, in China not everything 'West' is considered 'best'; the challenge in education is how to introduce 'Western' practices in teaching and learning without sacrificing local wisdom and traditions.

The terms 'East' and 'West' themselves are of limited value in a world of increasing interconnections and their use runs the risk of essentialising and stereotyping of individuals within these large civilisations and cultural systems. The boundaries between 'East' and 'West' are becoming increasingly fuzzy and less useful as analytical frameworks. Shijing Xu in her chapter is critical of the dichotomised 'East-and-West' thinking and the tendency that goes with this of seeing China's rise as a threat to the West, especially in economic and political terms. Instead, she points to the potential of China's social, cultural and educational values as points of learning for the West, particularly the potential for mutual understanding and adaptation. This last point is a central question and quest of this book; the possibilities for better understanding and dialogue between the world's great civilisations and intellectual traditions.

China has a long history of valuing academic excellence and rewarding successful students through their examination performance. Areas in which Chinese students have traditionally excelled such as Mathematics have attracted interest worldwide and have led to an eagerness in some quarters to learn more about China's education system. Equally, China recognises that there are many areas where it has not excelled and is acutely aware that its students need newer skills of problem-solving and creativity in order to operate successfully in a globalised world and workforce. It was concerns such as these that provided the original impetus for the curriculum reform programme and there is no doubt that there have been significant achievements in these areas.

About this book

This book examines the many facets of China's contemporary education provision and curriculum reform. It does this by working through a number of inter-connected levels, from curriculum policy and practice, the quality of education and access to it, educational values and beliefs and individual disciplinary areas and their future trajectories. It also examines the possibilities for mutual learning and adaptation that have arisen as a result of the increased movement between and interest across national and international systems. In this volume we make visible the connections and strands that cross the world, physically through the movement of people, and socially and academically through the ideas, knowledge, experiences and identities that are both brought to this process and that are changed through this process. Many of the chapters look at the same issue but from different cultural perspectives, that is, either the 'Chinese' or the 'Western' experience of the same phenomenon. This in itself can help to foster greater mutual understanding, dialogue and respect. The diversity of these accounts and the varied backgrounds of the contributors with their different values and viewpoints demonstrate and celebrate the power of such diverse perspectives and the learning that can arise from them.

The chapters in this book provide a picture of steady and often impressive, although uneven, progress across a range of areas in education provision and quality though those most closely involved in the reform process readily admit that there is still much to be done. The accounts in this book, often by those most closely involved in the reform programme either at the policy or practice levels, demonstrate these successes but also frankly document the tensions and challenges and the formidable work that lies ahead. They provide sobering reminders of the continuing tensions and challenges between and within these cultural systems and amongst those who work and study within them but also positive and inspiring accounts of those who successfully work at these intersections of cultures and ideas. The contributions from the Chinese writers are imbued with a sense of purpose and optimism, often missing from external critiques of China, though they readily admit the enormity of the task ahead. These accounts tell a story of continuity and change, but are generally imbued with a sense of optimism and enthusiasm about future possibilities.

This book aims to provide both an 'insider' as well as an 'outsider' view of educational developments in China. Many of the authors of the chapters in this book have crossed cultures in one way or another and have experienced the transformative effect of this on their lives and their thinking. All have personally engaged in intensive cross-cultural interactions and communication, often devoting their personal and professional lives to improving and enhancing understanding between cultures. Many are pioneers at the cutting edge of new and innovative practices and such accounts of their first-hand knowledge and experiences have not been previously available to English-speaking audiences. Many are working at the 'chalk face' of curriculum reform in China, and others are involved in ongoing collaborative work in China. Chapters provide a range of both Chinese and Western perspectives, including from educational practitioners through to eminent scholars who are internationally recognised as leaders in their fields.

This book begins from the perspective of exploring the benefits for all parties of respectful and mutual engagement across cultures and knowledge systems. Too often, engagement between Chinese people and Westerners is inhibited by out of date stereotypes of China and the 'Chinese learner' that bear little resemblance to the contemporary realities of China and the pace of change that it is experiencing. The contributors to this book reject the 'binary divide' view of culture and instead examine the ways that cultures and those within them have common goals and aspirations. This book examines more complex and nuanced aspects of cultural differences and commonalities, both within and across cultures, with the aim of re-theorising and re-positioning the ways that cross-cultural dialogue and engagement occur.

Origins of this book

The idea for this book arose from an international conference on education reform in China held at Keble College at the University of Oxford in March 2009. This conference brought together expert scholars as well as newer members of the academy including postgraduate students, and crucially, education practitioners working 'in the field'. Participants included professors, school principals, district level consultants, government officials, school teachers, university lecturers, students and the general public as well as educational administrators from China and the United Kingdom. What united the participants was a common interest in the future of education in China and its educational relationships and partnerships with the world.

The conference was a 'bi-cultural' event aimed at demonstrating a mutuality of regard and communication. It not only physically brought together Western and Chinese scholars and educational practitioners, but also resulted in a meeting of 'minds' and 'cultures' to generate new understandings, knowledge and relationships. It aimed to exemplify one of the central tenets of this book, the possibilities for combining the best of 'East' (here China) and the 'West'. It was an attempt to avoid the phenomenon of international conferences on education held in China where English is the only language used and is dominated by Westerners talking about China, or of conferences in China with parallel streams in Chinese and English and little overlap in attendance. It also sought to avoid the simple dichotomisation of 'East' and 'West' as, while themes and topics did acknowledge local and national differences, they also pointed to common challenges and aspirations.

Some of the challenges in this approach included the very real dilemmas of cross-cultural communication where a language is not shared or concepts are unfamiliar. Several conference participants spoke no English, for some it was their first time outside China, and for others it was the first time they had presented in English. Several presentations were in both English and Chinese, for others colleagues interpreted for those around them, and many of the presenters were from bicultural teams of researchers or education practitioners. The fact that so many of the research teams were multicultural and members spoke both English and Chinese (including Chinese-speaking Westerners) demonstrated the impacts of accelerated mobility across national boundaries and cultures and the possibilities for different ways of working and interacting that this provides. It also meant that there was a sensitivity about when concepts or expressions needed further explanation or translation as presenters were aware of areas of their own culture or ideas and concepts that would be unfamiliar to the audience. This cultural 'meta' sensitivity helped all of those involved to not only understand and communicate but to increase their own intercultural knowledge and skills.

What all had in common was an interest in education in China and the increasing educational contacts between China and the world. Although the conference was held somewhat symbolically in what could be described as a bastion of the Western academy, the University of Oxford, the conference truly was one 'with Chinese characteristics' such as social and cultural events and the conference ending with songs, a musical performance and group photos. This meant that not only did the conference have a 'mind', it also had a 'heart', giving it a very Chinese 'holistic' flavour but also imbuing it with the atmosphere of traditional Western intellectual excellence.

Editor's reflections

Editing this volume has not been an easy task, especially in the many challenges of translation from Chinese to English in ways that make sense for an English-speaking, Western audience but also provide fidelity and integrity to the original intention and meaning. Any errors of translation are my own. This effort has been well-worthwhile, however, in giving voice to those who would not normally be heard in Western learning contexts and has been enormously personally rewarding and an opportunity for further learning.

During this process I have been able to re-discover the highs and lows of the cross-cultural experiences of my youth when I spent two years as an international student in China in the early 1980s trying to survive not only the daily challenges of living in another country and culture, but also of studying in another language. This experience was a formative one; it changed my life and my world view and came to define me as a teacher and a researcher. This journey to learn more about China and its people and culture profoundly changed me; I hope that this book does justice to demonstrating the possibilities and potential for the transformation of knowledge and perspective that internationalisation can now more easily provide. A precursor to the transformation of world views, however, is a desire to gain reciprocal knowledge and learning. To date, this has mainly been one-way as Western educators are for the most part content to teach Chinese international students in ever increasing numbers without feeling the need to learn more about their backgrounds and experiences. Now, as China moves towards superpower status and promises to be the economic powerhouse of the twenty-first century, this requires a new stance by the West to learn about other cultures and paradigms.

Students and scholars from around the world now have greater access to the opportunities of cross-cultural study and collaborative research and Chinese students have taken up these opportunities in ways that mean that they are far more 'internationalised' than their Western counterparts. As China and its students and teachers change and adapt to changing world conditions so too must those with whom they engage.

I have felt privileged to be a part of the international collaborative research project described in the first few chapters of this book. I thank all of those responsible for this experience and especially the many teachers I have met as part of this project and the many others with whom I have worked in international education in China.

General outline of this book

Part I of this book is an account of the historical and contemporary issues involved in such a vast undertaking as China's current curriculum reform programme. It looks especially at education and curriculum reform policy and practice at the level of primary and secondary education. Part II looks at the quality of education, tackling the difficult issue of how to assess learning under the new curriculum reform programme. It also looks at educational provision in less-developed areas such as Tibet. In Part III, broader issues to do with cultures of learning and concepts of teaching and learning in China are explored, examining issues of change as well as continuity in the endurance of traditional Confucian values and beliefs. Part IV looks at particular disciplines and the ways that these are being reconceptualised in the context of the broader reform and internationalisation of education worldwide. Finally, Part V looks at the opportunities for learning about China and its culture through the learning of Chinese as well as the opportunities for mutual learning and adaptation through the movement of Chinese people across the world.

Part I   Curriculum policy and practice

This first section looks in depth at curriculum reform of K-12 (kindergarten to Year 12) education and documents this process from the very beginning of the reform programme. It does this from the perspectives of those most intimately involved in this programme, including at local, district, provincial, national and international levels.

Chapter 1 sets the scene for the book and the chapters to follow. Written by two key initiators and organisers of the reform programme, Changyun Kang and Jian Liu, it provides a unique insiders' account of the various stages of the reform as well as the tensions, conflicts and challenges that have arisen. It explains in detail the chronology, aims and processes of the education reform programme. It marks the milestones along the way over a decade of reform and explains the processes that have been put in place to deal with the very real challenges and dilemmas facing all stakeholders in this mammoth and ambitious task. The scale, detail and level of consultation and participation by thousands of government personnel, policy makers, administrators, academics, principals, teachers, students and parents is astonishing to any educator in contexts outside of China and this account from Kang and Liu gives an insight into the extraordinarily complex processes involved at each stage of the reform programme. Despite admirable attempts to make the processes democratic and consultative inevitable tensions and conflicts arose such as the alignment of the curriculum aims with the assessment system, especially in a country with such high-stakes examinations and fierce competition for entry into each further level of education. Nevertheless, this chapter documents the valuable lessons that have been learnt and the progress that has been made, especially in the development of collaborative and peer professional learning communities for teacher research and inquiry that are essential for deep and enduring reform. Kang and Liu argue that, compared with previously, relationships between teachers and students are more harmonious, the classroom atmosphere is more democratic, students are treated with more respect, the curriculum content has moved closer to students' own experiences and knowledge acquisition is no longer the only goal of learning. The approaches to professional learning they describe allow teachers and students to follow their passions and develop their own expertise and knowledge and address the much larger question for nations engaged in such reform about how to prepare its young people for the future so that they can optimise their life chances and the nation's future.

Such a large undertaking of course is destined to encounter criticism and resistance. This frank and open discussion details the sometimes contested nature of the debates and the crucial issues at stake but it also shows the strength and endurance of the communities of practice that have evolved from the programme. The reform programme started by looking at experience overseas but the kinds of innovative and enduring teacher research and teacher inquiry communities and practices that have been developed, some of which are detailed in later chapters, provide valuable lessons to those outside of China also engaged in curriculum reform and teacher professional development. Such opportunities for two-way learning are already being grasped, as detailed in the following chapter which recounts how cross-cultural teams have played a part in this reform process. There are lessons in this account for educators across the world of this type of 'root and branch' reform which raises perennial issues for educators about how to maintain fidelity between the 'ideal' or written curriculum and the actual or 'enacted' curriculum and how to ensure a shared vision across complex systems and vast numbers of people and geographical areas. The reform began with research into education systems and curriculum reform abroad in an attempt to learn from the best examples and practices elsewhere. This did not involve the slavish adoption of Western approaches but instead carefully took into consideration the need to retain the best of China's long and rich intellectual traditions even though this balance is clearly an enduring challenge.

Chapter 2 follows from the previous chapter and describes the cross-cultural international research project referred to in the first chapter. Changyun Kang, Gaalen Erickson, Janette Ryan and Ian Mitchell give an account of the broader issues involved in major curriculum reform and the types of challenges and difficulties that can arise in any such massive undertaking. It draws from such experiences worldwide and points to the lessons to be learnt. It focuses particularly on the types of professional development required to support teachers in changing their pedagogy and curriculum to better align them with the aims of China's education reform programme, in this case as in the previous chapter, of the K-12 curriculum programme. It discusses the role that teacher research and support through professional learning communities can play in bringing about the required change and transformation in enduring and sustainable ways. The chapter uses complexity theory to analyse the limitations of the initial 'top down' approach to curriculum reform and documents a 'bottom up' project based on professional learning communities engaged in teacher research and inquiry. It shows how mutual respect and dialogue have been purposefully used in all levels of this project to create successful models of teacher practice and change and collaborative research. It illustrates some of the principles required for such work to be effective as well as some continuing challenges and provides details of how this project is progressively building successful 'nested circles' at the local, national and international levels. The next chapter provides an insiders' account of the Chinese research partners in this project and documents how the project and the approach works 'on the ground'.

In Chapter 3, Changyun Kang, Keqin Liu and Yuping Li provide authentic first-hand accounts of the challenges facing teachers and school and district educational leaders in the curriculum reform process. Their chapter uses a narrative style to illustrate their journey, its pitfalls and its rewards, as they have established a teacher professional learning community over the past several years. This professional learning community is actively and collaboratively supporting teachers to research and reform their own teaching and learning practices. This chapter provides an insight into the very dynamic and undoubtedly impressive work being done by teacher researchers and professional learning communities across China when teachers are positioned as key players in the reform process. It outlines in detail the challenges involved and the rich and myriad strategies those involved in the project are employing to support and empower teachers in bringing about substantial and enduring changes to their educational philosophies and classroom practices.

Part II Educational quality and access

Part II looks at how well education is being provided in terms of quality and access to education and educational resources. It examines some of the more complex and difficult areas of the curriculum reform programme including how to measure the quality of education in the context of the new curriculum and approaches to teaching and learning. A related issue to the quality of provision of education is the evenness of educational quality and resources nationwide, particularly in such a geographically vast and diverse country as China and increasing disparities between the cities and the developed coastal areas and the less developed areas in more rural and remote regions.

In Chapter 4, Sally Thomas and Wen-jung Peng discuss the critical issue of the evaluation of school and teacher effectiveness in order to improve educational quality, a major objective of the curriculum reform programme. This chapter gives an overview of efforts in other countries to measure and evaluate school effectiveness and educational quality. The authors report on several collaborative UK/China research projects which have examined the 'value added' approach to assessing school and teacher effectiveness. As with education systems elsewhere, they demonstrate that although there are debates and complexities surrounding issues of educational quality and student outcomes, such debates, and reliable data upon which to base these, are essential in order for schools and teachers and educational leaders to pinpoint the areas in need of improvement in their teaching and at their school. Evaluation of teaching and education has proven to be one of the most difficult areas of the curriculum reform programme to implement, but this chapter points to the ways that education systems, including those in China, can better judge the success or otherwise of the quality and effectiveness of its school education system through school effectiveness research.

Chapter 5 examines the provision of education in rural and remote areas, in this case in the Tibetan Autonomous Region. Gerry Postiglione, Ben Jiao and Melvyn Goldstein focus on recent progress and continuing challenges in providing education particularly for rural and nomadic communities. With its distinctive culture and religious traditions, Tibet comprises one-eighth of the land area of China but is the most sparsely populated, with the majority of the population spread across a vast geographical area. This chapter describes the historical, political and contemporary challenges in improving access to schooling and the quality of education for those in the most remote areas in Tibet, and provides case studies in several rural and nomadic areas. Despite very poor provision historically, there has been major progress in the last 20 years and in particular in the past decade. In 2008, 98.5 per cent of children attended primary school, compared with less than 20 per cent completing primary education in 1990. Despite increased funding to improve school facilities and the quality of teacher training, and the introduction of a range of government policies providing subsidies and other incentives to encourage school attendance and retention rates, the quality of education remains uneven especially in remote areas. Continuing barriers include opportunity costs for families who lose the labour of their children who need to board at school in order to attend secondary school, harsh physical conditions, remoteness, perceptions of the value of school-ing, the urbanisation of youth, relevancy of educational skills for rural and nomadic communities, changing economic and labour conditions, language challenges between the Tibetan language and Chinese, and perceived threats to nomadic lifestyles and values.

Part III   Educational values and beliefs

Part III looks at issues of continuity and change in the midst of the new cur-riculum changes looking at ideas and values that either endure despite these changes or that develop in response to, and sometimes as counters to, these changes. It highlights the fact that outward reform often fails to change individual ideas and beliefs and that these can sit alongside apparent out-ward reform and change. As shown by the empirical studies reported in both of the chapters in this section, individuals exercise an active agency in these reform contexts and appropriate, 're-fashion' or even resist such notions in the contexts of their own lives and aspirations.

In Chapter 6 Lixian Jin and Martin Cortazzi remind us of the import-ance and enduring nature of Chinese 'cultures of learning'. They argue that although the 'external landscape' of education in China appears to have undergone much change due to education reforms, the 'internal landscape' (held in the 'heads' and 'hearts' of students and teachers in China) of individuals' expectations, values and beliefs about teachers and learning continue to have significant impact. This points to the impermeability of underlying cultural values and the part they can continue to play even in the context of strong national policies and rhetoric and radical outward reform of educational systems and practices. They draw on a large body of data collected over several years of the metaphors that students use to illustrate their values and beliefs towards teachers and learning. The metaphors that they have found students using are far more nuanced than those stated or implied in official policy documents and statements. They conclude that although there is much continuity of the ways that students in China talk about and conceptualise teachers' roles and learning, there have also been notable changes over the course of the reform of curriculum that demonstrate more creative ways of viewing teachers and learning. Although they draw broad conclusions about continuity and change in students' views, they also point to the fact that there is much diversity and difference within cultures, hence their term *cultures* of learning.

In Chapter 7, Phan Le Ha, Paul McPherron and Phan Van Que draw on historical, sociocultural, and philosophical perspectives to reflect on the tensions in education between globalisation and cultural continuity. They focus on the cultural politics of English as an international language and the perceived roles of English language teachers in China and Vietnam. Drawing on qualitative data from interviews with university students in China and Vietnam they examine students' views of the 'good teacher' with their findings demonstrating interesting parallels with the ways that the students in Jin and Cortazzi's studies describe their 'ideal' teacher. In the Chinese and Vietnamese contexts studied by Phan and her colleagues, teachers are expected to act as 'moral guides' to their students; to educate students to behave 'morally' and to respect local values and traditions. This 'moral' aim of education is reflected in the apparently contradictory aims of the curriculum reform programme in China to prepare students for a more internationalised and globalised world while at the same time respecting and nurturing traditional values and practices. Phan and colleagues examine the challenges that thus arise for teachers such as how to connect students' local and global identities and worlds. They argue that it is through moral education that the state is attempting to maintain and 're-traditionalise' education according to Confucian principles and local philosophies and that some traditional values are re-emerging or being re-asserted despite the modernising aims of the curriculum reform. Values such as the role of teachers as moral guides persist in educational environments that are changing dramatically in other ways, and these attempts at continuity or the reclaiming of traditional values are perhaps seen as counter-measures to these changes. Moral education could perhaps be seen as an example of continuity in the context of, or perhaps even as an example of, resistance to radical reforms especially when they are Western-influenced. What is worth noting, however, as can be seen from the current discussion of values and citizenship education in both Western and Chinese education systems (as seen in the chapter by Tudball), is that there are many similarities in the traditional values and objectives espoused in both systems although perhaps different labels are used especially in terms such as morality or ethics or liberal education and service learning. The data analysed in this chapter show that traditional views of the roles of teachers are enduring but also demonstrate that these views can exist alongside efforts to reform curriculum and pedagogy in other ways; seemingly contradictory values and beliefs can exist simultaneously. Comments by the authors that contrary to their expectations students and teachers would be concerned about the imposition of inappropriate foreign models (echoing the concerns of Kang and colleagues in their chapter), it is the foreign researchers and teachers who are more concerned about notions of cultural imperialism through the introduction of foreign educational concepts than teachers and students in Vietnam and China. They appear to be not only more relaxed and welcoming of apparently foreign and sometimes contradictory concepts, they can in fact simultaneously hold these without apparent internal conflict. This may show that instead of internationalisation being something that is being 'done' to these students and teachers, they are using their own active agency to appropriate these concepts and refashion them in ways useful to them in their own contexts.

Part IV   Reform and internationalisation in the disciplines

The recurring themes of how to reform curriculum while retaining the best of traditional practices come to the fore in this section. The reform programme has proven contentious in many disciplinary areas in China, most notably in the area of Mathematics education. Chinese educators are keen not to lose what they see as China's competitive advantage in this area and are sometimes divided on how the new requirements of the curriculum reform programme can be met while maintaining excellence. Other areas of the curriculum are equally contentious where they seek to embody and maintain Chinese 'values' in the midst of efforts to internationalise education. The area of moral education, discussed in the previous section, is sometimes seen as a way to rejuvenate traditional Confucian values but more recent initiatives in the related area of citizenship education and efforts worldwide to reform and enhance this area of education are also discussed in this section.

Chapter 8 provides a rationale for the benefits of two-way learning between China and the West. Mathematics teaching and high student Mathematics achievement is an area where Western educators are looking at Chinese models to learn about best teaching and learning practices. Wee Tiong Seah argues that China's continued strong performance in this area should be of interest to both those within and outside China, due to China's growing

economic development (and its realisation of the implications of this growing strength) and the large numbers of Chinese students going overseas to
study. This chapter examines how this excellence can be maintained in China
in the context of the curriculum reform, the success to date of the curriculum
reforms in this area as well as some of the enduring tensions and challenges,
and how China can conform to broader international best practices in Mathematics pedagogy. Rather than simply focusing on aspects of numeracy
attainment, this chapter examines the social and cultural situatedness of
curriculum reform and foregrounds this with a brief history of school Mathematics education, reflecting on China's long history of valuing academic
excellence, before examining 'soft' learning (values that reflect social and
cultural imperatives and contexts) as opposed to 'hard' learning (cognitive
and affective processing). Seah argues that the articulation and debate of the
values underpinning the curriculum reform can help to bring about enduring
and empowering reform by capitalising on existing excellence in this area
while also being responsive to broader educational trends in China and internationally and respecting local, ethnic Mathematical practices that reflect the
diversity of a country such as China. The challenge, he argues, is to respond
to necessary curriculum reform 'without sacrificing the essence of local norms
and practices', a common theme in several chapters in this volume.

Rather than looking at differences between China and Western countries,
in Chapter 9 Libby Tudball examines the common challenges facing educators in countries such as China and Australia in preparing a new generation
of students for the twenty-first century. Tudball examines the area of citizenship education in both countries, arguing the need for further reforms of
curriculum in both countries to prepare young people for more a globalised
and inter-connected world. She provides an account of contemporary thinking
and curriculum initiatives in both countries, including a discussion of the
evolution of citizenship education in China, historically offered variously as
ideological/political and moral education. Concerns about the future and about
persistent failings in both systems to address issues such as rampant consumerism and selfish individualism has prompted debates within and across
these systems about 'values' and ethics within those societies. The contemporary reinvigoration of interest in Confucianism in China is part of a response
to these concerns and demonstrates the ways that current attempts are being
made to address them. This chapter provides an interesting perspective on
the curriculum frameworks required to support 'values' or 'moral' education;
these notions are themselves analysed in other chapters such as Chapter 7.

Part V   Mutual learning and adaptation

Part V documents the learning that occurs amongst those who make a 'physical' shift into different cultures and educational systems and have to negotiate
new ways of being and knowing, as well as those who want to shift their
'mental' or 'intellectual' outlook by learning another language, in this case

either English or Chinese, and so cross borders in other ways. Themes of cross-cultural learning and adaptation are explored more fully in this section in terms of the possibilities for more reciprocal and respectful interactions and learning arising from cross- and inter-cultural experiences. With China's economic and political rise, the beginnings of Western attempts to learn about China and to engage in two-way learning can be seen in the increase in the numbers of people worldwide who are learning Mandarin Chinese. Rather than a focus on how Chinese and Western educational values and practices are different, in the final chapter Xu provides a theory for mutual learning by drawing on great educational theories from the West and China to explore the similarities and parallels between Confucian ways of 'being' and Deweyian ways of 'knowing'.

Chapter 10 will be of interest to those concerned with second language learning and the potential benefits that can come from Chinese speakers learning English and English speakers learning Chinese, a phenomenon growing rapidly in both directions. Jiewen Zhong continues the theme of how learning in another culture and another language can improve learning overall and examines precisely how learning in another language can impact not only on the way that the learner learns within their first language but also in terms of the cultural knowledge and understanding gained through this process. Zhong describes how Western countries are now embracing the need to learn Chinese and whereas 'English fever' took hold in China several years ago, 'Chinese fever' is now growing in Western countries. Zhong argues that Western countries can learn from China's efforts to introduce more effective foreign language learning in order to engage more effectively globally, and describes China's recent efforts to promote the learning of Chinese around the world in order to play a more influential role in world affairs. Zhong explores the special role of morphological awareness (of internal word structures) in learning a foreign language, suggesting that there may be some benefits for English-speakers learning Chinese, and vice versa, in terms of improving their literacy overall. Foreign language learning has a secondary effect of learning about other cultures and contexts and is an important platform for adaptation and respectful dialogue and exchange. Zhong argues that this needs to be a mutual rather than just a one-way endeavour. Importantly, Zhong argues that learning another language and engaging with another culture also leads to a greater understanding of one's own language and culture and offers a new way of thinking about the world and is thus transformative for the learner in perhaps unexpected ways. This also shows that for those wanting to engage more successfully with China, it is necessary to gain linguistic and cultural knowledge as a foundation for this engagement. However, Zhong shows that despite the massive numbers of people outside China trying to learn Chinese, education systems in countries such as the UK are not providing the infrastructure and facilities for this to occur and perhaps still have much to learn about the value of foreign language learning for successful engagement and encounters in globalised contexts.

In the final chapter of this book, Shijing Xu explores the themes of change and continuity that recur throughout this book with an examination of the process of adaptation and learning experienced by the children of Chinese immigrant families in Canada. Xu talks about how values endure but change in new contexts outside of China in areas of large Chinese immigration to countries like Canada. The site of the research described in the chapter, a highly multicultural primary school in Toronto, has a majority of Chinese speaking children. Xu shows how Chinese grandparents, who play a pivotal role in the care of their grandchildren, play an important role in bridging the gaps between Western and Chinese cultures and demonstrates how reciprocal learning and understanding can assist newly arrived Chinese children in Western schools. As in several other chapters, the study demonstrates the continuity of Chinese cultural values in contexts outside of China through the passing of Chinese and Confucian family values through the generations, in this case by grandparents. Xu uses narrative inquiry to show how a 'WE' consciousness of diversity (West and East) is required and how Confucian 'continuity of being' and Deweyian 'continuity of knowing' can be used as unifying discourses to underpin this reciprocal learning. She concludes that Chinese immigrants into Western educational contexts can act as forces for change in their adopted communities and societies and a resource for mutual learning and understanding. She calls for a move away from simply one-way learning and adaptation from West to East and a dichotomised 'East/West' view of the world to instead a focus on mutual understanding and adaptation and two-way flows of knowledge and interactions. This chapter provides a fitting end for this book as it points to the possibilities for new theories and ways of being and knowing (to use Confucian concepts of 'being' and Deweyian concepts of 'knowing') of the increased transnational flows not just of capital and goods but also of people and ideas.

Part I

Curriculum policy and practice

1 Reflection in action: ongoing K-12 curriculum reform in China

Jian Liu and Changyun Kang

Written by two key initiators and organisers of China's curriculum reform programme, this chapter provides a unique insiders' account of the various stages of the reform as well as the tensions, conflicts and challenges that have arisen and the extraordinarily complex processes involved at each stage of the reform programme. It explains in detail the chronology, aims and processes involved, marking the milestones along the way over a decade of reform and explaining the processes that have been put in place to deal with the very real challenges and dilemmas facing all stakeholders in this mammoth and ambitious task.

The end of the last century witnessed the launch of China's eighth curriculum reform since the founding of the People's Republic of China in 1949. Regarded as a radical systematic reform which covers every single aspect of basic, K-12, education (Kindergarten to Year 12), including curriculum aims, structure, content and assessment as well as curriculum administration, the reform has also triggered a series of reactions in related areas such as teachers' professional development, teacher education, assessment systems and education administration. The national reform project has been proceeding for over a decade. The two authors of this chapter, as key players in this reform, describe here the unfolding picture of the education reform from our first-hand experiences. This description entails five overlapping and interlinked stages. We reflect openly and in depth on the processes, the influencing factors, the social mechanisms and the various systems involved, as well as on the voices from various sections of society. We offer distinctive solutions to the issues and challenges that continue to confront the process of curriculum reform in China. We firmly believe that although there is still a long journey ahead for the reform with its ongoing difficulties and its opponents, the achievements and significance of the reform to the future of China's education cannot be denied. Moreover, it is clear that the reform will continue despite these issues and challenges. We believe that the current and ongoing education reform in China will undoubtedly provide a unique and extremely valuable case for curriculum reform worldwide.

Background

China, with its five thousand year history and a population of 200 million students, is at a time of rapid transformation and revival. The end of the last century witnessed the launch of China's eighth curriculum reform since the founding of the People's Republic of China in 1949. This remarkable national education reform has made great progress over the past decade and it is still in the process of being implemented. This chapter reviews the past decade of reform chronologically by first examining its major events and significant achievements and then providing a reflection and evaluation of each of its various aspects.

Stage 1   Curriculum ideology and planning (1996–98)

Key events and significant achievements

Survey of the nine-year compulsory education curriculum

From June 1996 to 1997, with funding from the United Nations Children's Fund, the Basic Education Department in the Ministry of Education (MOE) organised curriculum experts from six key Chinese universities including Beijing Normal University, East China Normal University and the Central Education Institute, to carry out a survey of the national nine-year compulsory education curriculum. The survey involved nine provinces and municipal cities, 72 districts, over 160,000 K-12 students, 2,500 principals and teachers and more than 50 national government education consultants and government science, culture and health committee members. The survey covered aspects such as the implementation of curriculum goals, the appropriateness of teaching content, approaches to teaching and learning and examination and assessment issues.

   The vast amount of information and data generated demonstrated that there were a series of major problems in the current curriculum practices, which included: relatively outmoded educational concepts; a lack of connection between school education models and contemporary theories of child development and learning; moral education which was lacking in relevance and effectiveness; curriculum content that was out-of-date; and curriculum structures that were narrow with isolated subject systems which did not reflect innovations and developments in modern Science and Technology and in the Social Sciences. In addition, the school curriculum was isolated from students' lived experiences and social reality; many students were struggling with the traditional memorisation approach to learning and teachers were exhausted and bored with worksheet training. In terms of assessment, too much emphasis was put on students' marks and the processes of selection to the next level of education. Curriculum administration was so centralised that the curriculum could not address local economic and social development needs as well as the dynamic growth of students. In some areas, these problems were so common and so profound that they had started to inhibit the healthy development of the younger generation and crush their creativity.

International comparative research on curriculum development

Between 1997 and 1998, a large number of Chinese education researchers carried out research on curriculum development and strategies in other countries and regions looking especially at how their education systems were confronting the education needs of the new century. This included education systems and curriculum in England, America, Canada, Germany, Japan, Australia, Korea, Russia, Sweden, India, Brazil and Egypt as well as Hong Kong and Taiwan. This research helped to underpin the development of an understanding of curriculum development worldwide and resulted in the publication of a series of influential papers and books which provided information and background for the new round of basic education curriculum reform in China.

Development of the Guidelines on Basic Education Curriculum Reform

After exhaustive discussions and debates at hundreds of meetings, seminars and consultation events across China, the values, mission, map and timetable for the national basic education curriculum reform were outlined in a blueprint document which outlined the aims of the reform in six areas: curriculum goals, structure, content, implementation, assessment and administration.

Reflection and comments

This stage took over three years due to the need to get to grass-roots levels and also due to a lack of policy certainty and limited financial resources. This situation, however, also created a rich environment for scholarly investigation and the identification of important education values for the new century and for the new basic education curriculum development to underpin the regeneration of the Chinese nation and the individual growth of every student. The common vision, core values and general spirit generated through this early stage of the reform programme attracted people to engage in research and carry out various types of research projects.

Stage 2   Design, dissemination and experimental stage of the curriculum documents (1999–2001)

Key events and significant achievements

In the second stage of the reform programme, the MOE issued the *Confronting the Twenty-first Century Education Rejuvenation Action Plan* to champion the campaign for the reform of the curriculum system and its assessment mechanisms. Following approximately a decade of trialling and experimentation, the twenty-first century basic education curriculum textbook system was implemented nationwide. Thus, the eighth basic education curriculum reform since the foundation of People's Republic of China was officially launched in this period, issuing in a phase of widespread action and government and individual organisation-led participation. A Basic Education Curriculum Reform Expert Team was established in January 1999 comprising over forty experts from higher education institutes, local administration bureaus, renowned scholars and researchers in the fields of curriculum, education and psychology, as well as principals' and teachers' representatives. The expert team members held a series of seminars and consultations on the topics of basic education curriculum goals, structures and design, curriculum standards, examinations and assessment, as well as subject curriculum standards, rural curriculum reform and curriculum support policies. The research projects on curriculum standards in Chinese Literacy, Mathematics, Moral Education and Elementary Science were given priority with the aim of exploring and initiating a set of subject curriculum standards. After a year of deliberation by the Mathematics curriculum standards research team, and drawing on extensive research on the existing literature, 30,000 copies of the draft National Mathematics Curriculum Standards were formally published in March 2000 to seek public feedback.

At the same time, the basic education curriculum reform expert teams formalised their working processes for the curriculum standard research projects as follows:

- Conduct research on historical and contemporary literature on the subject's educational development, international contexts and comparisons, future outlook and trends, and the future requirements for public literacy and the learning needs of K-12 students.
- Based on the above research, develop major concepts, ideas and strategies for the curriculum of the subject.
- Develop draft curriculum standards for feedback.
- Invite feedback from elementary and secondary schools and the public.
- Respond to the feedback and suggestions received.

As mentioned above, the basic education curriculum reform programme was divided into a number of key projects which included a general outline for curriculum reform, curriculum goals, curriculum standards, curriculum structure, textbook composition and administration, curriculum implementation, curriculum assessment and administration policy. Documents on *Basic Education Curriculum Reform Programme Application, Adjudication and Administration Details* and *Curriculum Reform Basic Education Project Outlines* were developed and disseminated and invitations to undertake projects were issued to some of the normal (i.e. Education) universities, research institutes and provincial education administration bureaus. The end of

December 1999 witnessed the opening of a national Basic Education Curriculum Reform: Workshop and Project Bidding Conference. In less than three months, 261 research proposals were received involving more than 3,000 education experts and scholars. The proposals were evaluated between April and June 2000. The project evaluation teams, which were composed of experts from the fields of education, curriculum, pedagogy and the subject area, conducted two initial and one final assessment of the proposals received. The committee considered principles of fairness and equity and used exhaustive selection processes to select the project principal investigators and co-investigators and finalise the proposals for each project bringing together the strong points of each proposal. By June 2000, a total of 11 categories and 40 key projects had been identified, which covered the national standards for K-12 curricula and guidelines for local curriculum administration and development, school curriculum administration and field activities, as well as processes for assessment, curriculum and textbook assessment, and teacher research and training. The research projects were fully implemented by July 2007.

To ensure the quality of the curriculum standards research projects and their effective implementation, apart from requiring the project teams to seek wide feedback during the research process, the Ministry of Education also employed a dozen local education bureaus, in Shenzhen (Guangzhou), Yulin (Guangxi), Xiamen (Fujian), Suzhou (Jiangsu), Dalian (Liaoning), Shijiazhuang (Hebei) and Wuhan (Hubei), to seek feedback on the standards from local teachers. It also commissioned Southwest Normal University, Northwest Normal University and Fujian Normal University to seek feedback from Southwest China, Northwest and Fujian province, respectively, and the Shanghai Educational Science Institute Intellectual Development Department was asked to seek feedback from large- and medium-size enterprises on the curriculum programme and standards. In May 2001 several well-known education academics including Zhou Yulin, Lin Qun and Zhao Zhongxian participated in the National Compulsory Education Curriculum Standards Adjudication meeting. Detailed adjudication comments were formulated for each project and subject and the leaders from the Ministry of Education considered the evaluation feedback for each subject.

The *Design and Launch of the Basic Education Curriculum Reform Guidelines* (Pilot Project), the *Compulsory Education Curriculum Design Pilot Proposal Guidelines* and each *Subject Curriculum Standards (Pilot version)* were then published and became cornerstone documents for this round of the curriculum reform programme, providing direction for the design of the new curriculum documents, the launch of the new curriculum policy and the processes for curriculum implementation. These clearly stated that the compulsory curriculum should provide each student with an educational standard that should be attained by the majority of the students, that curriculum content and aims should be explicit and should not be expanded or enhanced too liberally, that curriculum content should be developed with the focus on students' minds, healthy development and life-long learning, and that it should be centered on creativity and 'hands-on' learning. Emphasis should be given to students' ability to collect data, to acquire new knowledge and to be able to analyse and solve problems and to develop their skills of communication and collaboration.

In preparation for the new experimental curriculum work, and in order to apply and test the new curriculum, the first 38 state-level curriculum reform experimental districts were identified in early 2001, and training and professional development was provided for all the education administrators, teacher researchers, principals and teachers involved in the pilot work.

Reflection and observations

This stage of the curriculum reform process demonstrated the breadth and depth of the reform programme. Whereas previous educational reforms were limited to the adjustment of curriculum categories, revision of curriculum content and replacement of textbooks, this reform programme involved systemic and structural reform. It involved all dimensions of the curriculum including curriculum aims, structure, content, implementation, administration and assessment (see Figure 1.1 below) and entailed a transformation of perspectives of the curriculum nationwide.

The processes of systematic curriculum development involve the curriculum design process, the decision-making processes, the implementation process and the evaluation and feedback process (see Figure 1.2). This involves the development of the 'ideal' curriculum and the administrative arrangements required for implementation and then finally translating the curriculum into practice in the classroom. The processes required to minimise the difference between the transition from the stated 'ideal' curriculum to the actual, 'enacted' curriculum in the classroom was extremely important in order to avoid a simple 'passive execution' to more one of a 'mutual adaptation and accommodation'. The core theme that emerged from this phase of work was how to translate the shared vision of curriculum reform and also maximise motivation, initiative and creativity at the grass-roots level of schools and teachers.

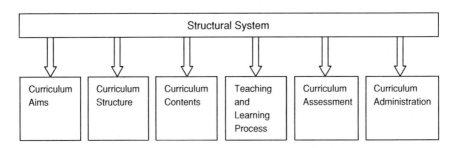

Figure 1.1

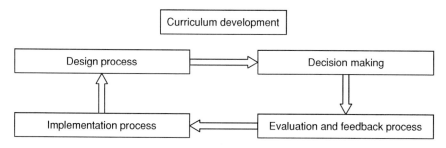

Figure 1.2

There was also a concern to ensure that the newly recruited curriculum design teams worked in ways that were scientific but also democratic. They worked closely together through a process of dialogue, consultations, weighing up of advantages and disadvantages of different approaches and finally by making overall judgements about the directions to take. There was a deliberate move away from formal hierarchies, institutional affiliations and academic 'authorities'. There was an effort to ensure that team members developed skills of negotiation and communication and constructive criticism, and that when disagreements or conflicts occurred, that the interests of the state and of the children were paramount. These efforts made a considerable contribution to democratic, equal and communicative curriculum development.

For the first time, the importance of standard teacher training programmes was recognised, and the expert teams developed a comprehensive model for teacher training based on principles of equality, dialogue and collaboration. At the research seminars organised for the new curriculum implementers, the organisers encouraged participants to actively contribute. They encouraged participants to bring their knowledge of the local environment, cultural traditions, education contexts, and their positive aspects as well as their real dilemmas to the seminars to share with colleagues and try to find strategies and solutions for the effective implementation of the new curriculum.

Stage 3   Compulsory education curriculum pilot and finalisation of secondary school curriculum programme (2001–2004)

Key events and significant achievements

The State Basic Education Curriculum Reform Pilot Taskforce meeting in July 2001 witnessed the launch of the new curriculum pilot programme and set forth the general goals and strategies of the new curriculum pilot programme, and mapped out the pilot programme implementation process and teacher training programmes. This signalled that the basic education curriculum reform had entered the third stage – the pilot and experimentation stage. The state and provincial level governments took the initiative in implementing the pilot programme followed by the steady expansion of the experimental curriculum through a process of exploration and experimentation. The curriculum implementation strategy was to first establish a programme, trial it and then carefully progress step by step towards its full implementation.

The experimental pilot stage then began to scale up. By 2001, there were about 270,000 grade one students participating in the new curriculum pilot programme, which represented about one per cent of students at that year level nationwide. About 110,000 grade 7 students (that is, about 0.5 per cent of the age group), 3,300 elementary schools and over 400 secondary schools were involved in this phase. By 2002, each province had identified its own pilot programme according to its own local situation. Overall, about 20 per cent of the Grade 1, 18 per cent of Grade 7 and 570 pilot districts embarked on the new curriculum. By 2003, 1,072 more counties across the country had introduced the new curriculum with a total student number of 40 to 50 per cent of the grade level. In addition to the pilot districts of 2001 and 2002, there were in total 1,642 experimental districts and 35 million students using the new curriculum.

Another feature of this phase of the reform programme was the establishment of a teacher research system that combined professional support with school-based inquiry. It became evident that a strong and effective professional support team provided crucial support to ensure the smooth implementation of the curriculum reform pilot projects. At the same time, the Ministry of Education set up a teaching and learning professional support team involving over one hundred scholars from 17 universities. The members of this team visited almost all of the curriculum reform experimental districts. The local educational bureaus at various levels attached high importance to the organisation and construction of these professional support teams and encouraged teacher research institutes, normal universities and other higher education institutes to establish professional support teams to deliver teacher training programmes and to provide timely and relevant professional support and assistance to teachers and schools. The schools and teachers in the pilot districts not only used this process to learn about and interpret the new curriculum but also as an opportunity to update their educational theories and philosophies. They worked to establish teacher research mechanisms that were based on school and classroom practice and were integrated with curriculum reform and teacher development. The content of the teacher training programmes was closely connected to teaching practice and research. The practice of individual reflection, peer communication and support, professional learning and innovation has become a valuable tool for the K-12 teachers in China who are trying to improve their professional development and address their own teaching and learning concerns in their own contexts.

A survey and appraisal of the pilot process was then carried out. During the periods from 23 to 28 December 2001, 4 to 12 March 2003 and 22 to 26 November 2004, the Ministry of Education carried out three rounds of comprehensive surveys and established appraisal taskforces for each of these evaluation rounds. In each taskforce, there were five to seven appraisal teams who went to different areas to carry out the surveys. Each appraisal team usually consisted of seven to ten people and included one educational leader (the head of the local education bureau or the president of a university), one coordinator from the Ministry of Education, two to three university researchers, two to three local educational administrators, principals or teacher representatives, and between one and three media reporters. These three appraisal programmes surveyed more than 20 provinces and cities covering about 50 pilot districts and 150 K-12 schools. More than 500 lectures and 300 seminars were held, with over 5,000 participants and over 10,000 questionnaires collected. During the appraisal period, the teams also randomly visited students, teachers and parents to gain a more complete picture of how the new curriculum was being received and implemented.

The next step in this phase included a survey of high school students' learning and the official announcement of the new high school curriculum programme and subject curriculum standards. In the middle of 2002 a large-scale nationwide survey was carried out to inform the design of the new high school curriculum programme. This covered ten provinces and municipal cities and over 14,000 high school Year 1 and Year 3 students and their teachers, principals and parents. Interviews were also held with a sample of local high-level administrators. By the end of 2002, significant progress had been made in terms of the design of the draft new high school curriculum, the specific new curriculum proposals and the pilot subject curriculum standards, and nationwide consultations to seek feedback on these began. The new curriculum structure and new administration system for high schools were officially announced in April 2003. These were then piloted in certain provinces and municipal cities.

Reflection and comments

A major feature of this phase of the curriculum reform programme was the recognition that school-based teacher research mechanisms were crucial to the establishment of a national pedagogy research system. While teacher development requires professional support, more importantly it needs personal practice and reflection. In terms of the depth and breadth of the practice and reflections of each individual, it showed that communication and collaboration among peers is essential and this in turn relies on teachers' professionalism and the culture of their professional environment. Therefore, the question of how to promote the formation of a professional learning community among researchers and classroom teachers became a crucial issue in the implementation of the new curriculum. The subsequent question of how the government could organise professional services to provide effective, timely and efficient professional support to the large numbers of classroom teachers became a major priority, as it became clear that simply relying on training initial pre-service teachers would never solve the overall needs for teachers' professional development.

Although we can say that at this stage there had been significant progress at the state and provincial pilot areas in terms of new curriculum implementation, we should also acknowledge that investigating and gradually establishing school-based teaching and learning research systems has played a fundamental role. The introduction of this system motivated principals and teachers to try out the new curriculum using their own initiative, passion and creativity. As the reform programme progressed over time, it was clear that even though the new curriculum had encountered strong criticism, questioning and even conflict and dispute in the years that followed, the concept of school-based curriculum inquiry has inspired the vast majority of educators to learn about and try the new curriculum and to pursue their own ideas and concerns. Most of all, it is this strong bottom-up 'counterforce' that has made the new curriculum programme irreversible.

A major challenge for this phase of the curriculum reform programme was how to ensure that curriculum development was proceeding in the desired way. This is an issue that no level of government or school could ignore. Each new round of curriculum practice needs to be reinforced by independent appraisal and evaluation with periodical feedback and reporting. This is an important task. However, the issue of how to structure an effective appraisal and monitoring system at the state level still needs to be explored.

There are many outstanding and important issues in secondary education that continue to need recognition and consideration however. Even now, there is still a general lack of understanding of the academic and practical support systems required to develop an effective secondary education system. High school students need to learn how to make decisions, identify their own interests, develop their own personality and plan their lives and their future. When they turn eighteen, they need to learn how to take on the responsibilities that a citizen should have for themselves, for others and for society. We know that we have a long way to go in this area.

Stage 4   Finalisation of compulsory education curriculum, nationwide implementation and the new secondary curriculum pilot (2004–2007)

Key events and significant achievements

By 2004, the new compulsory education curriculum had been put into effect nationwide. The first middle school graduates successfully passed the high school entrance exams under the new curriculum programme. The new curriculum pilot had been implemented for the three full years for the first cohort of middle school graduates of the programme. By Autumn 2005, the entering grades in elementary and middle schools were all required to study the new curriculum. The reform had entered the national implementation stage.

The high school entrance examination reform programme which was compatible with the new curriculum was put into effect in 17 pilot districts. The questions now became how could the high school entrance examinations better reflect the basic requirements of the subject curriculum standards, so as to demonstrate the quality of students' learning and development during their three years of middle school? How could examination results be used effectively in terms of recruiting high school students? These questions became topics for public debate.

A number of surveys demonstrated that, in general, the new curriculum pilot projects were viewed positively. The new curriculum had been welcomed by the teachers and students, as well as by the public. It was often commented upon by educators in the field that in those areas where the new curriculum was effectively employed, the initiative and motivation of the students was greatly enhanced and their curiosity and interest had been increased. Student inquiry and critical and reflective thinking had been encouraged and their sense of responsibility and collaboration significantly increased. What's more, in some inland and rural areas where the economy is less developed, due to the popularity of the new curriculum the drop-out rates decreased noticeably. School life had taken on a new look, and teachers and students were interacting and participating enthusiastically. It is now normal practice for many teachers to incorporate inquiry learning, active participation and 'hands-on' activities into their teaching and learning processes. The new curriculum has demonstrated a tremendous vitality. Even an independent nvestigation into the revision of the Mathematics curriculum standards revealed that despite previous opposition, the pilot standards have been well accepted by most Mathematics teachers. The high school entrance examination reform programme that is compatible with the new curriculum has been introduced and implemented in the curriculum pilot areas. The high school entrance examinations have been designed according to the curriculum standards and with an appropriate grading system. The self-governing rights of high schools on recruitment have been increased, which also provide assurance for students' individual and personalised development goals in accordance with schools' own priorities and operations.

In 2004 the new high school curriculum pilot project commenced at the level of university entrance with the first high school graduates undertaking the university entrance examination in 2007. The year 2004 witnessed the first four provinces of Shandong, Ningxia, Guangdong and Hainan employing the new high school curriculum, followed by Jiangsu, Fujian, Tianjin, Liaoning, Anhui, Zhejiang and other provinces and municipal cities. As with the compulsory earlier education stage, there were a number of difficult issues which arose. These included how to strengthen the organisation and leadership at various levels in education departments, how to guide the organisation of school lessons and lesson options, how to establish school-based implementation models, how to improve the capabilities and standards of principals and teachers in terms of implementing the new curriculum and in turn promote reform of the higher education admissions system, and how to establish effective communication with parents and the society more generally in the context of a culture of high-stakes university admission.

It is worth noting also that the new high school curriculum pilot has been positively received. In the past four years, quite a number of high schools have been exploring a range of different types of classes and subjects so that more options can be offered to students according to their needs and interests taking into consideration local contexts and teachers' expertise. Students can select options according to their own interests. The development of assessment portfolios has also been effectively applied in some schools. All of these initiatives have greatly motivated students and improved their learning. It is worth mentioning as an example of this the case of Shenzhen Secondary School which has structured its new 'real life' programme. This programme has four terms of ten weeks of which nine weeks are for lecturing and one week is for review and exams. The students study six Arts subjects simultaneously with each subject having two classes and four consecutive sessions per week. Students can select classes beyond their grade level and outside of their home class. This means that in 2008, for example, the 800 Year 2 students at the school had 734 curriculum options, so the number of options for thousands of students at this school has changed dramatically. The object of the curriculum design which involves the concept of 'Learning how to make choices and how to plan for life' has been turned into a reality through this initiative.

A further reform is the integration of school-based research and Internet seminars, in order to further improve the new curriculum implementation. In 2005, the Ministry of Education launched the New Curriculum Internet Seminar project. Among the curriculum reform expert teams that had been established since 1999 when the reform initially commenced, 37 project teams have set up interactive Internet spaces using a common platform. By 2007, there were experts online almost every day advising and guiding classroom teachers who were perplexed by or uncertain about certain common issues. These types of conversations and the sharing of a research culture have been very well received by the majority of teachers. In the meantime, following a successful pilot project in Hainan province, the 'K-12 Teachers New Curriculum National Online Seminars' have been offered to thousands of teachers simultaneously during the summer vacation. Since then, various kinds of online forums including blogs, video-blogs and virtual study and research spaces have been organised by local authorities, schools and non-governmental organisations and these have been welcomed by teachers and have become one of the main mechanisms for teachers to share their experiences and address and resolve their daily issues and dilemmas.

Under such interactive, equal and open Internet environments, a culture that is democratic, equal, dialogical, consultative and collaborative has emerged. Regardless of whether teachers are from rural areas or cities, or whether they are classroom teachers or educational experts, participants communicate openly and share their experiences and ideas, which has greatly promoted communication and dialogue among teachers and between academics and practitioners. These kinds of learning cultures will undoubtedly nurture teachers and permeate into each site of learning.

There are areas, however, where there has been dissent and opposition to the reforms. One area of strong disputation is the Mathematics curriculum standards. In 2005 at the People's Congress and the People's Consultative Committee meetings, a number of congress members and consultative committee members jointly proposed an immediately halt to the pilot Mathematics curriculum standards project. They campaigned through the press including the *Guangming Daily*, *Sichuan Daily* and the *Mathematics Journal* claiming that the new Mathematics curriculum standards have ruined a Mathematics system that has a history of over a thousand years and arguing that it is now difficult for teachers to teach and students to learn Mathematics and that the quality of teaching in Mathematics has dropped dramatically. In response to this opposition from the Mathematics community, the Ministry of Education directed a Mathematics Curriculum Standards Revision Taskforce to revise the Mathematics curriculum standards at the compulsory stage.

A comprehensive survey of the quality of the education system was also carried out in response to comments by leaders in the central government. In 2005, the Ministry of Education, together with the Central Propaganda Ministry, the Human Resources Ministry and the Social Sciences Institute carried out a year-long systematic review of the education system. Their final report stated clearly that this round of curriculum reform has drawn from the nation's intellectual and education traditions while also drawing on the experiences of developed nations. While highlighting the importance of cultivating students' innovation and practical skills it also pointed to the need to develop their initiative and creative thinking. It recognised the need to take into account children's interests and potential and to nurture their curiosity and passion for learning to ensure their healthy growth and development. It recognised that the basic education curriculum reform has brought about fundamental transformation of school education resulting in positive and profound changes in terms of teachers' teaching and students' approaches to learning.

Reflection and comments

What is NEW in the new curriculum?

Nearly every round of curriculum reform since the foundation of the People's Republic China has put more focus on physical changes, mainly including changes to curriculum subjects, the increase or decrease of class times, the updating of teaching content, adjustments to teaching requirements and the updating of textbooks. All of the material changes that resulted from these previous 'new' reforms have made us realise the limited impact of these reform programmes.

In the current curriculum reform programme, however, there is a concern to deal with much deeper and more fundamental questions. For our young people, during a learning journey that spans a period of six to nine years, or even 12 years, what does it mean to learn about the richness of civilisation? Does it merely mean finding a new way of being lectured to, memorising information and mimicking? Such approaches to learning in the long run will only mean that our youth are yet to grow mentally and intellectually. And what does this mean for a nation? We now know that it means that how to teach is more important than what to teach, and how to learn is more important than what to learn. This new round of curriculum reform has set as a priority the transformation of teaching approaches, learning approaches, assessment methods and administration systems. All these endeavours together comprise the true meaning of the new curriculum.

However, what we regard as most important for the new curriculum is the fundamental reform of curriculum culture, classroom culture, teacher research culture and the administrative culture. The aim is to establish new constructive partnerships and relationships between teachers and students, between students and their peers, between teachers and their colleagues, between teachers and administrators, and between schools and the public that are democratic, open, scientific, equal, dialogic and consultative. It is also hoped that through these curriculum reforms, schools will reform, and in turn, there will be an impact on the next generation by instilling in them a more progressive culture and in the wider community as well. We are confident that people who grow up in an environment that has combined the excellence of both Eastern and Western countries will develop strong confidence further enhanced with a sense of responsibility, collaboration and creativity. Their school life will be happier and they will have healthy personalities and a broader vision. A society that is filled with creativity is a society with a bright future. The closer we get to the core of the new curriculum, the stronger we will feel the profound impacts brought about through the new curriculum. Of course, the breadth and depth of the curriculum reform envisaged here will not be realised within three, five or even eight years; it may take twenty, thirty or even much longer.

It must be acknowledged that the new curriculum programme has been confronted with much criticism. Since the implementation of the new curriculum, especially at this period of time when people from across society are increasingly casting their attention to the quality of education, especially to students' academic results, a large number of teachers and parents have consciously or unconsciously compared the achievements of students under the new curriculum with the previous one in terms of academic marks. It is generally believed that students' foundational knowledge and skills are not as solid as previously, which has led to the conclusion that the quality of education has dropped. This criticism comes from not only the education sector; it also comes from the academic arena. These disputes about the new curriculum keep testing the wisdom and resolve of the various stakeholders, forcing everyone to ponder even deeper questions such as: What is the essence of education? What is the mission of contemporary basic education? Are we prepared for disputes and disagreements? Can we face such unexpected reactions while maintaining the principles of democracy and openness while trying to make objective and logical decisions?

So now we turn to the current state of play. Current concerns relate to the relationship between intellectual heritage and innovation, international perspectives and localised concerns, public education and 'niche' education, urban societies and rural communities, textbook knowledge and practical experience, teachers' roles and students as autonomous learners, as well as transmission-based learning and inquiry-based, collaborative and independent learning and thinking. All of these questions are being fiercely debated and are areas of disputation and contestation by Chinese educators, as well as replicating educational dilemmas in Eastern cultures going back hundreds of years. The crucial question is what is our nation's true educational position? This question is one that no Chinese educator can ignore. In the 1980s, because their children were doing poorly in literacy and mathematics, Americans responded by saying that their nation was in danger, and education reform was a must. Twenty-five years have passed since that time and in quite a number of international tests American students have improved significantly from the previous position of being last to now being in the middle or even above average. It appears that the education 'crisis' in America is on the way to being resolved. But what about China? How far are we from our stated goals? In terms of encouraging our students to be more autonomous, collaborative and exploratory, have we done too much or too little?

Stage 5   The new stage of re-reflection, re-interpretation and further implementation (From August 2007 to the present)

Key events and significant achievements

In 2006, at an assembly on the curriculum reform programme, President Hu Jintao stated that the transmission approach in education should be replaced with an innovative education approach. He argued that while the role of teachers should be respected, more focus should be centred on cultivating students' innovation and creativity and encouraging critical thinking. Children should be freed from the heavy burdens of schoolwork to inspire their curiosity and exploration, so that their youth can be fully developed based on the exploration of their interests and potential. In August of the same year, at a seminar of the Central Political Bureau 34th Congress, President Hu once again emphasised this position by saying, 'to implement quality education, the key is to solve the crucial issue of what kind of person we want to educate and how to educate them, this should become the theme of our education cause. We should inspire the inner motivation of students' development and enhance their innovation and hands-on ability'. In 2007 the Party's 17th Congress report appealed for 'updating education concepts, deepening reforms in the areas of teaching content and approaches, examinations and recruitment mechanisms and the quality assessment system; the schoolwork in K-12 schools should be lessened while overall quality should be enhanced'. In recent years, on various occasions, Premier Wen Jiabao has expressed his expectations for education by saying

> we should employ enlightened education by putting students as the centre of the teaching, so that in the whole learning process the students will take the initiative, ask questions proactively, thinking proactively, discover proactively and explore proactively. The core of enlightened education is to cultivate students' independent thinking and innovative ideas . . . What should be minimised is lecturing to children but instead guiding them more to discover, in this way the children will learn gradually how to study independently and their ability to learn autonomously will be enhanced.

The new high school curriculum pilot programme has been scaled up. The beginning of the school year in 2007 and 2008 saw the implementation of the new curriculum in ten provinces including Beijing, Heilongjiang, Jilin, Shanxi, Hunan, Jiangxi, Shanxi, Henan and Xinjiang. The involvement of Beijing municipal city, in particular, attracted the attention of the public and among academic circles. To some extent, this is viewed as an important signal of the further implementation of the new curriculum. Meanwhile, in 2007 Shandong provincial government commenced the compulsory implementation of the new curriculum province-wide. Administrative control by government was reinforced and stricter regulations were put in place in terms of the operations of schools. The message was 'a new high school curriculum, Shandong starts again'. Such measures have supported the deepening of the curriculum reform nationwide. In addition, in 2007 a conference on high school curriculum reform involving the collaboration of a number of major cities advocated that the whole education system nationally and all schools at various levels should robustly implement the curriculum reform and accelerate the reform of university entrance exams so that a positive social environment and public setting for the new curriculum implementation is established.

In 2008 middle school graduates nationwide faced the high school entrance exams under the new curriculum. The Ministry of Education issued a document ('File No 6 [2008]') further reinforcing that 'the practice of using the sum of subject marks as the sole recruitment standard should be changed. Changes should be made in terms of middle school graduates' academic examinations, comprehensive quality assurance and high school recruitment'. It recognised that 'to different degrees, in some districts and schools, there still exist incorrect practices of instruction according to what is to be examined, stereotyped training, recruitment based on marks alone, unethical competition amongst candidates and using graduating rates as the sole criteria for evaluating schools and teachers.' All these have led to excessive workloads for students and impair their health mentally and physically. They have also misinterpreted the direction of the teaching and learning reform in the K-12 schools and have affected the overall development of the curriculum reform. The document further stated that during the previous four years, in the process of implementing the high school entrance examinations reform program, the local authorities have followed the Ministry of Education's requirement to change the practice of using the simple sum of subject marks as the only recruitment criteria and have consequently endeavoured to make real achievements in reforming academic examinations, quality assurance and high school entrance recruitment. Through proactive experimentation and progressive implementations, they have generated a number of practical solutions to conform with the requirements for quality education, which have led to the re-structuring of high school entrance examinations so that they are aligned with the new curriculum and lay a solid foundation for nationwide implementation of the high school entrance exams reform programme.

The university entrance examination system has also experienced substantial breakthroughs. The four provinces of Shandong, Guangdong , Hainan and Ningxia have consecutively issued university entrance examination proposals that are aligned with the new curriculum. Two-year pilot projects have demonstrated that the content of assessment is generally aligned to the required curriculum standards. The proposals have been well received by teachers and students and by members of the public in the piloted provinces. In Jiangsu Province, although this triggered some dispute at the level of practice, the university entrance examinations proposals and the direction of the reform have been regarded as 'symbolic'. In 2008, the Ministry of Education issued guidelines for the new university entrance examinations, asking the local authorities to expedite the high school examination reform and the system of assessment and enhance its credibility and accountability under the guidance of the central government and administrated by the provinces. Reform of the content of examinations was to be further expanded so as to link more closely with the new high school curriculum. It was also to link with real life and real issues and put priority on assessing students' ability to analyse issues and solve problems employing the knowledge they have acquired. A multi-level assessment method that realigns university entrance examinations, high school tests and quality assurance of school-based testing was to be further explored. The intention was to ensure that the university entrance examinations better accommodate the further deepening of the quality of education symbolised by the gradual implementation of the new high school curriculum to address the pressing need for innovative citizens to build the new nation and to meet the expectations of the public on education quality and equity.

Reflection and comments

How can the issues and difficulties that have arisen during the new curriculum implementation process be analysed? To be frank, there have been reservations expressed in academic circles about the goals, structure, contents, teaching and learning approaches, assessment and examinations reform as well as curriculum administration and policy systems. At a practical level, in the process of transforming the new concepts into educational practice, it has been not uncommon to have variations in actual practice. In addition, it takes time for the new concepts to be understood and achieved, and involves a long cyclical process requiring experimentation and experience, practical adjustment and reinvestigation and further practice. What has been more important is that everyone involved in the implementation of the new curriculum has developed and matured enormously in the context of traditional education environments and deep historic influences, so even if teachers can conceptually accept and appreciate the goals of the new curriculum, it is not uncommon for them to continue employing the old quality benchmarks to evaluate the new curriculum and hence come to the conclusion that the quality of students' learning has declined. Moreover, in some areas where the new curriculum is supposedly being implemented, the daily education administration policies, assessment systems, research priorities and teacher training models are still using old methods and approaches and this has severely impaired teachers' enthusiasm and initiative in employing the new curriculum. All these factors, in addition to problems of limited curriculum resources, teacher staffing levels, class sizes, as well as the general media environment and parents' expectations, have to varying degrees affected, diminished and even hindered the effective implementation of the new curriculum and its potential outcomes.

The question remains after seven years' implementation of the new curriculum of how to evaluate the K-12 education today. In districts and schools where the new curriculum has been solidly implemented, it is clear that, compared with school life of five or ten years ago, the new curriculum has provided real change in schools, classrooms and amongst teachers and students. Relationships between teachers and students are more harmonious, the classroom atmosphere is more democratic, students are treated with more respect, and the curriculum content has moved closer to students' own experiences. Knowledge acquisition is no longer the only goal of learning. The initiative and enthusiasm of schools and teachers have been further motivated by the unprecedented improvement in teachers' professional development.

However, in reviewing and re-evaluating the six goals first proposed in the pilot version of the Basic Education Curriculum Guidelines, it is hard not to feel despondent. In terms of daily teaching and learning, what are still areas of concern are the amount of knowledge grasped, the speed of the acquisition of skills, the processes and methods used, and the attitudes and values that still linger. Curriculum activities and initiatives in the areas of physical education and the arts are threatened as the majority of students' time is spent on drill work in literacy, mathematics and foreign languages. Some teachers remain enthusiastic about teaching in active, deep and sophisticated ways but the number of teachers who are comfortable with the basic requirements of the new curriculum standards is still relatively low. Those daily lessons that are not observed or watched, which account for 80 to 90 per cent, still use old fashioned methods of instruction such as drill work by students. Organised tests and evaluations and excessive requirements of the high school entrance exams are not uncommon and ranking of schools, classes and students according to examination marks is still commonplace. What is more, the question arises as to what extent have our schools and local authorities been equipped with the capacity for stronger curriculum construction and management? Has our nation set up a sustainable development mechanism for the curriculum?

The issues and comments above may sound harsh, but there is no doubt that they exist. The reason why we raise these questions here is in the hope that, in ten years' time, through the efforts of the various shareholders, these education policies and reforms will be able to make consistent contributions to curriculum mechanisms that are healthy, rigorous and sustainable, so that each student has the opportunity to grow energetically and dynamically.

One significant issue that continues to confront the curriculum development programme is how to set up a dialogue mechanism that embodies the spirit of democracy, equality and consultation, so as to forge a favourable academic environment to better promote the rigorous development of education. In recent years, the debates around curriculum reform, in particular the different and even opposing voices among the reform processes that are being enforced by the government, are in fact the hallmarks of social progress and intellectual prosperity. However, we should also clearly realise that there remains deep concerns, especially in terms of the fact that some important decisions are made subjectively rather than being based on facts and investigation, and some exceptional cases are exaggerated to be general. With the further development and the advanced implementation of the reform policy, a situation of 'one order, one voice' in the education domain no longer exists and, more importantly, our government, academics and the media need to learn how to jointly build an academic and education culture that is democratic, open, scientific, equal, dialogic and consultative. This is not only the main pursuit of this round of curriculum reform; it will also have profound historic implications for the nation's rejuvenation, economic progress and academic prosperity as well as for the healthy growth of individuals within it.

Conclusion

If there were no dilemmas, frustrations or hesitations that would mean that the reform has not yet set sail. If there were no questions or challenges that would mean that the reform is just superficial. If there were no disputes or even protests that would mean that the reform has not reached the core of the problems and issues. We know that real reform is accompanied by systematic restructure and that it will impact upon cultural traditions and will touch people's souls and beliefs.

Therefore, when confronting the various challenges involved in this significant curriculum reform that have been outlined in this chapter, what we need to do is to establish positions based on facts and realities while accommodating disputes and complexities, and resolutely move forward. We need to move forward courageously and discard inaccurate or ill-informed assumptions and viewpoints and steer away from areas of misunderstanding. Most importantly, we need to cultivate the ability to distinguish between what is right and correct and what is not.

2 Constructing a cross-cultural teacher professional learning community in the context of China's basic education curriculum

*Changyun Kang, Gaalen Erickson,
Janette Ryan and Ian Mitchell*

This chapter gives an account of the broader issues involved in major curriculum reform and the types of challenges and difficulties that can arise in any such massive undertaking, drawing from such experiences worldwide and pointing to the lessons to be learnt. It focuses on the types of professional development required to support teachers in changing their pedagogy and curriculum to better align them with the aims of China's education reform programme. It discusses the role that teacher research and support through professional learning communities can play in bringing about the required change and transformation in enduring and sustainable ways.

Introduction

China's Eighth Curriculum Reform was launched a decade ago and is regarded as the most radical and wide-reaching curriculum reform covering every aspect of K-12 education. As can be seen from the previous chapter, the reform is ambitious and wide-ranging, covering curriculum aims, structure, content, implementation, assessment and administration. The reform has had implications for several related areas such as teacher professional development and teacher education. As outlined in the previous chapter, the depth and breadth of this reform has meant that substantial changes are required to teachers' pedagogy and, in turn, this has highlighted the need for professional development support in order for both new and experienced teachers to be able to deal with the magnitude of the changes required in the contexts of their own classrooms and schools. Such an ambitious reform could never be easy to achieve and events have revealed some problems with the initial, top down strategies for implementation, especially in terms of promoting the necessary professional development for teachers to address the requirements of the new curriculum reform programme.

This chapter looks at an ongoing international collaborative research project that seeks to provide the types of professional development required by using a more bottom up approach based on the development of 'Professional

Learning Community' (PLCs) through a project called the 'Learning and Developing Community' (LDC). Taking advantage of a unique opportunity, the authors initiated a cross-cultural project in the context of this national educational reform project. In this chapter we describe the progress to date of this ongoing collaborative research and development project involving teachers, schools and district leaders from different regions in China working with Chinese, Canadian and Australian academics on changing teacher practices through professional learning communities. This model draws on the success of such communities in Australia and Canada in bringing about substantial teacher development. This project provides a vivid scenario of Chinese teachers' collective and collaborative efforts of developing 'hybrid' PLC models with the characteristic of complex nested and interconnected learning communities extending outward from student learning, to teacher learning, school level learning, district level learning, and finally cross-cultural level learning. Drawing upon four years of rich, descriptive data, we have employed a 'complexity thinking' perspective to elucidate and examine the conditions of the teachers' professional learning communities created by the project to enhance their professional development and to meet the educational changes in the context of Chinese culture and educational reform. This project also demonstrates the mobility of ideas about teacher professional development and student learning across cultural systems.

The professional learning communities in the LDC project described here enable teachers to engage in forms of collaborative inquiry into a variety of pedagogical issues that flow from the reform. This chapter reflects on the complexities of teacher change in curriculum reform especially one that demands such levels of teacher change. It concludes by describing the benefits of this project and the LDC communities for all of the stakeholders involved, including in terms of two-way learning between educators across cultural systems, and the necessary principles for effective cross-cultural work.

Teacher development in the context of ongoing curriculum reform

China's ongoing, large scale curriculum reform of school educational practices over the past decade is regarded as one of the most important events in China's educational system (Guan and Meng 2007, Liu 2006, Paine and Fang 2006, Zhong 2006, Zhu 2005, Yu and Kang 2003, Zhu and Kang 2002). The reform encompasses fundamental and extensive reform of curricular content and pedagogical approaches. These reforms were launched with the release of the Guidelines on Chinese Basic Education Curriculum Reform published by the Ministry of Education (MOE) in 2001.

Quality education, where each student reaches their full educational potential, is at the centre of this reform. This is in contrast to the former system (the 'two basics'), which was dominated by examinations and rote recall of information. The six major aims of the reform are identified as follows in the Guidelines issued by the MOE:

- Changing the teaching and learning focus from the 'two basics' (basic knowledge and basic skills) to broader overall aims including active learning, and developing appropriate attitudes and values.
- Developing a new balanced and comprehensive curriculum structure that has a better balance of teaching hours for different subjects and that caters for the needs of students with diverse background in diverse regions.
- Changing from an overemphasis on knowledge from textbooks to a greater focus on linking the students' learning with real life and the development of modern society, science and technology.
- Changing traditional pedagogy, advocating students' more active and engaged learning, and nurturing their ability in the areas of sharing, co-operation and communication.
- Establishing an assessment system that promotes students' all-round development as well as teacher's professional development.
- Implementing a three-level curriculum administration system that involves co-ordination and communication structures between and among national, local and school levels.

The speed of this systemic reform is immense. In 1998, the government organised education experts to formulate national curriculum standards for each school subject area. By 2001, the MOE had issued curriculum standards for Grades 1 to 9 and in 2003 for Grades 10 to 12. The new curriculum standards were adopted in 38 experimental districts/counties across the country in 2001. By 2005, every initial grade of primary and middle school was required to begin using the new curriculum. The new high school curriculum was piloted in four provinces across the country in 2004, then extended to 25 provinces, and was expected to be complete in 2010 (see Chapter 1 for further details).

The huge size of China and its population, together with the multiple levels of government suggests that achieving system-wide reform will be an extremely complex process with all stakeholders in the chain of whole system reform, particularly the teachers and school administrators, confronting significant challenges and difficulties.

Since the implementation of the new curriculum, three surveys were conducted in 2001, 2003 and 2005 respectively, to evaluate the outcomes in the pilot experimental areas by the expert groups organised by the MOE. The evaluation examined the implementation process and identified a number of important issues. The most significant issues and challenges include: the tremendous differences in needs and resources between the city and the rural areas in implementing the reform; the insufficiency of curriculum resources as well as financial resources; the fact that teaching practices and resources are inadequate in many of the districts surveyed (e.g. teaching practices still focused on textbooks and reliance on rote recall); the lack of professional development support for the teachers; overcrowded classrooms; and increased teaching workloads. All these findings point towards the importance of providing more resources for teachers' professional development to bring about the desired changes in teaching practices and educational outcomes.

To support this reform and ensure its sustainability, the MOE established 18 Research Centres for Basic Education Curriculum Reform at various universities and institutes across China to develop a supportive system of professional development for teachers. These centres act as a bridge between academic research and teaching practice to develop in-service teacher education programmes.

China is a country with all authority flowing down through successive levels of command. This situation means that the main implementation model was initially dominated by a 'government orientated and top-down' model. While the MOE recognised the importance of promoting school teachers' professional development, their approach was to design a series of training materials and models for the new curriculum implementation. The Ministry also strongly advocated school-based research, in an attempt to address the shortcomings of a purely top-down implementation model. In practice however, the executive model emerged as the primary vehicle for change.

The need for improved teacher education and teacher development to support the reform process has been recognised as a highest priority in China's 11th 5 Year Plan (2006–2010). There have been numerous attempts over the past five to ten years to improve teacher professional development (see, for example, Paine, Fang and Wilson 2003 and Paine and Fang 2006). Ma *et al.* (2009) surveyed several hundred teachers on their reactions to the reform and found that, while the teachers were generally supportive of the goals of the reform, they were finding it difficult to actually implement. More effective strategies and procedures need to be applied to further strengthen teacher training and professional development. Some Chinese scholars (Ma and Kang 2007) realised that teacher training is a long-term task, especially when confronting such an immense curriculum reform with multi-levelled focuses. In addition to teacher training programmes, more immediate models based on classroom problems and classroom-based teacher inquiry have been recommended (Yu and Kang 2003).

There are many examples of professional learning communities in China, including some in areas that are remote and economically deprived (see Hannum and Park 2007, Paine and Fang 2007, Sargent and Hannum 2008). Sargent and Hannum's (2008) study of PLCs in schools in rural Gansu Province (covering 656 teachers in 77 schools) found that PLCs operate even within remote areas but that they are constrained by a lack of support systems and leadership.

PLCs in China are generally used to disseminate new curriculum and pedagogy and share teaching strategies (ibid.) but very little detailed information exists that illustrates precisely how they work on the ground. As Sargent and Hannum (2008) point out, 'there is little systematic empirical research on factors that contribute to the strength of these communities. Even less is known about the role of teacher professional communities in rural China' (ibid.: 4).

The initial intention of launching the LDC project (which is described more fully later in this chapter) was, learning from the experience in Western countries, to construct and support teacher professional learning communities and to explore a bottom-up approach to better support teacher professional development in the curriculum reform context in China. In Western contexts, an important aspect of many effective teacher learning communities involves the active participation of university academies (Erickson, Mitchell, Minnes, Brandes and Mitchell 2005). How to construct and support teacher professional communities in this way in China is one important aspect of this project.

Teacher professional learning communities: a Western perspective

The above discussion about the uniqueness and complexity of the curriculum reform in China suggests that it will be difficult for foreign colleagues to imagine and is well beyond their experiences in their own cultures. Therefore the research experiences and models that work in Western society should not simply be imported to China; rather one purpose of our project was to explore this issue of mobility of professional development models.

Learning from the era of big curriculum projects

The period from the early 1960s to the late 1970s was an era of well funded, big curriculum projects in Western education. The approach taken involved eminent educators designing detailed curriculum materials based on their views about what should constitute good teaching. The Humanities Curriculum Project and the Nuffield Science project were two examples in Britain, Man a Course of Study (MACOS) was a prominent American example and the Australian Science Education Project (ASEP) a later Australian example. These materials typically included specific classroom activities, often including student workbooks; indeed the phrase 'teacher proof' was often used to describe these materials (Connelly 1980, Doyle and Ponder 1977) to reflect the extent to which the materials attempted to limit teacher independence and decision making and ensure that the same activities would be done in the same way in all classrooms. By the late 1970s, it was becoming clear to researchers on educational change that this approach had not worked (Fullan and Pomfret 1977, Fullan 1991).

The literature on educational change embodies a singular dichotomy. There is on the one hand, a voluminous collection of prescriptive literature – strategies for educational innovation that purport to tell practitioners how to accomplish change in concrete school settings. On the other hand, there is a growing body of descriptive studies which indicate that the actual amount of change in schools falls significantly below expectations.

(Doyle and Ponder 1977:1)

Fullan and Pomfret (1977) pointed out that the fact that a school or teacher reports that they have adopted a particular programme tells little about how this is actually being implemented and the extent to which the implementation is faithful to the intentions of the developers. They reported that frequently the way a programme was implemented bore little relation to the intentions of the designer and in fact represented little or no actual change in the teacher's practice.

With the wisdom of hindsight, there were (at least) three deficiencies in this approach. One was a lack of appreciation of the multi-faceted complexities of teaching. The materials focused on the tasks the students would be asked to do and the way the classroom was intended to be organised – typically from what was often called 'teacher centred' to what was called 'student centred'. There is more to teaching than this, but what are often subtle, albeit crucial changes in, for example, the way teachers and students interact were not seen as (at least) equally important aspects of the intended change and were not articulated. This left teachers without advice on what were necessary new skills or even awareness of their need. A second deficiency was a lack of understanding about teacher change. The materials gave no ownership or control to the teachers; not only is this a likely cause of resentment and resistance – teachers were just being told to teach differently – but it also denied teachers the opportunity to build meaning for what was intended. This was not the case with teachers who were involved in the trialling and developing phases of these types of curriculum change projects. They were operating as partners with the developers and the trialling phase often reported success that was not replicated with teachers who were just given the materials. A third deficiency was the lack of appreciation of the significance of the changes in how students were expected to learn, often in ways that involved much more independence and much more reflection on what was being done. There were unrecognised issues of student change and the need to support this that were just as important as the issues of teacher change.

These events and subsequent insights occurred in Western, not Chinese contexts, but we thought it quite possible that they might be useful in making sense of what was happening in the new Chinese context. Our project is situated in China's current curriculum reform, which has been implemented in a top down model that reflects China's traditional culture and unique size and government structure. Our intention is not to criticise what has happened so far, but to see if lessons from the West can inform the development of a Chinese version of a bottom up approach that gives teachers much more ownership and control of the change process.

Teacher knowledge and the role of teacher research

The research on system level change is a very different literature from the field of teacher research and the Western authors' experiences with teacher research were not in the context of enacting systemic reform of the magnitude envisaged in the Chinese reform programme. Indeed this goal was very distant from our experiences. In the 1980s, Mitchell and Erickson were both interested in research into student learning in Science that challenged existing classroom pedagogy and they soon realised that carrying this research further could not be done without rich and on-going interactions between this 'theory' and new practice. This would require teachers researching, developing and analysing such practice. It was Kang, with his central involvement in the development and commencement of the China reform, who identified the potential value of teacher research in enacting system level change, in what is the world's biggest educational system.

Teacher research has both product and process outcomes that are important for this project: the process outcomes are addressed in the next section. In terms of product, teacher research generates the sorts of new knowledge and wisdom needed in implementation of new curriculum and does this in highly authentic and contextualised ways. As mentioned above, achieving the intended changes of the 1960s and 1970s required a much broader range of wisdom of practice than was realised at the time. Teacher researchers, who have to confront these 'deficiencies' in pedagogical wisdom, are best placed to both identify what is needed (a critically important issue) and then to develop the necessary understandings.

As part of the LDC project, we have run focus group meetings in several provinces and districts with groups of teachers, principals, consultants ('resource teachers'), district level administrators and academics. While these many meetings can only reflect a tiny, and not even very representative sample of educators in China (we have had no meetings with teachers in remote rural areas, for example, apart from in Dongsheng in Erdos City in Inner Mongolia where several schools are part of the LDC network), there have been strong recurring themes. These meetings support the research of Ma *et al.* (2009) that the teachers are generally supportive of the overall goals of the reform. Indeed they are more supportive than any of our comparable Western experiences. Many teachers have said that China is developing fast and taking an increasingly important place in the world; they are proud of this and feel a personal responsibility to play their role in this development by developing their practice, a theme echoed by the teachers in Sargeant and Hannum's (2008) study. However one recurring theme was that the materials produced to support the reform did not identify or address critical questions of implementation. Questions such as: How do you get all students to participate in group based problem solving? and: What can open ended tasks look like in Maths? were raised repeatedly. Behind these questions (and generally not explicitly raised) were questions such as: What new student and teacher behaviours are required?

In general, we found that teachers were facing many difficulties and challenges in the context of this reform and the changes required to teaching practice. For Chinese teachers, the key issue is how to handle the transition from knowledge-centred and examination-orientation to a more student-centred and learning-centred classroom. Here we need the Western literature to support our view that teacher inquiry is the most effective way to promote teachers' transition, rather than the traditional unidirectional training programme. The value and fundamental function of teacher inquiry for teacher' professional development in the context of current China's curriculum reform is one of the major thrusts of this project.

Professional learning communities

Research is often framed as a dispassionate exercise, concerned with developing new knowledge, but the process of engaging in collaborative teacher research has turned out to be as rewarding as the product outcomes for the participants. It stimulates and sustains teaching innovation, positions teachers as the generators and hence owners of new wisdom and also develops teacher leaders.

Experiences in Australia and Canada demonstrate that effective and sustainable changes in teaching and learning practices at both the classroom and institutional level can be built through collaborative models that give consideration to local contexts and individual teachers (Samaras, Beck, Freese and Kosnik 2008). These models have been built through years of teacher-led research supported by school leaders and university academics working together in professional learning communities (Erickson, Mitchell, Minnes, Brandes and Mitchell 2005, Mitchell and Mitchell 2001).

Teacher research can be conceived as an individual process; there are several reasons why we have considered it essential that it be done collaboratively in professional learning communities. These can be summarised by saying that the process advantages of teacher research require a collaborative group, the group fulfils a number of roles:

- It encourages and supports risk taking. Crucial to change is that teachers regularly try and then build on things that are outside their comfort zone of existing practice. One of the findings from the research on the era of big programmes was that teachers commonly did not move beyond what they were used to doing. Trying something new is always risky, something not well appreciated by systems. Hearing accounts from colleagues of risks they have taken and the (commonly successful) outcomes of these encourages others to try something outside their comfort zone.

- Teaching is a very busy job dominated by daily (hourly) demands – the class is at the door and must be taught now. A regular meeting reminds teachers to continue to innovate and to actually implement their good intentions.

- Meetings also have an important role in affirming new practice. Teaching is a lonely profession in that teachers typically operate alone in their classrooms and have limited experiences of having colleagues respond to (or observe) what they are doing and picking up these ideas for their own practice.

- Researching collaboratively means that new wisdom is commonly socially constructed; ideas and insights emerge and develop gradually as different people react to accounts of practice and share their different applications and extensions of these – the whole is commonly greater than the sum of the parts here.

- Finally, having a group allows ideas to be tested and validated in a range of contexts. One criticism of teacher research is that what emerges from any one teacher's classroom must always be highly contextualised and hence of limited generalisability. If an idea from one teacher's classroom has been tried, extended and polished in several others, then this criticism is much harder to sustain.

What does it look like?

Following a visit to Canada in 2005 to find new models of curriculum reform (as part of the first stage of the curriculum reform programme, as described in Chapter 1), to address the dilemmas and challenges outlined above and in the previous chapter, and as a result of observing teacher PLCs, Dr Kang Changyun (the lead author of this chapter) established the first PLC, called the 'Learning and Developing Community' (*Xuexi yu fazhan gongtongti*). The LDC project was initially established in Beijing in one school, Beijing Zhongguancun Number 4 Primary School, in collaboration with the school's principal, Ms Liu Keqin. Ms Liu is also a leader in the curriculum reform programme and is a key member of China's National 1–6 Primary Mathematics Curriculum Standards Development Group. The success of the Beijing group not only attracted interest from schools in Inner Mongolia, and led to the establishment of an LDC network across Inner Mongolia (now including the very remote ethnic minority area Eqi District), networks have since also spread to several other regions and provinces such as Shandong, Xinjiang, Hubei and Guangdong, and involve school and district level leaders and teachers.

In the LDC project, teachers meet and share goals, innovative practice and reflections on these. Over time they build richer shared meanings for all of these. This means that the discourse is often at a fairly specific level, relating to a particular classroom event for example. However critical to the process is that the discussion does regularly move to a more general level;

to help make sense of what may seem to be rather different events. In Western experiences these new insights typically emerge discontinuously and often unexpectedly. The following example, from Du Haijing, a Grade 4 Mathematics teacher and a member of the LDC, illustrates a teacher developing more general insight from a specific experience.

> *In the past, I would instruct like this: firstly, I would present the situation, followed by the Math question. Secondly, I would ask the students to think about the question and then do group work and share their ideas. I would observe and then ask the students with different solutions to come up and write their answers on the blackboard. Finally, I would share my solution with the class or ask a student who understands my method to do this.*
>
> *I have been teaching in this way for a long time before I realised that, during group work, most of the time there is the scenario of one speaking, the rest listening, some kids are even wandering around as they already know the answers and don't need to listen to others. Conversation with other colleagues ignited my passion for trying a new approach. I asked each group to begin with the question: How many solutions does your group have? My purpose was to promote student collaboration after thinking of individual solutions.*
>
> *Then I started to observe the effectiveness of learning and collaboration among the students. I noticed that, after independent thinking, they began a thorough discussion because they needed to find the differences and relationship among the solutions, in order to categorise them. The collaboration now involved one speaking, others listening, pondering, reflecting and providing feedback. No student was isolated. A better learning result was achieved.*

Collaboration between teachers and academics and the roles of academic colleagues

In Western contexts, the role of academic collaborators has been important. However this has meant a rethinking of the traditional top down relationships. It has been essential that the two groups have been seen as bringing different but equally valued sorts of expertise to the collaboration. In particular this has meant the academics recognising that there are important types of knowledge about practice that are not well represented in the traditional literature and which can be just as sophisticated and profound as other types of wisdom in education. This does not mean, however, that the academics have not had important roles. One is the apparently simple one of providing affirmation, stimulation and support. Academics are typically well placed to affirm teachers work by highlighting the new aspects of wisdom and the potential value of these. Another is helping teachers reframe what is being done in ways that allow generalisations to emerge. This involves choosing moments to shift the thinking to a bigger picture theme that links apparently disparate experiences. Over time, the teachers build this skill, but initially it is one that is more familiar to academics whose work involves looking for underlying themes. As a project matures, another academic role has been to identify new challenges that build on and extend what has gone before, but continue to sustain innovation. Finally, the different work situations of academics mean that they can more easily convey the wisdom of a group to broader audiences to link different groups and provide links to different levels in the system.

Elements for making cross-cultural collaboration work

We have identified several principles that we think are important for this type of cross-cultural collaborative project, at least in the Chinese context:

- recognition of *local contexts* and *teacher agency and commitment*;
- *leadership* from school principals;
- *support* from district and regional governments;
- *guidance and encouragement* from local and international university *academics*;
- partnerships and relationships based on *mutual respect and genuine dialogue*.

In an ideal world, we would be able to extract general principles from all of the factors that have made the cross-cultural aspects of this project successful, but this is not the case. In what follows, we report some more idiosyncratic factors that have been crucial to this project; we must leave readers to decide if and how they could be relevant to projects of their own.

For this project, Kang played a crucial role in organising the school communities and recruiting key players such as the school principals and district consultants. Without his knowledge and professional relationships with the participating schools and school districts, this project would not exist. Furthermore, he is the primary connection with the rest of the international project participants, although all of the project team members, as described below, have participated in a number of meetings and conferences involving the teachers and administrators. Put more generally, although the driving ideas about goals and process originated in Western experiences, this project was led and directed by Chinese. With hindsight, it is relevant that, unlike many projects in third world contexts, the Western partners did not 'arrive' with substantial (any) funding for which they would be accountable. Had this been the case, the way early decisions were taken may have been different in ways that would probably have been detrimental. The design and growth of the project is detailed below, but the initial plans were general intentions that guided Kang and his Chinese colleagues in reacting to and capitalising on events whose specifics could not have been predicted. The growth and progress was regularly discussed with the Western partners who offered reactions and sometimes advice, but never anything resembling shared control. A consistent feature of the project, from the perspective of the Western partners has been how quickly the Chinese partners have been able to understand and adapt to Chinese contexts thinking from a wide range of interconnected areas. A mantra has been to 'go with the flow' and trust the sense of the decisions taken – this is really an elaboration of the last dot point above.

There was one stage where the early interactions were a little different. In their first visits to China, there were several occasions when Mitchell, Erickson, Kang and his colleague Li Yuping ran joint sessions where we were presenting aspects of the project to different groups. The notion of these being interactive, involving activities such as case discussions and workshops of teaching activities was not part of the Chinese experience. As this was directly involving Mitchell and Erickson's practice, they were persistent and insistent about aspects of session design. The sessions were successful and this approach rapidly became part of the personal practice of Kang and Li; as has happened so often in Western contexts, they needed to experience practice outside their comfort zone of familiarity to build meaning for it.

Design features of the project

One of our primary interests in creating and participating in this project was to explore how the development of teachers' professional learning communities can promote teachers' understandings and practices to address some of the pedagogical challenges arising from the educational reform in China. In our early conversations, we discussed some of the Western approaches that were used to create teacher PLCs and how they might be used to design a programme to assist the teachers and administrators in China to cope with the difficulties and challenges encountered in the reform. While most of Western team members' previous experience was restricted to establishing teacher groups, we knew that if we were going to try to address the more general systemic aspects of the reform agenda in China that we had to conceptualise a process that consisted of a series of inter-related systems and not focus just at the classroom level. Hence we have described our overall approach in the project in terms of a series of nested learning communities or systems as shown in Figure 2.1.

We have described the above concentric circles as nested 'learning systems' drawing in part upon the language and perspectives in the emerging field of 'complexity thinking' (Davis and Sumara 2006). While our earlier discussion of a professional learning community is still relevant, the broader framing of inter-dependent learning systems has some distinct advantages since it allows us to put the learning system of the school student at the centre, given that this ought to be the primary aim of all educational systems. It also enables us to point out that there is a high degree of inter-relatedness between the various levels of practices. In LDC our initial work was at the school and

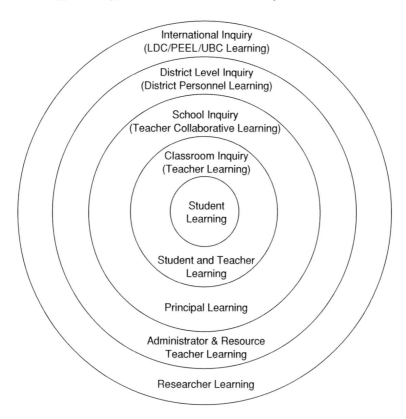

Figure 2.1 Nested Learning Systems

classroom levels but with the clear understanding that student learning was at the heart of our various inquiries and pedagogical activities. Our subsequent activities have extended to developing connections and exchanges between schools and teachers in different districts and have initiated some district level inquiry projects. As we look to 'scale up' our activities there will have to be a number of other clusters of schools, districts and academics created to form a type of network of associated learning systems across different districts and regions in China. The international research team makes connections with and between these learning systems at the international level, by sharing and discussing ideas about effective professional development models, curriculum and pedagogical practices in other contexts.

An important condition for the effective functioning of a learning system is diversity (Davis, Sumara and Luce-Kapler 2008) and this characteristic is very much in evidence in each of the learning communities that we have worked with and studied. For example, the participants in the school level communities in our project have a wide range of interests and backgrounds as they include the teachers, administrators, district level educational consultants and university academics. Each of these participants brings to the community differing concerns and practices: teachers being more concerned at pedagogical issues at the classroom level, like adapting their approaches so that they are more student-centred, in accordance with the new curriculum; school administrators and researchers focus more on approaches to enhance teachers' capability to creatively carry out the new curriculum based on local teaching conditions, as well as how to set up a supportive evaluation system; and academics may focus more on how to enhance the creation and dissemination of teachers knowledge and wisdom generated by the practices of the learning communities.

The scope and complexities of the curriculum reform in China have meant that achieving them is not easy. As in Canada and Australia, and in other countries experiencing major curriculum reform, it takes some time for these reforms to be implemented in local contexts and it requires much effort and fundamental re-thinking of ideas and perspectives about teaching and learning by teachers and school leaders. Consequently our work in the construction of these professional learning communities will be affected by many factors. As argued above, our endeavours to create and support a model of teachers' professional development must take into account the diversity of interests and practices of educators at all levels of the educational system and recognise the inherent relationships and inter-dependence of these issues and perspectives.

Creating and sustaining the LDC project

In this section we will focus on some of the features related to the establishment and subsequent nurturing of the LDC project. We begin with the important feature of leadership and how it was 'distributed' among the various participants. This notion of 'distribution of control' is another key feature of a complex learning system. We then move on to examine three phases of the project as it has emerged over the past four years.

Shared leadership and responsibility

There are several levels in terms of the leadership of the project, given the broad spectrum of stakeholders ranging from Chinese school-based educators to Chinese academics to foreign university academics. Given the nested structure of the project, each level has different goals and responsibilities. An important consideration in projects of this nature is to develop communicative structures that provide for some degree of coherence and co-ordination across these nested learning systems.

Right from the beginning, as the project was being conceptualised by the authors, a decision was made to begin our work with one school in Beijing. This would allow us to explore the viability of the 'professional learning communities' approach to teacher development in a Chinese educational context and, if successful, it would serve as an exemplar for other schools and districts. Kang selected a school where he had some previous professional contact with the school principal, Ms Liu Keqin. He then recruited another Chinese educator, Mr Li Yuping, (a teacher development consultant in Dongsheng school district in Inner Mongolia who was independently engaging in a more informal process of teacher inquiry) to come and work part-time at Zhongguancun No. 4 Primary school in Beijing with Principal Liu and her teachers.

As with the project as a whole, there was a form of distributed leadership at the school level. Li Yuping and Liu Keqin played a key role in initiating and subsequently supporting teacher inquiry into a variety of classroom practices and then creating teams of teachers to address larger issues of concern to the teachers and the school community. As the project progressed, a number of teachers began to take on greater leadership roles within their own teams and took on responsibilities for organising a school-wide conference to present the findings from their inquiries to a broader audience including community members and parents and university academics. As described in the next section, in the second year of the project these teachers were instrumental in organising and running a major conference in Dongsheng, the first annual conference of the LDC network, where over one hundred teachers made presentations on their inquiry projects to an audience of over 900 teachers, district personnel, and university educators.

Another form of leadership must occur at the project level where the issues are more focused on larger scale systemic change and maintaining the coherence of the project through the creation and management of communicative structures. Because the project is located both physically and culturally in China, Kang has played a key role in initially setting up the project in Zhongguancun No. 4 Primary School and in spending considerable time at the school with the principal, the teachers and Li Yuping explaining his ideas and vision for the project. While Kang, in the latter two years of the project has spent much more of his time in Canada at the University of British Columbia, he maintains close contact with all of the Beijing and Dongsheng participants and his academic and MOE colleagues through email, and other forms of electronic communication such as discussion forums and blogs. Clearly, Kang is the primary interface between the Chinese participants and the rest of the project team and has had the responsibility for initiating most of the Chinese publications that have emerged from the project to date (see Chapter 3 in this volume for the accounts of the project by Kang, Principal Liu and Li Yuping). Other project team members have also provided leadership in a number of different capacities: they have consulted and co-planned with Kang regarding overall project goals and approaches; they have maintained contact with teachers, school and district administrators and Chinese academics through a number of visits to China to consult directly with the teachers in their schools and to attend conferences; and they have taken primary responsibility for written accounts of the project for English audiences (see Erickson, Kang, Mitchell and Ryan 2008, Ryan, Kang, Mitchell and Erickson 2009).

As alluded to earlier, the communicative structures are essential to maintaining contact and coherence for a project where the four of us are situated in three different countries (Australia, Canada and England) and the educational context for the project is in China. It would not have been possible to even contemplate such a project, given the huge geographical distances between our respective home sites, were it not for the opportunities afforded us by the new digital technologies. Hence we have used extensively the electronic media – email, discussion forums, blogs, and video conferencing with Skype and other conferencing programmes. These have been essential tools, especially for Kang, to maintain contact with the many Chinese educators currently involved in the project. However, this claim is not meant to dismiss the importance of face to face contact and communication. We think that it was essential at the outset of the project for all of the team members to meet with the Chinese educators in their schools and classrooms to get to know them personally and professionally. These personal visits to schools and subsequently to conferences being organised by our Chinese collaborators in the project were critical in getting a much better sense of the educational and personal contexts in which these educators work. It was also crucial for the Chinese educators to see and converse with us regarding our perspectives and thoughts about many of the issues that they were addressing. And finally it is only through this type of personal contact that we were able to affirm their inquiries and work (as outlined above) and to create the conditions for 'mutual respect and genuine dialogue' – one of the principles for cross-cultural collaborative work that we stipulated above.

A developmental project

We can describe the LDC project to date in terms of several phases. In the first phase we launched the idea of a 'learning and developing community' (LDC) with the principal and teachers at Beijing Zhongguancun No. 4 Primary School, as outlined above. For the first six months Kang, Li, and some academic colleagues from Beijing Normal University worked with Principal Liu and her teachers. The priority in this phase was to set up teacher collaborative research teams at the school level that involved both the university academics and school-based educators to identify and then systematically address problems of practice that the teachers considered to be important as they adapted their teaching approaches to better align with the curriculum changes that had been introduced to them earlier by the Ministry of Education. Because of Li Yuping's joint appointment with the Dongsheng school district, after about six months a number of educators from Dongsheng visited the Beijing school and decided to join the LDC project. This was an important development, as it involved a commitment at the school district level and a number of schools became involved, thus moving the project to the next level of our nested communities and on to the second phase of the project. This second phase is characterised by the creation of a network of schools, connected by some common purposes and a desire to publicly share their inquiries and teaching approaches with other educators. This sharing occurs through the use of communicative structures such as discussion forums, common meetings and conferences, as well as published accounts of their inquiries in the form of published books.

Future directions

The third phase of the project is currently underway and it constitutes an important move to begin to 'scale up' the learning communities model to other school districts and to begin to involve more university academics in other regions of China. In addition to the intensive work in the Beijing Number 4 Primary School and a number of schools in Dongsheng school district, many schools in Shenzhen, Xinjiang, Shandong and Hubei have joined our project. These schools represent a diverse range from economically developed districts to developing districts; some are in cities and some are in more rural areas. It is worth noting that much of the work being done with teachers and school administrators in other districts and regions of China is being undertaken by teachers who have two or more years of experience with creating learning communities and inquiry projects in their own school. These 'teacher leaders' are now much more confident and have a good understanding of how these approaches can be carried out in classrooms and hence often have greater credibility with other teachers than would university academics, who typically have to make recommendations for teaching from theory or second-hand experience. Thus one of the original goals of our project, which was to increase the capacity of teachers to take on leadership roles with other teachers, is being realised much more quickly than we had anticipated. Our experience in Western contexts with this transition from a classroom teacher to confident and competent teacher leader in professional development contexts takes roughly four to five years, rather than the one or two years that we have observed with the Beijing and Dongsheng teachers.

We are also beginning to examine the ways in which teacher preparation programmes in China can be incorporated into the network structure. For example, two types of activities related to our project could be easily and quickly implemented in a teacher preparation programme. The first would be the use of the teachers' journals and writings about their inquiries in the coursework portion of a programme focusing on teaching and learning approaches. The second would be the placement of prospective teachers in classrooms of mentor teachers in our project schools where they could learn first hand about the nature and the value of teachers inquiring into their own and other teachers' practices. This is already happening at Beijing Number 4 school.

Further discussion

This project is a work in progress; as it proceeds the participants are researching in each of the circles in Figure 1. At the time of writing we have learnt quite a lot about the inner circles; as the project moves into its third phase we have as yet unanswered or imperfectly answered questions about the outer circles.

We have found that collaborative action research has been helpful and relevant to addressing both goals and challenges associated with the system driven curriculum reform. Substantial numbers of teachers in many schools have proved willing and able to engage in this practice and enhance their professional development. They have further proved to be proactive in dealing with the challenges that have arisen in the classrooms with the support of a professional learning community. This has demonstrated that the teacher can take an active role in the implementation of curriculum reform rather than being merely a passive implementer.

We have also found that ideas can cross-cultural boundaries. As discussed above, ideas about teacher research, professional learning communities and teacher learning and change that came from the West have proved useful in guiding what we have done. However, as discussed earlier, it has been crucial that the governance of the project has been led by the Chinese partners. We have also found that classroom issues of learning and ideas for teaching also cross-cultural boundaries (Erickson, Kang, Mitchell and Ryan 2008). However the professional conversations about all of these issues must be two way, not one way.

To a significant degree, the specific details of the development of this project have involved reacting to events that were often unpredictable, nevertheless, the development has followed the broad directions laid down at the outset. It has grown from one school to another and then more than one school district; there are features of Chinese culture and education culture that seem to be providing fertile ground for what has been very rapid growth. China is so huge that further scaling up will move well beyond the experiences of the Western participants. As multiple districts become involved in more parts of China, new types of 'networks of networks' will be needed that provide communication and mutual critique. The diversity of contexts within China means that it is likely that there will be diversity in the issues that matter most to the teachers and in how the networks operate. Nevertheless an important challenge will be to retain coherence without trying to retain central control. The objects of focus that will prove attractive and useful to teachers, school and districts leaders and other Chinese academics will need to be developed and refined in response to events.

References

Connelly, F. M. (1980) 'Teachers' roles in the using and doing of research and curriculum development', *Journal of Curriculum Studies* 12(2) 95–107.

Davis, B. and Sumara, D. (2006) *Complexity and education: Inquiries into learning, teaching and research*, Mahwah, NJ: Erlbaum.

Davis, B., Sumara, D. and Luce-Kapler, R. (2008) *Engaging minds: Changing teaching in complex times*, 2nd edn, New York: Routledge.

Doyle, W. and G. A. Ponder (1977) 'The practicality ethic in teacher decision-making', *Interchange,* 8(3) 1–12.

Erickson, G., Kang, C., Mitchell, I. and Ryan, J. (2008) 'Role of teacher research and cross-cultural collaboration in the context of curriculum reform in China', in C. Beck and C. Kosnik (eds), *Learning Communities in Practice*, Rotterdam, Netherlands: Sense Publishers.

Erickson, G., Mitchell, I., Minnes, C., Brandes, G. and Mitchell, J. (2005) 'Collaborative teacher learning: Findings from two professional development projects', *Teaching and Teacher Education*, 21(7) 787–798.

Fullan, M. (1991) *The new meaning of educational change*, New York: Teachers College Press.

Fullan, M. and A. Pomfret (1977) 'Research on Curriculum and Instruction Implementation', *Review of Educational Research*, 47(2) 335–397.

Guan, Q. and Meng, W. J. (2007) 'China's new national curriculum: Innovation, challenges and strategies', *Frontiers in Education in China*, 2(4) 579–603.

Hannum, E. and Park, A. (2007) *Education and Reform in China*, Abingdon, Oxon: Routledge.

Liu, K. Q. (2006) *Engaged education*, Beijing: Beijing Normal University Press. (in Chinese)

Ma, Y. P. and Kang, C. Y. (2007) 'The implementation and assessment of China's ongoing curriculum', Presentation in University of British Colombia, China.

Ma, Y. P., Yin, H. B., Tang, L. F. and Liu, L. Y. (2009) 'Teacher receptivity to system-wide curriculum reform in the initiation stage: a Chinese perspective', *Asia Pacific Education Review*. Online. Available HTTP: <http://www.springerlink.com/content/3295u1g904523626/> (accessed 12 May 2009).

Mitchell, I. and Mitchell, J. (2001) 'Constructing and sharing generalisable statements of teacher knowledge from context-specific accounts of innovative practice', American Educational Research Association Conference, Seattle, April 2001.

Paine, L. and Fang, Y. P. (2006) 'Reform as hybrid model of teaching and teacher development in China', *International Journal of Education Research*, 45: 279–289.

Paine, L. and Fang, Y. P. (2007) 'Challenges in reforming professional development', in E. Hannum and A. Park (eds), *Education and Reform in China*, Oxford: Routledge.

Paine, L., Fang, Y. P. and Wilson, S. (2003) 'Reform as hybrid model of teaching and teacher education', *International Journal of Educational Research*, 45(4–5) 279–289.

Ryan, J., Kang, C. Y., Mitchell, I. and Erickson, G. (2009) 'China's basic education reform: An account of an international collaborative research and development project', *Asia Pacific Journal of Education*, 29(4) 427–441.

Samaras, A., Beck, C., Freese, A. and Kosnik, C. (2008) (eds) *Learning Communities in Practice*, Springer.

Sargent, T. and Hannum, E. (2008) 'Doing more with less: Teacher Professional Learning Communities in resource-constrained primary schools in rural China', Conference on Poverty, Education, and Health in Rural China, University of Oxford, Oxford, 15–16 December 2008.

Yu, W. S. and Kang C. Y. (2003) 'The meaning of ongoing China's curriculum reform project', *Journal of The Chinese Society of Education*, 2003:11.

Zhong, Q. Q. (2006) 'Curriculum reform in China: Challenges and reflections', *Frontiers in Education in China*, 1(3) 370–382.

Zhu, M. (2005) 'A report on the current state of the basic education reform in China', A presentation at an invitational conference on University, Schools and Government in Educational Reform: International Perspectives held in October, 2005, Beijing.

Zhu, M. and Kang, C. (2002) *Approaching the New Curriculum: Dialogues with curriculum participants*, Beijing: Beijing Normal University. (in Chinese)

3 Collaborative narration: our story in a cross-cultural professional learning community

Changyun Kang, Keqin Liu and Yuping Li

This chapter provides an authentic first-hand account of the challenges facing teachers and educational leaders in China's curriculum reform. Written by key players in the reform programme, this chapter provides an insight into the dynamic work being done by a network of teacher researchers and professional learning communities across China. It outlines the challenges and pitfalls of this project and the rich and myriad strategies those involved in the project are employing to support and empower teachers in bringing about substantial and enduring changes to their educational philosophies and classroom practices.

This chapter is a narrative account of China's basic curriculum reform programme from the perspectives of three Chinese researchers, from a school, a school district and a university, respectively, and relates our personal experiences in an on-going cross-cultural teacher professional learning community project.

Over the past five years, we have been co-ordinating the teachers' Learning and Developing Community (LDC) project in Beijing, Inner Mongolia and other areas in China as part of a three country (China, Canada and Australia) collaborative Professional Learning Community project. The purpose of the LDC is to establish a professional research and learning community in order to assist and support teachers as they attempt to change their teaching and learning practices in line with the aims of China's curriculum reform programme as outlined in the previous chapters. In this chapter, we reflect upon the value of collaborative action research involving all participants in the context of curriculum reform and describe the characteristics and structure of the community in which teachers are positioned as the key players. Our research also reveals the importance of trans- and cross-cultural learning and how it can facilitate teachers to improve students' learning and the professional development of teachers as well as the advancement of schools and school districts in China.

Introduction and background

As can been seen from the existing literature on the curriculum reform programme in China, the voices of teachers and educational practitioners are relatively weak compared with those of academic researchers. The three authors of this chapter come from three different educational levels: one is from a primary school, one is from a school district and one is from a university. Here, our dialogue is based on our friendship developed in working together in the curriculum reform programme and our research collaboration over the past five years.

Dr Kang has been a visiting professor in the Faculty of Education at the University of British Columbia since 2004 but has retained his position as the Associate Director at the Research Centre for Science Education at Beijing Normal University. He was previously the executive Deputy Director of the Research Centre for Basic Education Curriculum which was set up by the Ministry of Education (MOE) to facilitate China's curriculum reform. He has been a key figure nationally in the curriculum reform programme since its inception.

Ms Liu Keqin is Principal of Beijing Zhongguancun Number 4 Primary School. She is Secretary-General of the Primary Education Committee in the Chinese Society of Education (CSE) and a key member of China's National 1–6 Mathematics Curriculum Standards Development Group. She is also a part-time Professor of Education at the Management College of Beijing Normal University. Principal Liu started her teaching career after graduating from teaching college many years ago. In the 1990s, she joined the 'Subject Research of Primary School Students' Project, collaborating with Beijing Normal University. It was this research experience that helped her to make the transition to become a teacher researcher. She was invited to participate in the research project that established the Standards for Mathematics Education in Compulsory Education and is the only teacher representative on this committee.

Mr Li Yuping is Associate Director of the Teaching and Learning Office in the Ministry of Education in Dongsheng District in Ordos City in Inner Mongolia. He is a senior teacher researcher with many years experience as a primary school teacher, principal, and curriculum facilitator. He is currently working as an education consultant and senior adviser on curriculum and pedagogical reform in Inner Mongolia and Beijing. He comes from the City of Ordos in the southwest of Inner Mongolia. He graduated from high school in 1981 and he became a 'minban' (community) teacher, teaching in a remote village in Inner Mongolia for ten years. He then taught in Haibowan District in Wuhai City in Inner Mongolia (located on the Yellow River between the Gobi and Ordos deserts) for five years, and worked as a teaching director for three years. Later, he worked as a teacher researcher for two years and as the Director in the Office of Teaching and Research for a further five years.

Context and aims of the project

In this new millennium, the 'old' China is experiencing an era of restoration, revival and prosperity. China's education is also experiencing a period of rejuvenation through the Eighth Basic Education Reform introduced since the People's Republic of China was established in 1949. As the Deputy Director of the Curriculum Research Centre for Basic Education at Beijing Normal University, Dr Kang was a key organiser and co-ordinator of this reform and has participated in the entire process of the reform since its inception. In 2004, Dr Kang visited the University of British Columbia and met the former director of the Teacher Education Research Centre at the University, Professor Gaalen Erickson, as well as the founder of the Australian PEEL (Project for the Enhancement of Effective Learning) teacher research project Dr Ian Mitchell and later, Dr Janette Ryan, who worked at that time in the Faculty of Education at Monash University with Dr Mitchell. Professor Erickson had been working with teacher professional learning communities in Canada for several decades and Dr Mitchell was the co-founder and co-ordinator of the PEEL teacher research network in Australia. Dr Ryan lived in China for several years and was interested in cross-cultural research and teaching and collaboration. We started our transnational research project from here. With guidance and support from Professor Erickson and Dr Mitchell, Dr Kang, Principal Liu and Li Yuping initiated the LDC project (Learning and Developing Community for Teachers) in Beijing and Inner Mongolia in order to support the introduction of the new curriculum reform programme amongst teachers and schools. In this chapter, we share our experiences in this project and outline how it has changed our work and that of the teachers working together with us in the LDC network.

The LDC project began at Beijing Zhongguancun Number 4 Primary School in the Haidian District of Beijing, in which more than 60 higher education institutions and research institutions are located. It is the heart of Chinese information technology and is called China's 'Silicon Valley'. The school has been established for six years and has 1,200 students. This relatively new school faces many challenges in this time of education reform. The curriculum reform advocates self-direction, self-exploration and co-operation in learning. However, like teachers in many Chinese schools, the teachers are accustomed to a 'systematic lecturing' approach to teaching so sometimes teachers can feel lost when students express different views in the classroom. On the one hand, many of the teachers in the school wish to participate in the curriculum reform; on the other hand, they are worried about a possible negative impact on students' test performance. Principal Liu is concerned to create an imaginative space for teachers to let their wisdom and knowledge shine through their teaching and to alleviate teachers' anxiety about education reform. The LDC project is serving the school well to meet this goal. At the beginning of this project, Principal Liu did not have a concrete goal; she merely hoped that teachers could learn to undertake research into the curriculum reform through this project. She hoped that teachers could cultivate their own capacity for learning, reflection, communication and co-operation in this project so that the school could develop into an effective learning community.

In 2000, at the beginning of the curriculum reform programme, Li Yuping was the Director of the Office of Teaching and Research in Haibowan District in Inner Mongolia. He supervised seven secondary schools and 13 primary schools and directed his colleagues to participate in this research project. At the initial stage, his colleagues were highly motivated and the educational administration office organised several training workshops. However, various kinds of conflicts and tensions began to emerge such as: Experts' ideas are good but how can we put these ideas into practice? All kinds of problems will come up in practice so who will help us to solve these problems? Will the reform have a negative impact on students' academic performance? Will parents and society more generally support the reform? How is the national curriculum reform effectively practised at the local district level?

Questions like these were raised more and more often as the reform was progressing and we realised that we had to reflect on our work and adjust our agendas. The LDC project was born in this context. Our experiences made us realise that teachers needed professional development in the context of the curriculum reform and that this needs to occur in a supportive environment and be supported by effective and co-operative research. Only when teachers become real practitioners of the curriculum is it possible to achieve success in any reform of curriculum, especially one that is so wide ranging and radical. We hoped to be able to solve not only problems but also to gain moral support through co-operative learning communities and effective co-operation between teachers and researchers.

How the LDC project works

Since August 2005, Beijing Zhongguancun Number 4 School has experienced three stages in this project. In the first year of the project, which we called the 'Enlightenment period', we communicated with teachers individually to arouse their research passion. We believed that real reform originates from teachers' transformation through research. Therefore, it was important to let teachers identify and work on their own questions and issues. The LDC research project groups teachers according to their shared interests with one professional researcher in every team. The professionals can thus provide different perspectives and cultivate teachers' thinking abilities. The biggest change teachers feel is that research is not remote from their teaching; research is part of teaching. In the second year, teachers started to become tired of the project; we called this period the 'Stagnation period'; the tension between research and teaching was obvious. It seemed that teachers could not see immediate changes arising from the research. The conventional administrative approach emphasises routines and conflicts with the research culture of innovation and uniqueness in teaching. We realised that we had to seek a balance between the stability of teaching routines and encouraging teachers' creativity. Meanwhile, we used the 'self-responsibility' model: teachers choose different projects according to their own interests. Many important projects are now using this model, such as the 'Document Research' project, the 'Teachers' Practice Knowledge' project, the 'School Environment Renovation' project and the 'Organisation of Student Groups' project. We adjust the models as we are using and practising them and revise our methods so that they are more effective. These relatively stable activities have meant that we have been able to develop more effective methods and make the research more meaningful for the participants. For example, we ask teachers to present their research at meetings and to make one-sentence comments in meetings, which is relatively easy for them.

The project has now entered into the third stage, the 'Development stage'. The teachers now enjoy communicating with each other and seek further exchanges of thinking and ideas and realise that all teachers have their own ideas to contribute. They communicate with their peers by seeking help and support for their problems in practice. More teachers actively seek more space and scope to improve their teaching and give students more freedom for their own development. In turn, the progress students are making gives teachers the motivation for further improvement.

In February 2006, the Dongsheng District of Ordos City in Inner Mongolia joined the project. It became the first school district to participate in the project and the project formulated a 'one school, one district' structure where individual schools and their school district become involved in the project. Now, in addition to Beijing and Inner Mongolia, many schools in Shenzhen, Xinjiang, Shandong and Hubei have joined our project. These include schools in economically developed districts and developing districts, in cities and in the countryside. So this is the basic structure for this project and it has been working very well to date.

A research network is also developing well. How do we get these schools to participate in this research? We have developed several different approaches that take advantage of a range of communication methods which are outlined below.

Internet-based research

1) Online discussion board: this is a conversation system based on the Internet. Our team members have a themed discussion once a week. The discussion is based on a real practice in schools. Every participant is an author. We learn from each other and build this online community together. So far, this discussion 'cafe' has hosted more than one hundred series of discussions and has become an important means of communication and co-operation among team members.

2) Team members build their own blogs and link to each other.

3) Electronic newsletters: every research site edits teachers' teaching stories and shares their leadership experience.
4) Project website: communication of information about the project takes place on this platform.

On-site communication in research bases

Online communication cannot replace the personal communication among project members. We make efforts to create an environment where teachers can easily and comfortably communicate with each other between and among the different research sites. These activities include:

1) Visits to different research sites and visits to classes: for example, two schools in Ordos have organised to regularly share their experiences.
2) Research classes: members work together for one or two weeks.
3) Annual conference: this is a large network event and all schools get together to share their experiences on an annual basis with teachers, principals, administrators, district and provincial officials, university academics and our international research project collaborators.

Teacher research and discussion forums

From the beginning of the project, we defined our conceptions of learning, reflection, practice, improvement, progress and communication in the context of teacher research. Teachers' research is different from purely academic research. It is research based on problems in practice and carried out with the aim of solving practical problems. Teachers focus more on doing research *through* teaching and doing research *for* teaching. The professional researchers involved in the project need to be able to understand the real situation of teachers and to be able to work together with teachers. Researchers are professional supports, not preachers. We work on this project using the following approaches. First, we encourage teachers to publicly share their experiences with others. For example, we have an academic discussion forum called 'Us as researchers' once every semester. Every teacher reflects on their own teaching experience and shares their stories with their colleagues. Another example is 'Discussion on Teaching Style Month' which is held once every academic year to encourage teachers to explore their own teaching styles.

At the beginning, teachers did not want to share their experiences or were afraid of not doing well in the discussions. We not only encourage teachers' participation but also do our best as role models. We do not act as leaders or experts but encourage teachers to join our conversations at any time. Sometimes, we help teachers to prepare Powerpoint presentations and demonstrate that an ordinary case or story can be unique and helpful to others through teachers' reflections. Later, we found more strategies and ways of working, such as everybody has to say something but cannot repeat others' opinions; they have to give an immediate one-sentence comment; lead the meeting by turns; share taking the meeting minutes, etc. These methods also help to improve teachers' communication with each other. Gradually, teachers have become used to opening their minds to others and to sharing stories and experiences with each other.

Second, we encourage teachers' collaborative work. We explore the most effective methods to encourage teachers to collaborate with each other. For example, we organise teachers to find the same topic and carry out research jointly. We write the school development plan collectively and carry out analysis, reflection and written summaries together at the end of the semester; and we discuss the particular cases of individual students and make diagnoses to find solutions together. These are the various ways that teachers are able to develop a collaborative identity.

Third, we engage in 'project recruitment'. Based on one project, we allow teachers to voluntarily make groups according to their own interests and expertise. For example, we introduce our school to guests who visit us; organise small meetings; and conduct joint research based on a topic. These activities help teachers to learn through collaborative and co-operative work. In our approaches to working co-operatively with all parties, we have teacher–teacher co-operation and teacher–student co-operation, we have class–class co-operation and school–family co-operation, and we have school–school co-operation and school–district co-operation. These diverse co-operative approaches help teachers to feel the excitement and rewards of collaborative work.

Fourth, we open our school to the outside. We invite our university colleagues to come to the school and communicate with teachers face-to-face so that teachers can develop new perspectives and learn new knowledge. We encourage teachers to invite university researchers to come into the classroom. Although teachers may not gain much information this way, the information they get is relevant to their daily teaching. Teachers also agree that this open-door teaching approach is very helpful. We believe that teachers can only gradually develop their own teaching knowledge and wisdom in the long run, rather than being 'crammed' full of knowledge and skills.

In terms of the topics and content of our research, we proposed 'three small' foci for the content of research: focus on 'small' phenomena; seek 'small' strategies; collect 'small' stories. 'Small' phenomena mean concrete problems, such as effective peer tutorship among students, students' participation in class, and finishing homework on time. 'Small' strategies are concrete and applicable methods to solve these 'small' problems, to help students participate in the class discussion. We use methods such as 'round talk', 'don't repeat', 'write on the blackboard'. 'Small' stories reflect these experiments and are written down for everyone to share. These 'three small' strategies reflect teachers' concerns and they are easy for teachers to accept. Compared with the traditional approach to research, this type of research is more accessible for teachers. Teachers often start their research without being aware that they are even doing research.

When we find relevant points, we improve our research methods. For example, in terms of effective observation techniques, we use methods such as 'focused' observation, class observation schedules, theme-based observation and student interviews. In terms of in-depth observation, we use 'risk prediction', 'new perspectives', 'case comparison' and 'three-round inquiry'. In terms of effective sharing, we use 'thinking while doing', 'theme-based sharing' and 'home visits'. When we improve our methods, we also improve their effectiveness and impact.

Cultivating a research culture is an important part of our research. We advocate building a democratic classroom for students but in fact our teaching and research have not been open. We advocate learning by doing, but our classroom teaching has been mechanical indoctrination. Teachers themselves haven't become the object of research before. We look forward to seeing our teachers standing on 'centre stage' as many are increasingly doing in presenting their own research at the annual LDC project conferences and even at national and international conferences.

The project content, format and culture are the 'seeds', the 'sunshine' and the 'soil' of this learning development community. With these three ingredients and conditions, our community gains life. Now, our job is to promote the idea of 'being a leader' among the LDC members and 'doing through communication and discussion'. The discussion is not limited to the school; it also includes discussion among schools. It is not limited to just among teachers, but also happens between teachers and researchers. We make friends first then we do research together. Teachers improve their work by collaborating with university colleagues and university researchers connect their work in more meaningful ways through collaboration with teachers.

Reflections on our work

The nature and value of the learning community

The nature of this learning community is to enable everybody to learn, engage in self-reflection and share others' experiences and excellence. In this community, information is exchangeable. Everybody actively seeks to collaborate and co-operate, to improve and to share the benefits and these practices and attitudes have become the norms of this community.

The value of this learning community is that it makes everybody feel that they are not alone in the challenges that they face. They have colleagues who share the same interests but they are also able to pursue their own unique interests. It is a platform where everybody enjoys participating and enjoys finding one's self. It is also a kind of 'gas station'; a source of energy; we get nutrition from the research and feel refreshed in our practice. We find inspiration from this community and create our own knowledge and wisdom.

It is also a source of motivation for everyone to study and research and to keep everybody feeling a sense of fulfilment and enjoyment.

The structure and character of an effective learning community

This learning community is very diverse. Inside the school, teachers develop this community with their colleagues from different grades, different subjects, different experiences, and different positions. It is also a united group formed by teachers, researchers and administrators; the more diverse it is, the broader perspectives it can provide. Members in this community are all equal; professional researchers, administrators, and teachers are different, but everybody is considered equal in the research activities. Only when we are equal can we all benefit from this community. The development of this community should be a gradual and open process. It is normal that members will have some conflicts because of their different ideas and ways of doing things. It is also normal that we will not always be at the same level of understanding. We need to tolerate and work with these differences rather than just seek short-term returns. But how do we support and cultivate this learning community for teacher professional development?

How to nurture a teacher learning community

First, we need to discover and value teachers' practical wisdom; teachers are the best people to comment and speak up. We need to provide opportunities for teachers to raise their own ideas and to exchange their ideas. It is also important that we do this continuously and over time. Second, we need to de-emphasise administrative power but cultivate a culture of discussion, conversation and sharing amongst the teachers. We need to engage in discussions with teachers as equal participants, to discuss the 'small' problems and provide options and opportunities for teachers. Third, we need to encourage teachers to learn how to reflect and learn new knowledge. Finally, we need to value everybody's contribution. We create larger spaces by including every individual member's knowledge and wisdom.

What we have learnt from foreign colleagues

Professor Erickson, Dr Mitchell and Dr Ryan not only bring their academic knowledge to us but also bring us new perspectives. The latter is even more important. We are very impressed on two points: one, they respect every person on any occasion. Two, their advice is concrete and manageable. I remember one occasion when we were having a small meeting teachers were able to join us when they didn't have a class. Every time when new teachers joined us, they briefly introduced them to what we had discussed before. Newcomers then could easily follow the discussion. So the message was to not ignore anyone, respect every teacher's creativity and contribution, and organically combine teachers' routine practices with innovation. We could easily see them practising these concepts from this occasion. This is an era of internationalisation and globalisation so conversations between the East and the West are more and more important. We are trying to absorb information from civilisations from all parts of the world and apply it to China's old but dynamic education development.

Our different roles

Our different experiences set up a quite high level of difficulty at the beginning. As the project has developed, we find that we are co-operating better and better all the time. Now, no matter who proposes an idea, we can understand each other without the need for much explanation. We often discuss together how to choose a perspective to communicate with teachers before each meeting. We all find that we bring something different to the project and the discussions. Yuping is firm but gentle; he always carefully listens to teachers. Once he discovers good teaching cases from teachers, he helps them to summarise and develop them. With his rich teaching and working experience he communicates well with teachers. Dr Kang's openness and passion influence teachers. His sensitivity and his theoretical framework on education help teachers to develop their teaching experience into teaching wisdom. As a Principal, Liu Keqin can provide leadership and professional guidance. In her school, she tries her best to introduce this project into every aspect of its daily teaching activities; it has become an organic, natural combination of teaching and research. Her role also helps her to communicate with other principals. Some people say we are a 'golden team', some say we are an 'iron triangle'. We share the same education values and the same educational pursuits. We have different roles and different experiences but we share the same ideas. As an old Chinese saying goes, our team is made by the universe, that is, it is a 'match made in heaven'.

For Yuping, compared with the time before he joined this project, even though he never had a chance to enter higher education, he now has the feeling of being important and valued; he doesn't feel like an outsider to research and theories. And both he and Dr Kang have learned a lot from Principal Liu about school administration and leadership. Our co-operation represents a mutual and reciprocal learning model between a university researcher, a school-based researcher and an administrator. What we seek is close collaboration between theory and practice. The idea of 'harmony but not sameness' is also what we seek among the three of us, as well as among every member in this learning community.

Our challenge

Nevertheless, many challenges still remain. There are a lot of differences and even conflicts between the culture of the LDC and the traditional teaching culture. How do we further develop this new LDC model? How can we apply this model to different schools so that they will not repeat the mistakes we made? We need to seek more diverse and effective approaches in our research. The biggest challenge is perseverance. Professor Erickson once said that research projects can invite more people to participate, but should not let just a few feel overly-burdened. We need to continue our efforts to look for a research approach that is compatible with teachers' daily routines and practices and that is sustainable.

One other challenge is the different perspectives that teachers have. Teachers usually expect short-term effects and benefits so although they often work in a collective way they expect guidance from the administrators. But research is actually a process of teachers' self-reflection, of moving from knowing to understanding, from understanding to practice, and from practice to internalisation. This is a long journey and it is not easy to find a balance with daily routines and demands. Another challenge is the conflict with the traditional research culture. We aim to build a democratic, collaborative and egalitarian research culture, but the traditional research culture is authoritative. In reality, it is more difficult to get the local educational administrators to accept this culture than to change teachers.

Concluding remarks

In the past three years of our research journey, we have travelled a long way together. We were excited by our passion for the research at the beginning. But as we face various problems, and try to understand the nature of the problems and how to solve them, we often feel lonely. What support do we need to continue this research journey? We haven't found the answer to this question yet but what we are pursuing is the joy in seeking this answer; this is also the wealth that we feel the LDC brings us.

In these past five years of practice and improvement, we have experienced several cycles from simplicity to complexity and from complexity to simplicity. The project has fluctuated in this process, but it is also this uncertainty that makes this research vibrant.

In conclusion, it needs to be recognised that China is a vast country experiencing rapid development and it is necessary for the world to pay more attention to its educational development as well as its economic and political development. Compared with many Western countries, our basic education faces many more challenges and difficulties. We believe that our education system is much like our old but hopeful country: full of challenges but also full of prospects. In our limited space here, and from the forefront of teaching, we hope that we have provided a clear picture of these challenges and prospects for the future.

Part II

Educational quality and access

4 Methods to evaluate educational quality and improvement in China

Sally M. Thomas and Wen-Jung Peng

This chapter examines the need for new methods to evaluate educational quality and school effectiveness in China drawing on previous research and policy development conducted in the UK and recent research on school evaluation in China funded by UKAID and the UK Economic and Social Science Research Council. These developments build on the mainly Western tradition of school effectiveness and improvement research and in particular utilise statistical analysis and multilevel modelling to estimate the 'value-added' by different schools to their students' progress and examination scores. The chapter considers the relevance of these approaches in the Chinese context and the implications for reviewing current definitions of educational quality.

Introduction

Almost all countries – both developed and developing – aim to improve the quality of children's education given the evidence of clear links between educational quality on the one hand, and on the other hand poverty reduction, better economic growth and the changes needed to address the challenges of globalisation (Haddad 1997, McGinn 1997, UNESCO 2004, Zhang and Minxia 2006, Tikly 2006, Yu and Thomas 2008). Therefore it is not surprising that the new educational reforms in China over the last ten years have put a strong emphasis on raising educational quality, particularly in rural areas and for girls. As noted in the introduction to this book, systematic transformation of curriculum goals, structure and content, teaching and learning approaches, and assessment and administrative structures has occurred, and control has increasingly been devolved from the centre to provincial, district and school levels. Moreover the reforms are now accelerating, indicated by a key meeting in 2008 chaired by the Chinese Premier Wen Jiabao, where an action programme 2010 to 2020 was formulated to construct the 'Guidelines of the National Programme for Medium- and Long-Term Educational Reform and Development' (国家中长期教育改革和发展规划纲要). A 10 year long-term approach is being implemented and the main tasks of the guidelines are to:

1. establish strategic objectives of educational development for the new era,
2. propose major strategies and policy measures to improve quality of education and promote quality education,
3. define development ideas and major measures for different phases and types of education,
4. define overall concepts and key areas for education reform, and
5. improve the strategic environment and supporting mechanism to prioritise education (Chinese Ministry of Education 2009).

More recently at the 2009 National People's Congress, the Chinese Premier Wen Jiabao reiterated the need to prioritise educational development and outlined an initial focus on five key areas:

1. promote fairness in education,
2. optimise the education structures to develop vocational education,
3. improve the quality of teachers,
4. advance well-rounded education, and
5. implement a programme to ensure that all primary and secondary school buildings are safe and promote standardisation in the construction of rural primary and secondary schools (NPC 2009).

The issue of fairness in education is crucial and relates to equal opportunities but also to fair assessment of both students and schools. Therefore one important strand of the new reforms centres on improving pupil assessment as well as the methods used to evaluate quality and improvement in schools. Moreover, this has been an outstanding issue for over ten years: in the Ninth Five-Year Plan for China's Educational Development the Chinese government made explicit the need to improve performance measures as well as reduce performance differences between schools:

> Effective measures need to be taken to solve the problems of solely pursuing high continuation rate and of heavy burdens for students. More efforts will be devoted to those schools with poor performance to reduce the discrepancy between key schools and non-key schools.
>
> (Chinese Ministry of Education 1996)

In addition there are particular concerns about the exam-oriented nature of the education system in China, the need for curriculum and examination reform, and the lack of systematic methods to evaluate education quality. For example, exam eligibility requirements are seen to be problematic because only graduates of senior secondary schools with three years local 'hukou' (i.e. residential registration) can register for the Entrance Examination for Higher Education (EEHE) via the local senior secondary schools and there are substantial variations in university admission rates across different areas (Xie 2007, Jiang 2008, Jiang and Ma 2008).

To inform new policy developments in China, innovative methods to evaluate schools are needed to provide alternative frameworks for teachers and policy makers to identify more fairly and accurately best practice in teaching and learning in a variety of contexts. Moreover, similar to the situation in the United Kingdom in the early 1990s, alternative approaches are needed to reduce the temptation of evaluating school performance on the basis of raw examination scores alone (Thomas 2001, Thomas *et al.* 2007). The concept of 'value added' measures of relative student progress as an indicator of school performance, and related school effectiveness research in the UK, has played a very significant role in focusing the attention of educational policy makers in the UK on the potential for raising student achievement. The impact of new approaches to evaluation and accountability has been linked to improved student outcomes (Miliband 2004). Therefore, this chapter aims to examine the opportunities and potential for enhancing educational quality in China and successfully implementing the objectives of the curriculum reform programme via innovative school evaluation methods and school effectiveness research (SER).

In this chapter, we start by looking at the need for new methods to evaluate educational quality and school effectiveness in China drawing on previous research and policy development conducted in the UK and pilot research in China. These developments build on the tradition of work on school effectiveness and improvement since the 1960s and in particular utilise the substantial advances in statistical analysis and multilevel modelling to estimate the 'value-added' by different schools to their students' progress. This is followed by an overview of a new DFID/ESRC (UK Department for International Development/Economic and Social Research Council) funded study: Improving Educational Evaluation and Quality in China (IEEQC) which extends previous work on school evaluation in China and is being conducted in collaboration with the China National Institute for Education Research in Beijing. Finally we consider the potential implications for reviewing current definitions of educational quality.

The need for 'value added' approaches to school effectiveness and evaluation in China

In mainland China, raw measures of pupils' academic outcomes and entrance levels to higher education are frequently viewed as the key indicators of school quality. The phenomenon of 'war over student recruitment' between schools is not uncommon every year following the Entrance Examination for Senior Secondary Schools (EESSS) (Ding and Xue 2009) for example, by providing scholarships for the best students to increase the likelihood of getting higher outcomes for the schools in the Entrance Examination for Higher Education (EEHE). As a result schools with disadvantaged intakes tend to be judged unfairly, while complacency is possible amongst schools with more able pupils, and it is difficult to identify best practice. An alternative 'value added' approach aims to provide a fairer approach to accountability and evaluating school performance than the 'raw' examination results (Gray *et al.* 1986, Goldstein *et al.* 1993, Thomas and Mortimore 1996). Essentially this is achieved by adjusting for students' previous attainment and other relevant factors outside the control of the school to estimate their progress, in comparison with students in other schools. This methodology can be applied to any quantitative measure of student outcomes such as academic, attitudinal or vocational, although it has most commonly been applied to examination scores, and is now widely regarded as providing the most valid and accurate measures of school effectiveness. More specifically, value added measures estimate the relative progress made by pupils in a school over a particular period of time (usually from entry to the school until public examinations in the case of secondary schools, or over particular years or curriculum stages in primary schools) in comparison with pupils in other schools in the same sample. The method compares outcomes after adjusting for varying intake achievement and reflects the relative boost a school gives to a pupil's previous level of attainment in comparison with similar pupils in other schools. The concept of value added is, therefore, both an indicator of a school's effectiveness and a tool for head teachers and their staff to use to analyse the extent to which they have effectively raised pupil achievement.

Value added evaluation methods emerged from empirical studies of effective schooling and the background to this research can be traced back more than 40 years. Briefly, over this time period, SER in the UK, USA and other Western countries developed from research into the educational factors and process that correlate with effective schooling to practitioner orientated action research, and subsequently to school improvement research alongside improved evaluation methodology (Teddlie and Reynolds 2000). The latter developments involved the establishment of comprehensive and longitudinal datasets and sophisticated statistical analysis techniques (multilevel modelling) used to create 'value added' measures of school effectiveness outlined above. These SER developments have fed directly into identifying new approaches to evaluate school performance and subsequently to wide-ranging policy developments in school evaluation in the UK and elsewhere. For example, from 2006, contextualised value added measures have been included in the Department for Education and Skills (DFES) school performance tables for all English schools and school self evaluation is a central element of the new national inspection framework (DFES and OFSTED 2004, OFSTED 2005).

The beginnings of school effectiveness research in China

So far value added methods of school evaluation and empirical studies using the paradigms of school effectiveness research have only rarely been reported in mainland China (Tang and Liang 2005; Sun *et al.* 2010), although this situation is changing as demonstrated by the IEEQC project, which we will return to later. Mainland China is also notably missing from international comparative studies of school effects (e.g. Scheerens 2001). This is not the case in Hong Kong and Taiwan where several significant studies of school effectiveness have been conducted (see Cheng 1999). However, given the substantial differences in the education and assessment systems a review of research outside mainland China is beyond the scope of this chapter.

Interestingly some Chinese researchers have explored the concepts of SER (Chen 2003, Yu 2005) and below we outline the few relevant empirical studies we have identified. For example, in a small-scale exploratory study, Tang and Liang (2005) analysed the data collected from 244 students from six classes in one junior secondary school to look at the feasibility of using a value added approach to explore school and teacher effects over one semester on students' total scores of Chinese, maths and foreign language tests. More recently using a longitudinal approach and a much larger sample of over 8,000 students from 62 schools, Ding and Xue (2009) employed multilevel modelling to investigate the impact of student, class and school level variables, including prior attainment (on entry to senior secondary schools) on the 2006 total EEHE scores and we will discuss this study further in the next section.

The other studies we have identified examine class and school effects on raw student attainment at one point in time, but these studies are limited because the data employed are cross-sectional rather than longitudinal (Scheerens, Glas and Thomas 2003). Zhou and Wu (2008) reported a study employing a two-level multilevel model to look at primary school effects on migrant children's outcomes in maths and Chinese. Similarly, at the secondary level, Xue and Min (2008) adopted a three-level multilevel model to examine the effects of class and school on junior secondary students' scores in maths and Chinese in 20 Gansu counties and Jiang, Yang and Yao (2005) examined the class effect on the Chinese scores in EEHE of 751 randomly selected students in 20 senior secondary schools. However, due to the small-scale nature of most of these studies and unsatisfactory operational definitions of student ability, Chinese researchers have called for further empirical research, and the need to introduce prior attainment baseline measures such as EESSS and to systematically establish student databases across cities, provinces and even at national level to enable a fairer evaluation of school effectiveness (Jiang, Yang and Yao 2005, Tang and Liang 2005).

Thus researchers have sought to examine both the meaning and definition of school effectiveness in China (Sun and Hung 1994, Wang and Zheng 1997) and the development of SER methodology, particularly the concept of schools adding value to students' academic progress and the use of multilevel modelling to calculate measures of relative pupil progress (Nan 2003, Ren 2007, Zhang 1998, Zhang and Meng 1995, Yang and He 2008). The findings so far are intriguing suggesting that school effects may account for up to 40 per cent of the total variance in students' academic achievement and that in rural areas the equivalent figure may be much higher. Across a landscape as huge as China, more large-scale and representative studies in this area are needed. As an illustration, in the next section, we provide details of a pilot value added study conducted in China.

A pilot 'value added' project

In addition to the SER research highlighted above a pilot value added research project has also been conducted in China as part of a DFID funded British Council Higher Education (HE) academic link that focused specifically on innovation in school evaluation and strategies to improve quality of schooling in China between the Graduate School of Education (GSOE), University of Bristol (UOB) and the China National Institute for Educational Research (CNIER), Beijing (Thomas 2005, Peng *et al.* 2006, Ma *et al.* 2006, Thomas and Peng 2009). This pilot project provides a useful illustration of the kind of large-scale projects that would be possible if the appropriate datasets were available at regional or national level in China.

The pilot value added project involved 17 senior secondary schools in Baoding City in Hebei Province. Students' 2003 EEHE data was linked to their previous attainment in the EESSS and other pupil and school background information and the data was analysed using multilevel modelling to create value added measures for each school in three outcomes: total score, mathematics and English. The results, fed back confidentially to each school, indicated that the performance of senior secondary schools changed significantly when comparing raw and value added measures of the Higher Education Entrance Examination. After controlling for student prior attainment (i.e. EESSS scores) and other factors 20 to 30 per cent of the total variance and 30 to 40 per cent of the school variance in student outcomes was explained. Of the remaining total variance, 20 to 22 per cent was attributable to differences between schools and some school differences in value added performance were statistically significant in spite of the small sample size, thereby demonstrating a school effect (see Peng *et al.* 2006 for further details). Interestingly, these findings are supported by similar comparable results from a follow up pilot study in Baoding City (Ma *et al.* 2006) and the Ding and Xue (2009) study both of which employed a larger school sample. However, it seems the percentage of school variance explained was greater in these two later studies (40 to 60 per cent) possibly because more school factors were controlled for in the analysis.

Figure 4.1 illustrates the findings for mathematics. Each point (marked as a triangle) represents one school and the 95 per cent confidence interval is represented by the vertical line. Only those schools whose vertical line does not cross the horizontal reference line (at zero) can be interpreted as performing either above or below expectation in terms of value added performance.

The findings of the pilot study also revealed the issue of differential school effectiveness. In other words, in reality schools may perform differently in different areas of the curriculum. Figure 4.2 illustrates this issue for

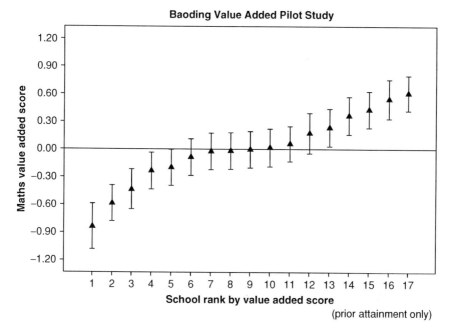

Figure 4.1 Schools ranked order by mathematics EEHE value added scores

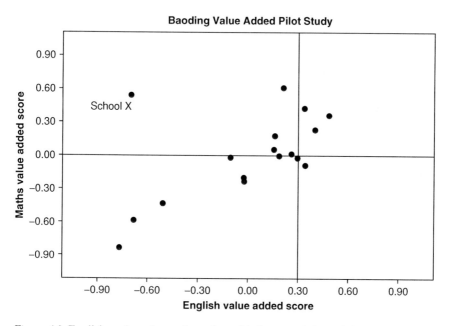

Figure 4.2 English and mathematics value added scores (adapted from Peng *et al.* 2006)

mathematics value added scores in comparison with English scores. Each point represents one school, and as an example, School X is performing below expectation in terms of its English value added score (i.e. negative score) but above expectation in terms of its maths value added score (i.e. positive score). These kinds of results are very useful to schools for self-evaluation and indicate that the issue of differential effectiveness may be concealed if only one overall measure is used to evaluate performance.

There is now growing evidence in several countries worldwide demonstrating similar findings. However, it is important to emphasise that if these methods are to be useful to evaluate quality in the Chinese context then it is important to be aware of both the limitations of the methodology (e.g. mainly a quantitative perspective) and the criticisms of school effectiveness approaches. In particular Morley and Rassool (1999), alongside other critics, have rightly questioned the transferability of Western education policies in diverse global contexts and emphasised that school effectiveness research needs to 'be contextualised within particular societies and specific conditions that exist' (134). They also indicate a need to look more closely at issues of power, poverty, deprivation and social exclusion when evaluating educational quality; as well as a broader range of educational outcomes and these important aspects are addressed to some extent as part of the new IEEQC project outlined below. Nevertheless, overall, the Boading pilot study strongly suggests the need for more robust quantitative evidence about the range and extent of school effectiveness in China. Such evidence is vital to inform initiatives aiming to enhance educational quality and student outcomes, particularly in rural and socio-economically disadvantaged areas (e.g. DFID Gansu basic education project, Chu and Liu 2005) as well as increase the SER international knowledge base (Teddlie and Lui 2008).

Thus, in the context of little relevant research, the impact of 'value added' approaches to improve the evaluation of educational quality in developing countries such as China is potentially very significant, but not necessarily clear-cut or straightforward, given the many different social, cultural, economic and political contexts and priorities – both between developed and developing countries and within developing countries like China with a large and very diverse population. Further research is therefore urgently required to identify innovation and best practice in educational evaluation in a range of different regional and country contexts. Evidence of this kind is essential to inform the rapidly changing education reforms in China and to establish the key lessons learnt for developing countries elsewhere.

The IEEQC project

To address these issues directly two linked research projects 'Improving Educational Evaluation and Quality in China (IEEQC)' and 'Improving Teacher Development and Educational Quality in China (ITDEQC)' are being conducted in collaboration with CNIER and funded by the DFID/ESRC programme (Thomas, 2010; IEEQC 2011). The IEEQC project aims are twofold. First, to extend current knowledge concerning the definition and measurement of secondary school effectiveness across a range of regional contexts in China, using a value added approach for different pupil outcomes. Second, to explore how 'value added' approaches to evaluating school performance and educational quality may have been adapted and developed by policy makers and practitioners in China to take account of local contexts and priorities: for example, in terms of the type of student learning and outcomes valued such as citizenship versus academic, preference for qualitative versus quantitative approaches, and the kind of contextual features that impact on student and school performance. Broadly the aims of the new project are to enhance understanding of the complex nature of school effectiveness in China – but crucially we also want to explore a more fundamental question – how local context may play a key role in determining definitions of educational effectiveness and quality.

Thus one key objective is to explore the way school, local authority government and higher education staff evaluates educational quality and improvement in the quality of schooling. Particularly with regard to school staff, this involves identifying the opportunities – via data feedback – for school and teacher self-evaluation. In these circumstances we want to explore how the key concepts and limitations of value added and other approaches to evaluation are understood by local authority officers and practitioners. By taking this approach, the purpose is to learn about the relevance of Western approaches to evaluating school performance in different contexts and how these methods may be actively adapted and transformed to take account of local priorities. This latter issue has been central to current debates regarding how appropriate it is to apply Western models of educational quality and evaluation to different country and regional contexts, especially in developing countries where expertise and resources to address these issues locally are often very limited (Stephens 2007). Moreover, school effectiveness and improvement research would be very much enhanced by a clearer understanding of why concepts of education quality, and approaches and methods of educational evaluation largely developed in the UK, Europe and the USA, may be viewed differently by policy makers and practitioners in different social, economic and political cultures such as Mainland China (Teddlie and Reynolds 2000, Scheerens 2001). Comparative evidence of this kind is also essential for UK policy makers and practitioners to understand how contextual and cultural issues may impact on educational values and priorities of both schools and individual students; for example, by contributing insights and possible hypotheses about the relationship between Chinese culture and the above average GCSE achievement of Chinese students in UK (Wilson *et al.* 2005).

In addition, by drawing on school effectiveness and improvement research findings and practical experiences in the UK and elsewhere, the IEEQC project plans to build on the pilot multilevel analyses outlined above to produce more robust and representative quantitative research evidence to feed into the development of alternative methods to assess school effectiveness in different rural and urban contexts in China. Thus the IEEQC project involves two complimentary research strands. Although still in progress, the first strand (study 1) is exploring the nature and extent of school effectiveness in China by using innovative quantitative methodology (multilevel modelling) to analyse examination, prior attainment and other pupil, class and school background data, collected from the 2009 student cohort of 120+ senior secondary schools in several district education authorities (LEAs) across western and eastern China. The second strand (study 2) involves the collection of new qualitative data – interviews and focus groups have been conducted with 90+ key stakeholders including headteachers, teachers, students, national and local policy makers – to explore the way educational quality is defined and evaluated in China as well as how international research on school effectiveness, evaluation and self evaluation may have been applied and adapted in the Chinese context. The study 2 research questions are as follows:

1. What are the views and experiences of key stakeholders in relation to the nature of education quality, values and priorities and the impact of local context on educational outcomes?
2. What are the views and experiences of key stakeholders in relation to school evaluation and self-evaluation, and specifically in relation to 'value added' approaches?
3. What are the key lessons learnt about building research capacity in school evaluation and self-evaluation in China and what is the potential impact on educational quality?

So far we are still analysing the IEECQ research data but below we reflect on some emerging themes.

Conclusions: Emerging themes about educational quality in China

Improving educational quality is a critical goal in China. However, underlying this goal and the IEEQC project are two fundamental questions which continue to be debated vigorously both in China and across the world. The first is how should educational quality be defined and the second is how should educational quality be evaluated.

Turning to the second question first, this relates largely to the methods of evaluation and we have argued in this chapter that 'value added' measures provide one essential methodological approach to enable a fairer evaluation of schools and students than raw examination scores. The IEEQC project findings when complete will provide detailed evidence from China on estimates of school effectiveness. However, it is important to note that value added approaches are not perfect and there are real limitations that apply, as for all numerical measures, which need to be well understood such as measurement error and statistical uncertainty. In particular value added measures should be interpreted as the school effect *plus* the effect of all other relevant factors not controlled for in the statistical analysis. Moreover, this approach to measuring educational quality reflects a fairly narrow definition of school effectiveness which is quantitative in nature and focuses specifically on pupil outcomes. Of course there are other more qualitative approaches to evaluating school effectiveness and educational quality, especially the quality of educational processes, and in support of SER critics such as Morley and Rassool (1999) we see these as both essential and complimentary to value added measures. In order to evaluate quality more comprehensively, for example as outlined by the UNESCO (2004) education quality framework, it is clear that both qualitative and quantitative evaluation methods are necessary. Early indications from the IEEQC study suggest that educational stakeholders in China are generally in agreement regarding this approach and frequently emphasise the need for new types of evaluation and a broader range of student outcomes. Interestingly, however, although recognising the concept of 'value added' many local stakeholders do not seem to be fully aware of alternative statistical methods to create and utilise value added measures in evaluating school performance.

Regarding the question of how should educational quality be defined – particularly in terms of the different aspects of school functioning and student outcomes that should be considered – there are clear signals that policy makers would like to see a broader definition of what is meant by education quality in China (State Council 1999). As explained by Hannum and colleagues:

> China's educational policy makers in the reform period have made quality a top-level priority. What quality means, however, has become broader than achievement on tests. There is a significant movement among policy-makers to promote learner-centered teaching approaches. The so-called 'quality education' (*sushi jiaoyu*) reforms are intended to develop the diverse skills of the whole child, not just promote test-taking skills, and to stimulate critical thinking. The reforms are meant to encourage students to consider multiple answers to the same question and multiple solutions to the same problem.
>
> (Hannum *et al.* 2007: 13)

This issue reflects similar concerns in both developed and developing countries to redefine quality education so as to ensure students have the knowledge, skills and key competencies needed to meet the employment and social challenges of globalisation. For example, UNESCO's announcement of 'Four World Education Conferences 2008–2009' declared:

> education for sustainable development (ESD) means learning throughout life to acquire values, knowledge and skills which help children, young people and adults find new solutions to social, economic and environmental issues which affect their lives.
>
> (UNESCO 2008: 5)

Going further Matsuura (2004) has argued:

> Quality is not just about academic knowledge and achievements, important though they may be. It is clear that the modern world is demanding much more of education – it is counting on education systems to build the foundations of a better world, one based on universal values of peace and equality.
>
> (Matsuura 2004: 6)

After reviewing different traditions of understanding and interpretation of quality, UNESCO (2004) has outlined a framework with four elements (learner characteristics, enabling inputs, context and outcomes) as a start for audiences to think about the key components of education systems and how they interact.

Earlier, UNICEF had similarly identified five aspects of educational quality (learners, environments, content, processes and outcomes) founded on 'the rights of the whole child, and all children, to survival, protection, development and participation' outlined in the Dakar Framework (UNICEF 2000: 4). Both the UNESCO and UNICEF approaches draw on the philosophy of the Convention on the Rights of the Child (UNESCO 2004) but also on school effectiveness research paradigms which first introduced the input–context–process–output model to provide a framework for understanding educational quality issues (Scheerens, Glas and Thomas 2003).

Specifically in relation to student outcomes UNESCO highlights two key areas as follows:

> Defining quality: Two principles characterize most attempts to define quality in education: the first identifies learners' cognitive development as the major explicit objective of all education systems. Accordingly, the success with which systems achieve this is one indicator of their quality. The second emphasizes education's role in promoting values and attitudes of responsible citizenship and in nurturing creative and emotional development. The achievement of these objectives is more difficult to assess and compare across countries.
>
> (UNESCO 2004: 17)

However, in spite of policy developments worldwide, in practice broader approaches to education quality are generally being emphasised more successfully in developed countries, than developing systems where the key indicators remain to be assessments of literacy and numeracy. The competition for admission to senior secondary school and higher education in China, as well as student performance incentives for teachers means that in practice the education system remains largely focused on examination results (Lee, Ding and Song 2008). As Hannum and colleagues pertinently note regarding the context in China:

Cultivating teachers who can offer high-quality learning experiences and produce successful test-takers under the new teaching model is a critical challenge.

(Hannum *et al.* 2007: 14)

Of course the same comment could be applied to many education systems around the world. Emerging findings from the IEEQC study indicate that stakeholders in China are critically aware of these quality issues and raise a number of key points regarding fairness, equal opportunities and the educational outcomes that should be evaluated in the context of schooling such as student values, employment potential, lifelong learning as well as examination success (see also, for example, the chapter in this volume by Tudball about citizenship education reform in China). It is clear that the Confucian ideal of an excellent well-rounded scholar remains a strong underlying influence in the Chinese education system that positively motivates the best students, although there are some indications that this ideal is not necessarily realistic or helpful for many children. The final IEEQC analyses aim to document the full complexity and range of perspectives regarding definitions of educational quality in China.

In conclusion, the UNESCO and UNICEF frameworks provide examples of the kind of conceptual models for educational quality that we will contrast against the final themes emerging from our qualitative data analysis of stakeholder views. Indeed the emerging issues identified so far from the IEEQC study can already be mapped onto these frameworks but it is possible that our findings – when complete – may suggest new ways or models in which educational quality in the Chinese context may be better understood and evaluated. In China both cognitive development and attitudes and values in education would be seen as important aspects in defining educational quality. However, cultural differences, for example, related to Confucianism (Cheng and Wong 1996) and the fact that the rural–urban gap is much more of an issue in China than other countries, in the UK for example (Teddlie and Liu 2008), may mean that these areas may be defined somewhat differently to Western countries. Thus it is crucial that further evidence is obtained to understand the impact of local priorities and context on definitions of school effectiveness and educational quality. We hope this chapter has provided food for thought concerning improving educational evaluation and quality in China as well as pointing the way for further essential research on this important topic.

References

Chen, F. W. (陈丰伟) (2003) 国外学校效能研究述评 'Review on external schools effectiveness' 江西教育科研, *Jianxi Educational Research*, 10, 33–34, 42.

Cheng, K. M. and Wong, K. C. (1996) 'School effectiveness in East Asia: concepts, origins and implications', *Journal of Educational Administration*, 34(5), 32–49.

Cheng, Y. C. (1999) Editorial, Special issue on recent educational developments in South East Asia, *School Effectiveness & School Improvement*, 10(1), 3–9.

Chinese Ministry of Education (1996) 国家教委关于印发《全国教育事业"九五"计划和2010年发展规划》的通知 'Notification of State Council on printing and distributing the Ninth 5-Year Plan for China's educational development and the development outline by 2010'. Online. Available HTTP: <http://210.28.182.158/edu/1/law/12/law_12_1082.htm> (accessed 15 July 2009).

Chinese Ministry of Education (2009) 教育部2009年第1次新闻发布会:介绍为制定《国家中长期教育改革和发展规划纲要》公开征求意见工作的有关情况 'The first Ministry of Education 2009 press conference to launch consultation on the Guidelines of the national programme for medium- and long-term educational reform and development'. Online. Available HTTP: <http://www.moe.gov.cn/edoas/website18/32/info1230081158575832.htm> (accessed 26 June 2009).

Chu, H. and Liu, X. (2005) *Independent review of the Gansu Basic Education Project (GBEP) on Impacts on Management*, Cambridge Education (CE) and Gansu Provincial Education Department (GPED).

DFES and OFSTED (2004) *A New Relationship with Schools: Improving Performance Through School Self-evaluation*, Nottingham: the Department for Education and Skills.

Ding, Y. Q. (丁延庆) and Xue, H. P. (薛海平) (2009) 高中教育的一个生产函数研究 'A study on the education production function with high school data.' 华中师范大学学报(人文社会科学版), *Journal of Huazhong Normal University (Humanities and Social Sciences)*, 48(2), 122–128.

Goldstein, H., Rasbash, J., Yang, M., Woodhouse, G., Pan, H., Nuttall, D. and Thomas, S. (1993) 'A multilevel analysis of school examination results', *Oxford Review of Education*, 19(4), 425–433.

Gray, J., Jesson, D. and Jones, B. (1986) 'The search for a fairer way of comparing schools' examination results', *Research Papers in Education*, 1(2), 91–122.

Haddad, W. D. (1997) 'Globalization of the economy: the implications for education and skill formation', *Prospects*, 27(1), 35–40.

Hannum, E., Park, A. and Cheng, K. M. (2007) 'Introduction: market reforms and educational opportunity in China', in E. Hannum and Park, A. (eds), *Education and Reform in China*, Oxford: Routledge.

IEEQC (2011) '*Improving educational evaluation and quality in China*'. HTTP: <http://ieeqc.bristol.ac.uk> (website accessed 7 March 2011).

Jiang, S. J. (姜世健) (2008) 高考移民现象的成因分析 'Institutional analysis of the phenomenon of the immigrants for NCEE', 教育发展研究 *Research in Educational Development*, 17, 16–20, 30.

Jiang, W. (蒋伟) and Ma, Z. Y. (马照云) (2008) 中国高考移民诉讼第一案追问 'Inquiry of the first litigation case of immigration for Entrance Examination for Higher Education', 政府法制 *Government Legality*, 12, 16–17.

Jiang, L. (蒋莉), Yang, Z. M. (杨志明) and Yao, S. Q. (姚树桥) (2005) 学生高考语文成绩影响因素的多层线性分析 'Analysis of influencing factors on the Chinese achievement test in the college entrance examination: a hierarchical linear model', 中国临床心理学杂志 *Chinese Journal of Clinical Psychology*, 13(4), 414–416, 419.

Lee, J. C. K., Ding, D. and Song, H. (2008) 'School supervision and evaluation in China: the Shanghai perspective', *Quality Assurance in Education*, 16(2), 148–163.

Ma, X. (马晓强), Peng, W. J. and Thomas, S. (2006) 学校效能的增值评价—对河北省保定市普通高中学校的实证研究 'School effectiveness evaluation with value added method: case study of senior high schools of Baoding, Hebei Province', 教育研究 *Educational Research*, 10, 77–84.

Matsuura, K. (2004) Opening Address, *47th session of the International Conference on Education (ICE): Quality Education for All Young People – Challenges, Trends and Priorities. Geneva, Switzerland, 8 September 2004.* Online. Available HTTP: <http://portal.unesco.org/education/en/files/33594/10947182863DG_geneva.pdf/DG_geneva.pdf> (accessed 2 June 2009).

McGinn, N. F. (1997) 'The impact of globalisation on national education systems', *Prospects*, 27(1), 41–54.

Miliband, D. (2004) 'Using data to raise achievement', *Speech at a conference of the education network, London, 11 Feb 2004.* Online. Available HTTP: <http://www.teachers.gov.uk/_doc/6280/Miliband%20speech%20at%20TEN%20Conference%2011Feb04.doc> (accessed 21 May 2007).

Morley, L. and Rassool, N. (1999) *School Effectiveness: Fracturing the Discourse*, London: Falmer Press.

Nan, J. W. (南纪稳) (2003) 教育增值与学校评估模式重构 'Value added by education and the reconstruction of a model for school appraisal', 中国教育学刊 *Journal of the Chinese Society of Education*, 7, 59–61.

NPC (National People's Congress, 全国人民代表大会). (2009) 温家宝作政府工作报告: 2009年3月5日在第十一届全国人民代表大会第二次会议上 Report on the Work of the Government delivered by Premier Wen Jiabao at the Second Session of the Eleventh National People's Congress on 5 March 2009. Online. Available HTTP: <http://www.xinhuanet.com/2009lh/090305a/wz.htm> (accessed 23 June 2009).

OFSTED (2005) *Conducting the Inspection: Guidance for Inspectors of Schools (HMI2502)*, London: OFSTED.

Peng, W. J., Thomas, S. M., Yang, X. and Li, J. (2006) 'Developing school evaluation methods to improve the quality of schooling in China: A pilot "value added" study', *Assessment in Education: Principles, Policy and Practice*, 13(2), 135–154.

Ren, C. R. (任春荣) (2007) 增值测量法:公平利用考试成绩评价学校效能的科学途径 'Value added method: a scientific approach of fairly using examination results to evaluate school', 中国考试 (研究版) *China Examinations*, 4, 12–16, 38.

Scheerens, J. (2001) 'Monitoring school effectiveness in developing countries', *School Effectiveness and School Improvement*, 12(4), 359–384.

Scheerens, J., Glas, C. and Thomas, S. (2003) *Educational Evaluation, Assessment and Monitoring: A Systemic Approach*, Lisse: Swets and Zeitlinger.

State Council (中共中央国务院) (1999) 中共中央国务院关于深化教育改革全面推进素质教育的决定 'Decision of the Central Committee of the Chinese Communist Party and the State Council on Deepening the Education Reform and Improving Quality-Oriented Education'. Online. Available HTTP: <http://www.moe.gov.cn/edoas/website18/14/info3314.htm> (accessed 22 July 2009).

Stephens, D. (2007) '*Culture in Education and Development: Principles, Practice and Policy*', Bristol Papers in Education: Comparative and International Studies. Symposium books.

Sun, H. C. (孙河川), Wang, X. D. (王小梿), Yuan, S. F. (袁书凤), Hao, L. L. (郝玲玲), Liu, W. Z. (刘文钊) and Liu, Y. (刘颖), (2010) 中国教育效能研究的近况、不足、发展、展望、发表于中国第二届国际教育效能与学校改进大会暨中国教育效能学术委员会第三届年会, 2010年10月22–23日, 沈阳、中国, '*An Overview of the Status Quo, the Weakness and the Development Tendency of Educational Effectiveness*

Research in China'. Keynote paper presented at the 2nd International Conference on School Effectiveness and School Improvement and the 3rd Meeting of the Educational Effectiveness Academic Committee in China, 22–23 October 2010, Shenyang, China.

Sun, M. T. (孙绵涛) and Hung, Z. (洪哲) (1994) 学校效能初探 'The initiative study of school effectiveness', 教育与经济 *Education & Economics*, 3, 1–5.

Tang, K. C. (汤林春) and Liang, L. L. (梁玲玲) (2005) 学校效能评价的尝试 'An exploratory study on school effectiveness using value added method', 上海教育科研 *Shanghai Research on Education*, 4, 24–26.

Teddlie, C. and Liu, S. (2008) 'Examining teacher effectiveness within differentially effective primary schools in the People's Republic of China', *School Effectiveness and School Improvement*, 19(4), 387–407.

Teddlie, C. and Reynolds, D. (2000) *The International Handbook of School Effectiveness Research*, London and New York: RoutledgeFalmer.

Thomas, S. (2005) 运用「增值」评量指标评估英国学校表现 'Using indicators of value added to evaluation school performance in the UK', 教育研究月刊 *Educational Research Journal*, 26(9), 20–27.

Thomas, S. (2001) Dimensions of secondary school effectiveness: comparative analyses across regions, *School Effectiveness and School Improvement*, 12(3), 285–322.

Thomas, S. M. (2010) '*Educational Quality in China: Concepts and Evidence*'. Keynote paper presented at the 2nd International Conference on School Effectiveness and School Improvement and the 3rd Meeting of the Educational Effectiveness Academic Committee in China, 22–23 October 2010, Shenyang, China.

Thomas, S. M. and Peng, W. J. (2009) 'Enhancing quality and capacity for educational research', in D. Stephens (ed.), *Higher Education and International Capacity Building: Twenty Five Years of Higher Education Links*. Symposium Books/Bristol papers in Comparative Education.

Thomas, S. and Mortimore, P. (1996) 'Comparison of value-added models for secondary-school effectiveness', *Research Papers in Education*, 11(1), 5–33.

Thomas, S., Peng, W. J. and Gray, J. (2007) 'Modelling patterns of improvement over time: value added trends in English secondary school performance across ten cohorts', *Oxford Review of Education*, 33(3), 261–295.

Tikly, L. (2006) *EdQual Annual Report to DFID 05/06*. 1 November 2006. Online. Available HTTP: <http://www.edqual.org/publications/ar0506.pdf> (accessed 23 May 2007).

UNESCO (2004) *EFA Global Monitoring Report 2005. Education For All: The Quality Imperative*, Paris: UNESCO.

UNESCO (2008) *Quality Education, Equity and Sustainable Development: A Holistic Vision through UNESCO's Four World Education Conferences 2008–2009*, Paris: UNESCO.

UNICEF (2000) *Defining Quality in Education*, New York, UNICEF.

Wang, X. R. (王新如) and Zheng, W. (郑文) (1997) 谈学校组织文化与学校效能 'Introduction to organisational culture and effectiveness of schools', 教育科学 *Education Science*, 3, 53–57.

Wilson, D., Burgess, S. and Briggs, A. (2005) *The Dynamics of School Attainment of England's Ethnic Minorities, Working paper No. 05/130*, Bristol: Centre for Market and Public Organisation, University of Bristol.

Xie, X. Y. (谢秀英) (2007) "高考移民" 政策限制的合理性分析 'On the rationality of policy restriction of "migration for the National College Entrance Examination"',

陕西青年管理干部学院学报 *Journal of Shaanxi Institute of Junior Managerial Personnel*, 20(1), 27–29, 35.

Xue, H. P. (薛海平) and Min, W. F. (闵维方) (2008) 中国西部教育生产函数研究 'A study on educational production function in western regions of China', 教育经济 *Education & Economy*, 2, 18–25.

Yang, H. Q. (杨会芹) and He, J. H. (何俊华) (2008) 多层线性模型在心理和教育纵向研究中的运用 'The application of hierarchical linear model in longitudinal research on the study of education and psychology', 石家庄学院学报 *Journal of Shijiazhuang University*, 10(3), 71–72, 102.

Yu, J. F. (俞继凤) (2005) 西方国家学校效能研究的反思及其未来发展 'The introspection and future development of school effectiveness research of Western countries', 外国教育研究 *Studies in Foreign Education*, 6, 1–4.

Yu, G. and Thomas, S. (2008) 'Exploring school effects across southern and eastern African school systems and in Tanzania', *Assessment in Education: Principles, Policy & Practice*, 15(3), 283–305.

Zhang, X. (张兴) (1998) 引进增值观念, 推进素质教育 'Introduction to value added for quality education improvement', 教育导刊 *Journal of Educational Development*, 2–3, 14, 81.

Zhang, Y. (张煜) and Meng, H. W. (孟鸿伟) (1995) 教育研究中的多层分析方法 'Educational research using multilevel data analysis', 教育研究 *Educational Research*, 2, 42–47.

Zhang, T. and Minxia, Z. (2006) 'Universalizing nine-year compulsory education for poverty reduction in rural China', *International Review of Education*, 52(3–4), 261–286.

Zhou, H. (周皓) and Wu, X. W. (巫锡炜) (2008) 流动儿童的教育绩效及其影响因素: 多层线性模型分析 'School performance of migrant children and its determinants: a hierarchical linear model analysis', 人口研究 *Population Research*, 32(2), 22–32.

5 Education in the Tibetan Autonomous Region: policies and practices in rural and nomadic communities

Gerard A. Postiglione, Ben Jiao and Melvyn C. Goldstein

This chapter takes an overview of educational progress in China's Tibetan Autonomous Region. It notes a rapid expansion of access to basic education, despite the harsh climate, rugged geography, dispersed population, and scarcity of resources. This has been achieved by an increase in qualified teachers, boarding schools, and improved classroom resources. Case studies of rural and nomadic regions reveal that two TAR educational policies – the 'three guarantees' and 'inland schools', provided households with an incentive to support compulsory schooling. The chapter argues that while the TAR is fast approaching full access to nine-year basic education for all, it lags far behind urban China in the level of instructional quality.

How does one of the world's most recognised centres of cultural heritage adapt and capitalise upon schools for the economic and social development of its rural and nomadic communities? Contemporary Tibet's main educational policies are set by the Beijing Central Government within the context of a socialist state adapting to market economics, while legislating a special status for education in the Tibetan Autonomous Region (TAR). This chapter provides a description and analysis of selected aspects of educational development in the TAR. It aims to identify the major successes and ongoing challenges. It begins with an outline of the context within which the education system is situated, followed by a general account of educational progress and problems, and a review of related measures to improve access to education for students from rural and nomadic communities.

The context of TAR education

Population and geography

The TAR faces an educational challenge. How can its schools become vibrant community-based institutions that transmit the core values of the society, yet contribute to household economy and a rise in living standards? The TAR is populated by Tibetans who live at altitudes averaging 3,600 meters above sea level, and possess a distinctive culture that has remained intact for over a thousand years, with a complex religious tradition and sophisticated writing system (Goldstein 1989, Goldstein and Beall 1990). At 1.2 million square kilometers, the TAR comprises 12.5 per cent of China's area. Although this chapter focuses on the education system of the TAR, Tibetans are also dispersed across a region of 3.8 million square kilometers that stretch beyond the TAR and into the surrounding regions of Kham and Amdo in the Chinese provinces of Sichuan, Qinghai, Gansu, and Yunnan.[1] When established, the TAR was about 99 per cent Tibetan. It is still far more ethnically homogenous than any other provincial-level ethnic autonomous region in China. Although the capital city of Lhasa has universalised access to basic education and has the best schools, less than half of the capital city is populated by its TAR Tibetans. About 82 per cent of TAR Tibetans live in rural and nomadic regions where both access to schooling and quality education vary across the vast expanse of the TAR.

Historical background: society

After the Chinese People's Liberation Army entered Tibet in 1951, the traditional theocratic structure of government, the organisation of monasteries, and traditional forms of landholding remained somewhat unchanged for a time (Goldstein 2007). About nine years later the Dalai Lama fled to India where he remains in residence a half century later. After his departure in 1959, land was redistributed from the upper elite to landless peasants. In 1966, all private land was taken into the commune system and communal production began. The TAR was officially established in 1965 (Grunfeld 1996). The Cultural Revolution, a 10-year political campaign aimed at rekindling revolutionary fervour and purifying the Chinese Communist Party, soon followed and tore into the fabric of Tibetan life with devastating results, including a massive destruction of temples. Class struggle became the order of the day, and the quality of teaching and learning in schools worsened. Where they remained open, schools became predominantly an ideological arena for propaganda and self-criticism. Class warfare took precedence over academic affairs, and any mention of cultural heritage became associated with feudalism and was severely criticised. The People's Communes were not abandoned until 1981, after which rural reforms, specifically the household responsibility system, put the focus back on the family as the unit of production. This led to a drop in school participation rates as the need for children to labour at home became more important.

Historical background: education

The first 'modern' school in Lhasa was established in 1952 (Zhou 2002). The Seventeen Point Agreement signed in 1951 stated that: 'the spoken and written language and the school education of the Tibetan nationality shall be developed step by step in accordance with the actual conditions of Tibet' (Sino-Tibetan Agreement 1951). This agreement permitted monasteries to continue operating. Though they were never educational institutions for the masses, they continue to transmit the religious culture of Tibetans to the next generation of monks. Before 1959, there were also some small private schools for children in towns of Lhasa, Shigatse, and Gyantse. Like elsewhere in China, the masses had little access to schools, and for those that did attend, the focus was on basic literacy. The newly established government schools in towns like Lhasa drew some of these students away from these private schools. Some elite families agreed to allow a son to go for education in Beijing but others continued to send children to India for education (Mackerras 1994, 1995). Nevertheless, by 1959 the educational system was brought more into line with the rest of China. While most children did not attend monasteries, research confirms that the traditional emphasis on recitation of the scriptures still exerts an influence on teaching methods in schools, in the same way that Confucianism still exerts an influence on teaching and learning in most parts of China (Mackerras 1999, Palden Nyima 1997, 2000, Zhang, Jiao and Postiglione 2006).

The Preparatory Committee for the Establishment of the TAR in 1956 eventually came to emphasise the rapid expansion of community (*minban*) schools, many of which closed later due to poor quality (Xia, Ha and Abadu 1999). China's gradualist approach to ethnic minority education was abandoned during the Great Leap period. Expansion leveled off by 1978. According to Bass, reforms after the Cultural Revolution initially led more children to attend monasteries (Bass 1998: 215, Geng and Wang 1989). However, the dissolution of the communes in 1981[2] also saw more parents withdraw their children from school to labour at home under the new household responsibility system.

China launched its economic reform and opening to the outside world in December 1978. In 1979, Tibet had about 6,266 primary schools, 55 middle schools, 22 technical secondary schools, eight worker schools, and four colleges (Wu 1995: 81). Due to the severe lack of qualified teachers and administrators, as well as buildings, equipment, and textbooks, schooling was chaotic at best, and instructional quality was minimal (Zhou 2002: 84). Between 1978 and 1985, a consolidation of schools took place that more than halved the number of students enrolled in primary schools from 262,611 to 119,939. It became possible to see a slow recovery between 1985 and 1994 with enrolments growing steadily back toward the 1978 level in 1994 when the total number of primary schools, including teaching points,[3] was about 3,300 (Wu 1995: 94–95).

By 1990, less than 20 per cent of the TAR Tibetans had completed a primary school education; few had much more, and the number that had joined monasteries was only a few thousand. Rapid progress followed so that by the end of the century, illiteracy and semi-literacy stood slightly above 50 per cent, and enrolment in junior secondary school stood near 25 per cent.

Urban school enrolment was high, but some remote regions only had universalised 3-year compulsory education (N.A. 2001). By 2000, the TAR had more than 4,000 schools: 820 primary and secondary schools, 3,033 teaching points (or incomplete primary schools), 110 regular and vocational secondary schools, and 4 institutions of higher education. These schools served about 360,000 TAR students in all forms and levels of education, and were staffed by about 19,000 teachers.

While official figures indicate that only 6 per cent of the region's population had achieved nine-years of basic education in 2000, 70 per cent had achieved 6-years of basic education. The remaining 22 per cent had achieved or nearly achieved 3-years of basic education (N.A. 2001). Although the TAR still had the lowest education levels of any provincial level entity in China, by 1999, the enrolment rate for all school-aged children in basic education increased to 83.4 per cent, surpassing the 80 per cent target set for 2000.

By September of 2006, the reform and consolidation of schools had produced a system with 890 primary schools, 118 middle schools, and a large dispersed system of 1,568 primary school level teaching points throughout its remote rural and nomadic areas (*Tibet Daily* 4 September 2006: 1) The total enrolment, while open to debate, was proclaimed to be 530,000, which encompassed 96.5 per cent of the school-age children. (*Tibet Daily* 30 January 2007: 1).

In 2008, the enrolment rate for school-age children in the TAR reached 98.5 per cent in 884 primary schools, and 70 of the 73 counties had popularised nine-year basic education, a figure that our research found impressive though somewhat doubtful since rural and nomadic areas are notorious for their inaccurate reporting of enrolment and attendance figures (*China Tibet News* 2009). Nevertheless, the increase in access to basic education in the TAR during the past ten years has been impressive.

From quantity to quality

Enrolment rates tell part of the story because as these rates rise, the work needed to sustain and retain students increases. In general, the early phase of popularisation of basic education sees a rise in both access rates and dropout rates. In cases when learning conditions provided by rural schools are still poor, then spending on teacher training is one of the most cost effective measures to sustain enrolment rates.

In the 1990s it was not unusual to see poorly constructed and maintained rural schools, dormitories with leaky ceilings and cracked walls, classrooms without light, students without dictionaries, and some classrooms without teacher desks or even chalk and blackboards. With much support from the Central Government, the financial burden of capital expenditures is still significant for the TAR government. However, substantial financial support for school construction also came from other provinces. There was also some minor support from Non-Government Organisations (NGOs) such as Save the Children and Hong Kong donors.[4] By 2001, it was possible to see a rapid improvement in physical facilities, including primary schools at the township level with modified Tibetan style architecture, standard classrooms with attractive facilities, and reliable supply of electricity. By 2007 two of the authors visited remote nomadic areas where townships schools were equipped with modern facilities, trained teachers, a standard basketball court, and an internet dish on the school roof to provide access to cyberspace.

Such rapid progress in providing high quality facilities and popularising basic education in remote regions is notable and deserves recognition. Yet, school facilities and trained teachers do not automatically equate with quality instruction and meaningful learning. This is also the case in some of the most developed regions of the country. That is no reason to expect less from education in the TAR. Education specialists from China and around the world would assert that quality also refers to an education that is student-centred and driven by the needs of the local community, school based curriculum that is relevant to the immediate community, a learning environment that is stimulating and attractive to students, classroom learning activities that are problem based and interactive, teaching methods that promote critical thinking skills, creativity, and innovative approaches to assessment and evaluation, and school based management that is responsive to social development needs.

Educational policies in rural/nomadic communities

Making schools function as vital institutions for Tibetan households aspiring to a higher standard of living should be a basic aim of rural and nomadic education programmes. The establishment of literacy and basic education is guided by a framework of national policies, and there are additional policies designed for implementation in ethnic minority regions. These include provisions for boarding schools, ethnic teacher training, bilingual education, and preferential admission (Ha and Teng 2001). The Education Bureau of the TAR has also promulgated specific educational measures to suit the TAR's special circumstances. Two examples are the three guarantees (*sanbao*) and Inland Tibet Schools (*neidiban*). Moreover, the education departments of prefectures or counties may also have their own special measures, including incentive arrangements for households or teachers, as described below.

The sanbao (three guarantees policy)

In theory, the compulsory education law of China requires that all children attend nine years of compulsory education. This also applies to the TAR; in fact, fines have been levied for non-attendance. However, such fines are generally ineffective as most poor households have no way of the paying the fines. In many cases a household would lose less money by paying the fines so their children could continue to herd sheep or goats instead of attending school. A number of measures are used to encourage children to attend school in poor rural areas. Groups of households sometimes pool their livestock and share the herding duties so children can attend school. One of the most well known measures aimed at raising attendance rates in rural and nomadic regions has been the *sanbao* or three-guarantees policy (Tongzhi 1994, Wu 1995). This includes measures designed to relieve families of the financial burden associated with schooling. It includes a guarantee to provide food. This usually means providing butter tea for children who live beyond two kilometres from school during the daytime and meals for those students who board at school. It also includes a guarantee to provide clothing. This can include school wear and a set of bedding for boarding school children. Finally, it guarantees accommodation, which means living accommodation for boarding school children.

The neidi xizang ban *policy*

Another major policy with implications for rural education is the *neidi xizang ban* (inland Tibet secondary schools and classes), which provides for sending primary school graduates to inland secondary schools across China (Wang and Zhou 2003, Postiglione and Jiao 2010). The TAR government selects and recommends primary school graduates of 12 to 13 years old for these inland schools. The majority of the students attend segregated classes in urban secondary schools. The policy began in 1985 when Beijing, Lanzhou, and Chengdu established *neidi* schools, and by the end of 1986 there were 16 such schools. A 1993 working group on Tibet called for long-term support for *neidi* boarding school education. The perceived success of the *neidi* schools led to the establishment of similar schools for students from the Xinjiang Uyghur Nationality Autonomous Region in 2000 (Chen 2008). In 1985, about 20 per cent of Tibet's elementary school graduates were dislocated for junior secondary education. As the secondary school enrolment rates of the TAR continued to grow, the proportion but not the number being dislocated to China decreased. From 1985 to 2005, 25,000 students went to 89 *neidi* schools in 20 provinces and municipalities (Xiangba Pingcuo 2005). Most of the students came from urban cadre families. In 1992, Beijing's *neidi* school set an 80 per cent quota for rural and nomadic region students from all parts of Tibet. While the early cohorts were dominated by urban children of cadre families, the aim was to shift enrolments in favor of children from rural and nomadic regions. Although there are no reliable figures to assess the outcome of the policy favouring children of families from rural and nomadic regions, research indicates that at least half of the students were from cadre households (Postiglione and Jiao 2010). The boarding schools are clearly preparing an elite stratum, with about half of the children already from elite households and the rest aspiring to that category.

Continuing challenges

School attendance inevitably involves opportunity costs for rural households since most rural and nomadic children will have to leave their villages and live in school dormitories away from home. Village parents sometimes express concern about the value of schooling at county secondary schools because of the risk to youth caused by urbanisation and leading to value separation from home farming communities. Completion of county level junior secondary school has not provided youth with knowledge and skills that open doors in the non-farm labour market, leaving many of them between the status of urban unemployed and dislocated rural returnee.

Although opportunities for vocational education have been increasing, there is still a critical need for vocational skills training, a need identified by long-standing NGOs in the TAR, such as the Tibet Poverty Alleviation Fund. While this need is more for training (i.e. repair of transport vehicles, restaurant and hotel work, etc.), than for education, this kind of training is closely linked to basic education because such training is most effective for Tibetans who have already attained literacy through basic schooling. Although vocational training programmes help Tibetans compete with newcomers from other parts of China for non-farm labour jobs, these pro-grammes are far from reaching their full potential (Wang/Gyamtso 2009). With the move away from a planned economy, the senior secondary specialised schools (*zhongzhuan*), which were run under the authority of particular ministries and which led to stable jobs under ministries, have been reduced in scope (except in teacher training and policing). At the same time, oppor-tunities for regular senior secondary vocational education under the authority of the TAR education commission has improved but are still far from ade-quate. Given the probability that there will be continued changes in the skills required for the TAR economy, a senior secondary vocational education also needs to emphasise adaptability of skills for a changing labour market.

At the tertiary level, enrolment rates of Tibetans at TAR universities have not reached parity with their proportion of the general population. Moreover, the shift from guaranteed job allocation to market forces has been especially hard on college and university graduates who are from rural and nomadic areas. In 2005, for example, about 2,730 Tibetan graduates of three-year colleges faced the job market and about 700 were still looking for work. In Lhasa, 356 graduates, about one-third of that year's total, were still looking for jobs (*China Daily*/Xinhua 2006; Xinhua 2006). Since that time, new measures have been introduced for unemployed college graduates. The Tibet Branch of Bank of China introduced loans for unemployed college graduates in Lhasa, Shigatse, Nyingchi and Lhoka. The loans are to be used to start businesses, but are only available to college degree holders who had not found jobs within five years, a fact that indicates the depth of the problem. The Education Bureau of the TAR in 2009 cited the number of college graduates last year as 11,118, with 88.95 per cent having found jobs.

Among the new measures said to be responsible for the decrease in the unemployment rate are: services for job-hunting college graduates, including free consultation on employment regulations, guidance on recommendations for top students; launching non-profit, large-scale and diversified job fairs; and encouraging graduates to go online for recruitment opportunities. Colleges and universities in the TAR also established an intern system for graduates (Xinhuanet 2009). The main problem confronting tertiary education is also one of quality and external efficiency – increasing the relevance of tertiary education for finding a job in Tibetan society.

Overall, education in the TAR followed a pattern of zigzag development since 1950, with major progress in access rates and impressive improvements in facilities and teacher qualifications over the past ten years. Educational development remains behind the rest of the country, but the provision of good facilities and trained teachers has now placed TAR schools with the capacity and potential to conduct more experimental programmes and implement innovations to improve the quality of the learning environment.

Case studies of educational practices in rural/nomadic communities

The TAR is the most sparsely populated region in China, with 2.26 people per square kilometre and a total population of about 2.6 million, of which only about 20 per cent reside in urban areas. The other 80 per cent live in both rural and nomadic livestock breeding areas. Most of the population is concentrated in the southern and eastern parts. The rest of this chapter will cite selected aspects of case studies in two rural counties (Benam and Lhundrup) in 1998 to 2002 and two nomadic prefectures (Nackchu and Ngari) in 2007 so as to highlight policies, practices, challenges and possibilities.

Rural areas

Rural and nomadic families are larger on average, and it is not always the case that every child in a family will stay in school for the full six years (Lu 2007). In areas such as Penam and Lhundrup counties, school attendance rates are a key concern of the county governments (Postiglione, Jiao and Gyatso 2005, 2006). In the villages of these rural areas, fees have been eliminated, including the cost of books. Accommodation in boarding schools are provided, along with some food and clothing, if the school is far from home. For some families, opportunity costs associated with school are still steep, in particular, the loss of household labour. Some communities have tried to pool household labour, for example, by combining herds for grazing to free-up children to attend school.

As the TAR moves to increase enrolments in secondary schools, county leaders visit township schools to encourage parents to send their children on to junior secondary school. Household that have two to four or more children sometimes feel the need to keep at least one of their children at or close to home. However, this is no longer considered acceptable for exempting attendance in secondary school.

Students who attend schools in the countryside have Tibetan language textbooks for all subjects except Chinese and English which are taught as separate subjects. Most rural community (*minban*) school teachers who cannot speak Chinese have been phased out or replaced by regular (*gongban*) or substitute (*daike*) teachers. Interestingly, about half of those returning from the secondary schools for Tibetans that are located in Chinese cities [inland schools (*neidi ban*)] become school teachers. Of these, some are placed in township primary schools. These teachers usually have a good knowledge of Chinese language, though school principals sometimes comment about their inadequate level of Tibetan which is needed in rural settings where little Chinese is spoken.

Local incentives

In the early 1990s, the Penam county had many village schools in Sogang and Mag that were in many ways like their counterparts in other parts of rural China during the 1980s. Village schools were run down buildings without lights or electricity. Of the seven schools in Mag township, for example, five were the poorest buildings in the villages. The fortunate schools had chairs, desks and blackboards. Chalk, pens, papers and dictionaries were another matter, and these were often difficult to acquire. Many village schools had no library or sports equipment at the time. Although the qualification of teachers gradually improved, teachers seldom developed school based curriculum, used discovery methods or problem based learning, or stressed critical thinking skills in their teaching. However, the Sokang village school taught Tibetan, Chinese and Mathematics. Village teachers in the 1990s typically organised instruction for a non-age graded one room school house. Some rural areas like Mag township have begun to close the many small village schools and consolidate them all in the township central school. This can have the effect of improving costs and efficiency, but it also means that many children will have to board at school beginning at a much younger age.

When there was a need to raise access rates, innovative incentives were introduced. In the case of Penam county, a certain portion of village school teachers' salary was withheld by the county education authorities each year, and that portion was awarded back to teachers based upon attendance rates and students passing examinations for promotion to the next level of school.

In general, there is a continuing need to strengthen the capacity of teachers, provide better working conditions, and more in-service teacher training focused on problems specific to particular regions and school communities. Much of such training for village teachers is organised at the township central school where top teachers are identified and used to promote better teaching performance.

In the late 1990s, almost two-thirds of the parents we surveyed believed that Tibetan was the most useful subject, which was two to three times the proportion who believed it was Chinese. Nevertheless, households with at least one member who migrated for work to an urban area were aware of the importance of being able to speak Chinese, though this in itself did not guarantee urban job acquisition.

Measures to improve access and equity in primary schools remain a concern and education officials mobilise resources and parents to improve school attendance. It is notable that the proportion of girls to boys is higher than in many other parts of rural China.

Building parental support

Education officials stressed the importance of convincing parents of the benefits brought by schooling. Attendance rates were low in the early 1990s when some poor households even ignored fines levied for non-attendance at school. The government had in fact discontinued the three guarantees (*sanbao*) policy and only reinstituted it in 1999. When we revisited in 2002, families had less reason not to send their children to school (Shao 2004).

In September of 2002, parents with one child not attending school were called to the school grounds to meet with a delegation of county education leaders. Parents could plead their case for keeping one or more of their children at home. A villager with four children, three of whom were in school, wanted an exemption for his oldest son who had just graduated from the township primary school but was scheduled to attend the far off county boarding school. If this son was away at school, he asked, who would tend the livestock, and keep it from grazing in other fields? Exemptions were rare, however, and usually only granted for children with disabilities.

Village households

Most rural villagers have few skills outside of basic farming and animal husbandry. A small number have skills in carpentry, weaving, masonry, and painting. Some areas had farm tractors that could be used in an educational sense to provide teachers with simple but practical examples of benefits from science and agricultural technology. Most parents recognised the benefit of their children learning to read and write Tibetan and do simple mathematical calculations to maintain records and accounts, for example when selling their products or taking loans. Some associated schooling with having a better life and as a path to becoming a local government official.

To improve school attendance in the late 1990s, Penam county had established a point system for rewarding school attendance and penalising truancy. Each awarded point was worth two mao (20 cents) and households could actually earn money for their children's school attendance. This measure was instituted as an interim measure when the attendance rates were extremely low.

Other measures included the three guarantees and adjusting the school calendar to agricultural work. In the busy spring and fall seasons, when children's help is urgently needed for planting and harvesting, schools have instituted a system whereby students can be sent home for up to seven days.

These point measures for teachers and households, including the three guarantees policy, coupled with improved school resources and more qualified teachers resulted in a significant improvement in school enrolment rates. With the approach of 2010, rural counties like Penam and Lhundrop have schools facilities and resources that are compatible with those in many comparable rural regions of China. The provision of basic conditions means that the opportunities have been increased for more innovative approaches to improve classroom learning.

Rural families increasingly recognise the relevance of schooling to an improved standard of living. Tibetan teachers are able to better articulate the link between schooling, cultural values, improved standards of living, and community development. Preparing Tibetan children to compete with the increasing number of TAR outsiders puts schooling in a different light. Young men returning to their villages shared their experiences about urban Tibet and reported that speaking Chinese could increase job opportunities, even if discrimination toward workers from rural and nomadic areas still existed. It is increasingly apparent that school represents a path to non-farm jobs. Rural Tibetans would probably look more positively upon schooling if they could see a more direct economic return in the non-farm labour market.

Nomadic areas

The major nomadic regions are mainly in the west and northwest and account for most of Tibet's land area. This area includes eastern Ngari and western Nakchu and has one of the lowest population densities in the world, about 0.23 person per square kilometre. Among Tibet's 73 counties, 14 are nomadic and 24 semi-nomadic. Unfortunately, Tibet's statistics only distinguish between urban and rural areas and do not further differentiate between farming and nomadic areas. Therefore, when doing a survey of the available data, we have to consider Nakchu and Ngari Prefectures as approximately equal to nomadic areas, and make other prefectures, except Lhasa, generally equal to rural areas. The following provides a brief comparison of basic education in the two major nomadic prefectures of Nakchu and Ngari.

Basic education in two nomadic prefectures: Nakchu and Ngari

Basic education in Nackchu

By 1978, Nakchu had increased its provision to 72 public primary schools with 648 teaching and administrative staff and 7,100 students. It also had

1,360 community-run teaching points and schools with 1,359 teachers and 27,424 students. Beyond that, there were two middle schools with 52 teachers and 887 students, and a trade school with 19 teachers and 127 students. In 1984, Nakchu increased the number of public schools and introduced the three guarantees (food, lodging, clothes) policy mentioned above. The Pachen County Middle School was established in 1984 and by 1988, there were 194 schools in total, including 70 public primary schools, 120 private primary schools, three middle schools and one teachers college, with a total enrolment of 9,595. The Prefecture Vocational Secondary School was set up in 1997. By the century's end, 40 townships had achieved the goal of three-year compulsory education (Wang 2000). There were 138 schools in total, including a vocational secondary school, 10 middle schools and 127 primary schools. The total enrolment was 34,300 with 64 per cent of school-age children enrolled. However, only 66 per cent of teachers in primary schools and 83 per cent of those in middle schools were qualified.

Basic education in Ngari

In 1986, barely 16.1 per cent of school-age children in Ngari were enrolled. According to the 1989 Tibet Commission of Science and Technology (CST) statistics, there were 8,624 school-age children between 7 and 11-year-old in Ngari, but only 1,492 were enrolled, a rate of 17.30 per cent and a retention rate of 80.6 per cent. In 2001, there were 58 schools, 13 complete primary schools, 25 junior primary schools, 12 teaching centres, three junior middle schools, one complete middle school, and a kindergarten. In contrast to Nackchu, about 90 per cent of the teachers in middle schools and 86 per cent in primary schools are qualified (Geju Jiandzan 2001).

Comparing school access in Nakchu and Ngari

The enrolment rate for the Tibetan Autonomous Region (TAR) in 2000 was 85.8 per cent. The enrolment rates were 64 per cent for Nakchu and Ngari, far behind Lhasa with 97 per cent. In a 2005 article, Wangdui of the Tibet Education Ministry stated, 'The enrolment rate of school-age children in nomadic areas fell 10 to 20 per cent behind the TAR average . . . Eleven counties which could not achieve the goal of nine-year compulsory education by 2007 were entirely nomadic counties' (Wang 2005).

Perspectives in Nakchu and Ngari

There are a number of reasons why the promotion of school access has been a challenge in nomadic regions. First, the nomadic areas of Nakchu and Ngari are all above 4,500 metres. Together, Nakchu with 420,000 square kilometres and Ngari with 345,000 square kilometres account for 64 per cent of Tibet. Tibet's population in 2004 was 2.59 million, but Nakchu's (387,200) and Ngari's (77,800) population accounted for only 18 per cent of that. The population density, respectively, is 0.92 and 0.23 persons per square kilometre, far below Tibet's average of 2.16 persons per square kilometre. Needless to say, altitude and population density make for adverse conditions when popularising basic education. While the service radius for primary schools in rural areas of Tibet is 15 to 20 kilometres, it can be 100 to 150 kilometres in nomadic areas, and 150 to 200 kilometres for the county junior middle schools. Therefore, over 95 per cent of students and teachers need to board at school (TASS 2004: 254). All this makes it difficult to attract good teachers to remote nomadic schools for long periods, and those that do stay on find that the lack of information access and communication takes its toll on the quality of their work (Liu 2007).

Second, labour demands may affect school access. While almost all rural households have livestock, their herds are tiny in comparison with that of nomads. Although the current practice in rural areas is for several families to herd one another's livestock, this is not always feasible in nomadic areas. A year in nomadic areas is generally divided into life in a home base campsite where they spend most of the year and a Fall pasture site where they move with their animals and tents for three to four months. While at their home base site, they also sometimes move some of their livestock to satellite tent camps to provide better pasture. Per capita livestock can range from 15 to 70 (Wang 2005). Throughout the year, school age children would be useful for herding as nomad families typically divide their livestock into two to four herding units, for example, their milking sheep/goats, non-milking sheep/goats, female yaks, and stud sheep/goats.

Third, nomads have traditionally not held a very positive view of the commodity economy and professional businessmen and traders. They generally did not measure wealth with money or cash, and instead perceived differences between wealth and poverty by their number of livestock and especially women's clothes. They may have had flocks of cattle and sheep, but were not cash rich. In the new China where goods can be bought with money and they can receive cash for their products, they fully understand cash and animals are measures of wealth. If they want to have money in the bank they could simply sell some of their animals. Some nomadic families live near areas rich in caterpillar fungus and make a fortune selling Cordyceps (a type of fungi). Most nomads seldom migrate to urban areas for work, and those who do are handicapped by language barriers and custom taboos, as well as a lack of start-out cash and of work skills. Sending children away to school can affect household production in the sense that other family members would have more work to do. Despite the 'three guarantees' policy that provides free schooling, accommodation, and food, parents may have to provide children with some pocket money. As schooling becomes more widespread, nomads calculate the value of school attendance against the probability that schooling will lead their children to become a cadre or county official, or go on to university (Du 2006).

Fourth, it is still difficult for nomads to recognise the long-term value of schooling. They send their children to schools with the hope they might become cadres and have stable salaries, rather than with the expectation they will gain useful knowledge that will spur the household economy (Tenzin Norbu 2005). Albeit, parents do mention that knowledge of basic arithmetic and literacy skills which could be acquired in a few years of schooling is an advantage. Education officials, school principals, and classroom teachers visit families to persuade them of the value of the new government initiatives in education, usually pointing out the long-term benefits to the community as a whole and to their children as part of the next generation. Poorer nomadic families find such notions difficult to understand as they struggle to sustain a basic standard of living. Households that have gained some benefit directly from specific government initiatives for land use, herding rights, flood relief, health care, etc. are more likely to adhere to the plea of local leaders to send children to school.

Fifth, the language of instruction in rural and nomadic primary schools is Tibetan. However, it abruptly changes to Chinese in junior middle schools, despite the fact that there is virtually no Chinese language environment in Tibetan rural and nomadic communities. The capacity for Chinese language teaching in rural and nomadic areas is limited and generally poor (Chen 2006, N.A. 2005). After completing primary school, nomadic students might not even be able to have a simple Chinese conversation, or read basic Chinese sentences. The medium of instruction issue is highly complex and differs across different Tibetan areas (Upton 1999, Postiglione, Jiao and Manlaji 2007). There are many multilingual places in the world where the medium of instruction becomes an emotive and politicised issue and the same is the case for Tibetan regions (Nyima 1997, Bass 1998, Upton 1999). Few Tibetans advocate not learning any Chinese and most realise that Chinese is needed in a market economy. Dual track education (Tibetan and Chinese) is generally available in the urban areas, but after the primary school grade three, there is a shift toward Chinese as the medium of instruction, with only language and literature courses taught in the Tibetan language (Xiangba Pingcuo 2005). From an educational point of view, unless a student has achieved a threshold level of competency in the second language, its use as a medium of instruction can severely limit the potential for academic success and can lead to other deleterious effects noted by sociologists of education. While many parents may be in favour of Chinese as a medium of instruction due to its currency in the job market, they may not be aware of the countless studies showing that students do not learn well unless they have achieved a level of competency in the second language so as to be able to learn school subjects effectively (Baker 2001, Street 2001). In short, learning should take priority in schooling and while the national language must be studied, it is the responsibility of the school that students learn in the most efficient manner, whether that is in the national language or the language of Tibet (Dai, Teng, Guan and Dong 1997, Zhou 2000). Moreover, students may have a sufficient level of competency in Chinese for effective learning, but unless their teachers are able to teach competently through Chinese, student learning will be affected. In many nomadic counties, there is a shortage of Chinese language specialists, in which case teachers of other subjects who are unqualified as language teachers, will take on the role of teaching Chinese as a subject. In short, the low achievement level in education for Tibetans has a great deal to do with the language policy. China has done a great deal to produce school textbooks in ethnic minority languages, including Tibetan and about 21 other languages. The five province/region Tibetan learning materials leadership group has facilitated the production of Tibetan language learning resources and has visited other countries to learn about how bilingual education is undertaken elsewhere. However, the Tibetan language school textbooks in mathematics, science and other subjects are often direct translations of Chinese language materials. Moreover, the updating of Tibetan language textbooks is slow and costly. Meanwhile, Tibetan medium of instruction is often viewed as a hindrance to advancement as TAR secondary school graduates soon discover when they have to compete for jobs with the thousands of TAR students returning with a good grasp of Chinese from their years of study at the inland (*neidi*) schools.

Finally, usually only primary education and secondary education are available in nomadic areas. Pre-school education, vocational education, and special education are far less developed.

Conclusion

Impressive advances have been made in expanding access to basic schooling. National policies, laws, and regulations are guiding the establishment and development of basic education in the TAR. Many households are dealing with the effects of an intensified market economy. As in other parts of rural China, household nutrition and health indicators have a major impact on enrolment and achievement (Yu and Hannum 2006). In many regions, policies such as the three guarantees have helped relieve the financial burden on households. In order to improve access and equity in basic education, county education bureaus have experimented with incentive systems aimed at families and teachers. Intensified teacher training, phasing out of community (*minban*) teachers, recruitment of younger teachers (including *daike* teachers) and graduates of inland (*neidi*) schools accompany the popularisation of basic education. However, improving the quality of teacher training remains an urgent need. As access rates increase, dropout rates also increase for a period of time until regular attendance is sustained. At the local level, school planning is not yet a community driven process, though local governments have initiated a number of meetings with families at the village and township level to encourage them to send their children to school and keep them from dropping out. Given the level of resources now available to rural and nomadic schools, and the rising qualifications of teachers, there is a growing potential to experiment with a variety of new methods to improve the quality of teaching and learning in rural and nomadic regions. In short, instructional quality remains far behind the rest of China, though there are signs that given the right conditions, it could catch up quickly.

Notes

1 The education focus of this chapter will be largely on the TAR, although similar developmental challenges may exist in other Tibetan areas as well.
2 To this day, one commune still exists in the TAR.
3 Teaching points are usually located in remote villages where one or two teachers will provide primary school age children with instruction.
4 One of us facilitated two donations from the Hong Kong Save the Children fund for dictionaries, school library, and a generator for dormitory lights.

References

Baker, C. (2001) *Foundations of bilingual education and bilingualism* (3rd edn), Buffalo, NY: Multilingual Matters.

Bass, Catriona (1998) *Education in Tibet: Policy and Practice since 1950*, London: Zed Books.

Chen, B. S. (2006) 'Discussion about the status quo of education quality in rural and nomadic areas', *Tibet Education Journal*, 2.

Chen Yangbin (2008) *Uyghur Students' Social Recapitalization as a Response to Ethnic Integration*, New York: Lexington Books.

China Tibet News 1 June 2009 Online. Available HTTP: < http://english.chinatibetnews.com/news/Society/2009-06/01/content_251688.htm> (accessed 1 June 2009).

Dai, Q. J., Teng, X., Guan, X. Q. and Dong, Y. (1997) *Zhongguo shaoshu minzu shuangyu jiaoyu gailun* (Introduction to bilingual education for China's minorities), Liaoning: Nationalities Press.

Du, S. Y. (2006) *A Study on the Development of Gansu – Qinghai Tibetan Modern Education*, National Education Press.

Geju Jiandzan (2001) 'The developing Ngari education', *Tibet Education Journal*, 4.

Geng, Jinsheng and Wang, Xihong (1989) Xizang jiaoyu yanjiu (Research on education in Tibet), Zhongyang minzu xueyuan chubanshe (China Nationalities Institute Press).

Goldstein, Melvyn C. (1989) *A History of Modern Tibet, 1913–1951: The Demise of the Lamaist state*, Berkeley: University of California Press.

Goldstein, Melvyn C. (2007) *A History of Modern Tibet*, Vol 2, 1951–1955, Los Angeles, CA, University of California Press.

Goldstein, Melvyn and Beall, Cynthia (1990) *Nomads of Western Tibet, the Survival of a Way of Life*, London: Serindia publications.

Grunfeld, Tom (1996) *The Making of Modern Tibet*, New York: M.E. Sharpe.

Ha, J. and Teng, X. (2001) *Minzu jiaoyu xue tonglun* (A general survey of ethnic minority education), Beijing, Jiaoyu kexue chubanshe, Educational Science Publishing House.

Liu, Z. Q. (2007) 'Problems and coping strategies in the process of Tibet educational information', *Tibet Education Journal*, 6.

Lu, D. S. (2007) 'A comparison of the values of school education held by parents in agricultural and pastoral areas of Tibet – Taking B township and T township as examples', *Journal of Research on Education for Ethnic Minorities*, 4.

Mackerras, C. (1994) *China's Minorities: Integration and Modernization in the 21st Century*, Hong Kong: Oxford University Press.

Mackerras, C. (1995) *China's Minority Cultures: Identities and Integration since 1912*, New York: St Martin's Press.

Mackerras, C. (1999) 'Religion and the education of China's minorities', in G. Postiglione (ed.) *China's National Minority Education: Culture, Schooling and Development*, New York: Falmer Press.

N. A. (2001) *China Education Daily*, May 30, 2001. Available on-line, http://www.jyb.com.cn/gb/2001/05/30/zhxw/jyzx/3.htm (accessed May 20, 2006).

N. A. (2005) 'Xizang Shuangyu Jiaoyu Qingkuang' (The bilingual education situation in Tibet) Yuyong Wenzi Gongzuo Jianbao (Language Planning and Administration Working Newsletter) 151 (15 April 2005). Online. Available HTTP: <Document available on-line, http://202.205.177.129/moe-dept/yuyong/jianbao/151.htm> (accessed 15 April 2005).

Nyima, Palden (Nima, Baden) (1997) 'The way out for Tibetan education', *Chinese Education and Society*, (30)4, 7–20.

Nyima, Palden (2000) *Wenming de kunhuo: Zangzu de jiaoyu zhilu* (*The Puzzle of Civilization: The Way Out for Tibetan Education*), Chengdu: Sichuan Education Press.

Postiglione, Gerard A. and Ben Jiao (2009) 'Tibet's relocated schools: popularization reconsidered', *Asian Survey*, 49(5), 895–914.

Postiglione, Gerard A., Ben Jiao and Manlaji (2007) 'Language in Tibetan education', in Anwei Feng (ed.), *Bilingual Education in China: Practices, Policies and Concepts*, New York: Multilingual Matters.

Postiglione, Gerard A., Ben Jiao and Sonam Gyatso (2006) Household perspectives on school attendance in rural Tibet, with Ben Jiao and Sonam Gyatso, *Educational Review*, 58(3), 317–337.

Postiglione, Gerard A., Ben Jiao and Sonam Gyatso (2005) 'Education in rural Tibet: development, problems, and adaptations'. *China: An International Journal*, 3(1), 1–23.

Shao, Y. W. (2004) 'An analysis on the reasons and countermeasures for rural and nomadic children dropping out of schools', *Tibet Education*, 12.

Street, B. (ed.) (2001) *Literacy and Development: Ethnographic Perspectives*, London: Routledge.

Tenzin Norbu (2005) 'Investigation on initiative study habits', *Tibet Education Journal*, 11.

Tibet Academy of Social Sciences (TASS) China's Tibet Development Report (2004), Tibet People's Press, p. 254.

Tongzhi (1994) Approved regulations concerning our region's provision of the 'three guarantees', in Tibetan Autonomous Region Education Research Institute (2000) *Zizang zizhiqu jiaoyu falu fagui xuanbian* (A collection of educational guidelines and regulations of the Tibetan Autonomous Region), London: Tibet People's Press.

Upton, Janet (1999) 'The development of modern school based Tibetan language education in the PRC', in G. Postiglione (ed.), *China's National Minority Education: Culture, Schooling and Development*, New York: Garland Press.

Wang, D. (2005) 'Reflections on the educational work in Tibet nomadic areas', *Tibet Education Journal*, 4.

Wang, Z. B. (2000) 'The practice and exploration of quality education in Nakchu, *Tibet Education Journal*, 4.

Wang Chengzhi and Zhou Quanhou (2003) 'Minority education in China: from the State's preferential policies to dislocated schools', *Educational Studies*, 29(1), 85–104.

Wang Shiyong [Gyamtso] (2009) *Tibetan Market Participation in China*, A Doctoral Dissertation of the University of Helsinki.

Wu Degang (1995) *Zhongguo Xizang jiaoyu gaige yu fazhan de lilun yanjiu* (A study of educational reform and development in Tibet), Yunan: Yunnan Press.

Xia, Z., Ha, J. X. and Abadu, W. (1999) 'Xizang Zizhiqu Minzu Jiaoyu 50 Nian' (50 years of ethnic education in the Tibetan Autonomous Region) in Zhongguo Minzu Jiaoyu 50 Nian (50 years of ethnic education in China), Beijing: Hongqi chubanshe, 1995.

Xiangba Pingcuo (2005) *Education Annals of the Tibetan Autonomous Region*, Beijing: China Tibetology Press.

Xinhua (2006) 'China's last guaranteed jobs axed, Tibetan graduates face market', Online. Available HTTP: <www.chinaview.cn> (accessed 27 November 2006).

Xinhuanet (2009) http://news.xinhuanet.com/english/2009-02/12/content_10811748.htm (Accessed on 16 January 2011).

Yu, Shengchao and Hannun, Emily (2006) 'Poverty, health and schooling in rural China, in G. Postiglione (ed.) *Education and Social Change in China: Inequality in a Market Economy*, New York: M.E. Sharpe.

Zhang, Lifang, Jiao Ben, Postiglione Gerard A. (2006) 'Accounting for Tibetan university students' and teachers' intellectual styles', Paper presented at *Achieving Diversity in Tertiary and Higher Education: Cross-National Lessons, Challenges and Prospects*, Yunnan Province, People's Republic of China 15–17 November 2004.

Zhou, Aiming (2002) *Xizang jiaoyu*, Beijing: Wuzhou Chuanbo Chubanshe.

Zhou, Q. S. (2000) *Yuyan yu renlei* (Language and mankind). Beijing: Central University of Nationalities Press.

Part III
Educational values and beliefs

6 The changing landscapes of a journey: educational metaphors in China

Lixian Jin and Martin Cortazzi

As Chinese higher educational institutions move towards more learner-centred approaches, it is crucial to understand Chinese values and beliefs about learning. This chapter explores continuity and change in views of learning through a study of metaphors: we examine the official external landscape of English teaching in China and the internal unofficial landscape of students' ideas of 'learning as a journey'. We show how the learning journey is elaborated as a constant, determined effort in bitter-sweet travel from hell to heaven, in which teachers direct, guide and show devotion and sacrifice. This is an insightful model for teachers and learners anywhere.

The external landscape of the current system and organisation of education in China can be characterised by the enormous scale of mass learning with widespread enthusiasm and a series of recent developments, changes and reforms. However, the internal landscape of the cultures of learning in China has arguably changed much less. This is not surprising if we understand that cultures of learning comprise the implicit expectations, values and beliefs of teachers and students underlying the interpretation of practices, since culture changes more slowly in education than policy or curriculum requirements. On the other hand, it can be expected that the current extensive developments and changes in practice will influence cultures of learning at some point: the continuity of socially transmitted values will be influenced or modified by the challenges of applied innovations and the demands of new situations.

This chapter focuses mainly on the inner landscape held in the 'heads' and 'hearts' of students and teachers in China. In general we are asking: what are the values and beliefs of students regarding teaching and learning? Specifically, we examine a large corpus of students' metaphors to investigate their interpretations of 'teacher' and 'learning', especially their ideas of journeys in learning. Our research shows that this metaphor of 'Learning is a journey' is commonly characterised as a journey 'through hell to heaven', a bitter-sweet journey of ups and downs towards ideals and dreams of future success. We take English language teaching (ELT) as a specific case of educational change and rapid development and, although the data relate to all learning not just ELT, we ask how far ELT in China has gone on a parallel journey through 'hell to heaven'. We draw on two key concepts: cultures of learning and theories of applied metaphor research. These are briefly explained before we turn to the external landscape of ELT in China and then to our main focus on the internal landscape of students' metaphors of learning as a particular journey.

Cultures of learning and metaphors

We have developed the concept of 'cultures of learning' over a number of years to draw attention to the often implicit values, expectations and interpretations of learning and teaching which frame ideas and pedagogic practices (Jin and Cortazzi 1993, Cortazzi and Jin 1996a). Cultures of learning are socially transmitted in family and social contexts and especially in classroom practices and are distinct from personal or individualised ideas. Cultures of learning embrace beliefs about what constitutes a good teacher or student, what their roles and relationships should be; about preferences, expectations and interpretations of classroom interaction, materials and outcomes; and about how classroom learning relates to broader issues of the nature and purposes of education. Chinese cultures of learning (we pluralise the term to include diversity and difference within a broadly understood consensus) have arguably evolved through a Confucian heritage, but they have changed (Cortazzi and Jin 2001, Jin and Cortazzi 2006). An underlying assumption is that by looking at 'other' cultures of learning, we can gain insights into different ways of interpreting learning and teaching and reflect on those which are more familiar. In intercultural contexts we can investigate whether there are common features or gaps in understanding between different communities and whether different expectations of cultures of learning may be bridges or barriers. This is tricky because they are bound up with collective and individual identities and because a researcher's preferred culture of learning may implicitly frame intercultural research issues and interpretations of practices (Jin and Cortazzi 1998, Cortazzi and Jin 2002). If researchers work in teams whose members come from complementary cultural backgrounds (as we do, and as do other research teams writing in this volume) and are familiar with a range of international educational contexts, this may resolve this issue.

Metaphors and images of teaching activities are part of a culture of learning. The analysis of metaphors for teaching held in common among participants in a Chinese culture of learning can be shown to be coherent with observed representative classroom practices or with photographic and video data of classroom interactions, and with the outcomes of research by survey questionnaires or interviews (Cortazzi and Jin 1999, Jin and Cortazzi 2008).

This chapter uses applied metaphor research (Cameron and Low 1999) which extends investigations of metaphors for Chinese teachers (Cortazzi,

Jin and Wang 2009) to those for journeys of learning. Metaphors are devices for comparison in everyday speech: one thing in the 'target' domain, which is often relatively abstract, is compared to another in a 'source domain', which is often derived from familiar everyday experience. Collecting large numbers of metaphors and analysing them shows clear patterns revealing underlying concepts. Thus, the metaphor of 'learning is a journey' examines the relatively abstract experience of 'learning' (the target domain) in terms of a journey (the source domain) over an area, space or landscape. This 'journey' in ordinary student–teacher discourse has characteristics of direction, movement and speed (*going forward rapidly, forging ahead, moving on, going up, reaching upper levels, making slow progress*), goals (*getting there, arriving, attaining the target*), and a path (*following a route, staying on track, on course, following guidelines*), with demarcations (*stages, steps, levels*) and features of a landscape (*climbing a mountain, reaching a peak, going downhill*) and perhaps guidance (*having a map, following a guide*).

Similar features of a journey can be seen in the etymology of 'curriculum', which is 'running', 'the course to be run', 'a race' or 'race course' (from Latin curro: 'run', 'hasten' or 'move quickly'; curriculum: 'a race', 'a course', 'a chariot used in races', 'a lap' or 'career') so that in the first Oxford English dictionary 'curricular' meant 'pertaining to driving of carriages'. Accordingly, in discourse about a curriculum there is a cluster of expressions which illustrate 'a journey round a course': *a starting point, a goal* or *destination; direction, movement, speed* and *pace* through *stages* or a *sequence*; and, sometimes, *a competition* with test or exam results and *winners* and *losers, celebrations* and *disappointments*. Such expressions about learning and the curriculum are so commonplace in both ordinary and professional talk that they are easily overlooked, but they show a coherent pattern which may guide or constrain discourses of learning and how we think about learning.

Metaphors have 'entailments': these are the underlying reasons and the points of comparison (how the source domain and target domains are linked), according to the provider of the metaphor. By analysing patterns of metaphors with their entailments, researchers can identify cognitive patterns (Lakoff and Johnson 1980, Lakoff 1987, 1993), or socio-cultural and linguistic features of the community in which such metaphors are common (Berendt 2008), or socio-cultural features of educational discourse (Cameron 2003). Here, we use 'landscape' as an over-arching metaphor (a meta-metaphor) to include many other metaphors for learning which are expressed as 'hills, mountains, rivers, seas, trees and plants', and other features of a landscape to group these together to analyse key beliefs and values underlying metaphors and then construct a model for these within Chinese cultures of learning.

The external landscape of ELT in China

ELT in China is characterised by its massive scale: nationally it is linked with modernisation and with global development, but popularly it is linked with perceptions of success for many learners (Cortazzi and Jin 1996b, Jin and Cortazzi 2004). China has the world's largest education system and in both formal and informal spheres there are more learners of English than in any other country. This represents a journey of numerical success. Authoritative estimates of the numbers of learners of English in China were 200 million in 1995 (Zhao and Campbell 1995) but 300 million in 2009 (British Council 2009). Numbers of teachers of English have increased too, but they lag behind those of students: in 1957 there were only 843 full time middle school teachers of English in the whole country (Ross 1992) but about 400,000 in 1995 (Cortazzi and Jin 1996b). Nationally, 100,000 teachers of English are now needed annually at all levels – and there is a current shortage (British Council 2009). Increasing numbers of the over 20 million children attending kindergartens (aged 2–6), at least in urban areas, are now learning English. Of around 120 million attending primary schools, those from grade 3 are now mostly learning English and often the younger ones are too. English is overwhelmingly the dominant compulsory foreign language among around 70 million attending junior middle and vocational schools and another 30 million or more attending senior middle schools. In higher education institutions (HEIs) English is again the dominant foreign language for 10 to 12 million students. For most students English has a gate-keeping role: it is necessary to achieve well in tests in English to enter university and to graduate, and students see that English opens doors to professional success and career progression (see also the discussion of this gate-keeping role and the problems of ELT at the higher education level in China in Stanley 2010). This helps to explain the popularity of around 50,000 other ELT institutions in China which teach increasing numbers of adult learners and often children. Apart from preparing for exams and tests or to achieve qualifications in English, many learners see English as a language of aspiration: they envisage higher social status, using English in work contexts or to improve their career prospects, particularly through oral English skills.

Changes in university requirements for College English show current directions and demands (see Figure 6.1) which are consistent with changes in emphasis in schools. It is envisaged that College English courses will be more flexible and more individualised, and that they will make considerable use of Information and Communication Technology (ICT). While these features accompany the development of more student-centred, autonomous and independent learning, and attempt to meet the huge demand and rising expectations, they are also designed to offset the problems of large classes and limited resources and staffing. The new emphasis on practical skills and the ability to use language is in line with ELT internationally, but in China it also counters long-standing criticisms that teaching is 'duck-stuffing' and that learners emerge from college as 'deaf mutes' in English because of emphasis on grammar, vocabulary, texts and tests. There have been parallel reforms in English in schools (Ministry of Education 2001 and later) which include developing learners' active participation, their thinking skills, a 'creative

	Previous Guidelines (1995, 1999)	**New Requirements** (2004, 2007)
Requirements	Standardised for students at all levels in all HEIs	More individualised and flexible; can be locally adapted
Approach	Separated language skills; focus on grammar, vocabulary and reading, knowledge of language, exam performance	Emphasis on practical skills, communicative ability and oral skills, use of language, development of whole-person and learning capacity
Curriculum	Focus on form, structured content	Focus on meaning and use, more flexible content
Pedagogy	Teacher-centred; transfer of knowledge	More student-centred; develop more autonomous, independent learning; more interactive teaching; incorporate ICT
Other features	Develop students' effort and discipline	Develop students' motivation, collaborative and creative thinking, critical thinking and problem-solving, intercultural learning

Figure 6.1 Reforms in university teaching of English in China based on Ministry of Education Guidelines (1985, 1999) and the New Requirements (2004, 2007)

spirit', and new elements of cultural awareness and intercultural communication skills, with uses of multimedia and ICT.

These developments in ELT in universities and schools represent a quite radical stage in the qualitative journey of English. Older teachers of English have experienced the historical drama of this journey in China with shifts in the value, purposes and methods of ELT (see Figure 6.2, which draws on Buley-Meissner 1991, Cortazzi and Jin 1999, Lam 2005, Adamson 2007). Developments are not purely linear, however, and might be better characterised as overlapping waves. Aspects of grammar-translation, though widely deprecated as outmoded, still continue (translation is regarded as a fifth skill, with listening, speaking, reading and writing). Classroom activities still often centre on the 3Ts of the teacher, text and test, though more interactive uses of pair and group work are often integrated with them. The 3Ts are often still the basis of actual class uses of technology (with CD-Rom, Powerpoint or multi-media). While the New Requirements are challenging for many teachers, for some others they simply match current movements towards forms of bilingual education (Feng 2007) and e-learning (Spencey-Oatey 2007).

The historical landscape is heavily contoured with ups and downs, which are reflected in metaphors for teachers that were widely promulgated in official documents. Many of these now seem outdated; they evoke smiles among

Periods of National Development since 1949	Features of the journey of English language teaching	Official metaphors for all teachers, including English teachers
Reconstruction (1949–1957)	Neglect of English; Russian favoured	*gardeners, brain-power labourers*
First Five Year Plan (1953–1957)	Some English for science and technology using Russian pedagogic approaches; grammar-translation methods	*people's heroes, advanced producers, engineers of the soul*
Great Leap Forward (1958–1959)	Shift back to English for the economy; English as transmission of knowledge; grammar and vocabulary	*obstacles; common labourers*
Retrenchment (1960–1965)	English for international engagement with caution; some audio-lingual methods	*machine tool makers, engineers of the soul, 'red and expert'*
Cultural Revolution (1966–1976)	Foreign learning repudiated, English suspended, then some English for renewing international ties in 'reform and opening up'	*freaks, monsters, or stinking number nines; warriors, weapons in the class struggle, red thinkers*
Opening Up 1980s	English strongly promoted in drive for modernisation; debate communicative and eclectic or mixed approaches; centre on teacher, text and test	*technicians, machinists, people's heroes, 'red and expert', 'teach the book, cultivate the people'; performers*
Market economy, Reform 1990s	English for international status; rising popular demand; schools and colleges focus on exams and English for study but make efforts to develop communication	*candles, lamps, golden key-holders, engineers of the soul, 'plunging into the sea', 'stir-fry night'*
Millennium economic development 2000s	English for global roles; huge popular demand; reforms of pedagogy; applied skills; emphases on developing thinking, creativity and uses of technology	*conductors, directors; cultivators of talents and ability; nurturers of creativity and future professionals*

Figure 6.2 Some features of the journey of ELT and official metaphors for teachers

Chinese teachers; they are museum metaphors but are not part of a contemporary scene (see Figure 6.2).

These metaphors reflect public attitudes and track changes in perceptions of teachers (Cortazzi and Jin 1999). Most periods show a positive evaluation of teachers in socialist terms: *labourers, producers, warriors and weapons* or *red thinkers*. Some are mechanistic or technical: *tool-makers, technicians, machinists*, but it is important to recognise humane aspects of this, as in the recurrent metaphoric expression, *engineers of the soul*. The meanings of some other expressions are more holistic than may be apparent: *red and expert* signifies moral worth and exemplary behaviour to balance technical subject expertise, and while *teach the book* (*jiao shu*) seems to indicate a didactic book-centred approach to teaching, the partner expression *cultivate the people* (*yu ren*), indicates a more holistic and humane approach. Noticeable deprecations of teachers are seen in the low points of the Great Leap Forward (teachers as *obstacles*) and particularly in the Cultural Revolution (*freaks, monsters*), when many teachers were held to represent bourgeois groups or feudal aspects of Confucianism, which at that time was severely criticised. English teaching was repudiated. English teachers were likely to be regarded with suspicion as having links with the West and held to be *stinking number nines* – a category which put teachers in the ninth place in a list of 'enemies of the people' who were publicly shamed and often exiled to the country-side for 're-education'. In this harsh educational landscape, schools and universities were closed for long periods; however, a few teachers were *weapons and warriors* in the class struggle. Since then, the landscape for teachers has steadily improved through the rising uplands of the 1980s to the hills of the 1990s and millennium peaks.

While features of the ELT landscape look largely like transmission, the teacher as a *performer* has expertise not only in knowledge *per se* but brings this knowledge to students through a performance of demonstrating and explaining with carefully thought-out classroom examples, and in how the teacher predicts learners' problems with any given concept (Cortazzi and Jin 2001). Metaphors of the 1990s reflect a market economy and a period of low teachers' salaries: *plunging into the sea* (*xia hai*) meant going into private business, as a second job (particularly English teachers), while references to *stir-fry night* (*chao geng* – *geng* means both 'a dish of food' and 'night')) or *using a sieve or net* (*lao wai kua*) showed some teachers moonlighting for extra money. Since then, teachers' salaries have much improved. Teachers are again *candles*, a metaphor of light and sacrifice (to be discussed later), and *cultivators* or *nurturers of talents, ability and creativity* or, in universities, *cultivators of professionals*. Such metaphors with Confucian resonances are used with scientific-technical overtones in educational reform and 'rejuvenation' (Li 2004). Teachers are also *conductors* and *directors*, with management and guidance functions rather than being transmitters of knowledge. They are masters who have the power to guarantee the success of their students, if their students make efforts.

Internal landscapes: metaphors for teachers and learning

The metaphors for teachers cited above are from official documents, representing a view from the top. This view was, however, at least partially derived from common sayings of the time. To investigate how these compare with the views on the ground, we elicited 2,882 metaphors on 'teachers' and 3,235 metaphors on 'learning' from 1,140 university students in two major universities in China by asking them to complete a form requesting three metaphors for teachers and three for learning (Cortazzi, Jin and Wang 2009). Students were also asked to write reasons for their metaphors (i.e. the entailments). Students were given a non-Chinese example to illustrate what was meant by metaphors and reasons. Most students wrote metaphors in English but some wrote in Chinese and while some found the task difficult many gave thoughtful examples and showed aspects of creative and reflective thinking in both languages, though more elaborately in Chinese. This demonstrates that a proportion of students have some competence in the direction required under ELT reforms (Figure 6.1) although many lack confidence. Students were free to write practically anything in this open format so any patterns which emerge strongly may be important themes in cultures of learning. These extensive data were grouped, classified and analysed inductively by first building up categories and then analysing the entailments. This second step is an essential requirement to investigate the student's beliefs rather than impose those of the researchers. For instance, *a teacher is a robber* would be perceived negatively in the West because it equates teachers with criminals, but the student giving the metaphor specifies in her entailment a positive moral rationale of the teacher 'robbing our bad things so that we can do everything to perfection'. This example would thus be categorised with positive metaphors and grouped with others which show that the teacher has a 'cleansing' or 'purifying' function. The analysis needs care because one metaphor given by a number of students may have several entailments, while a classification of entailments shows that one entailment may be realised in several metaphors. To inductively construct a model, such as 'learning is a journey from hell to heaven', we use only metaphors given by at least several students, with at least two network links in the overlapping inter-relations between metaphors and entailments; this method ensures that the analysis is not biased by a few students or rarer metaphors or entailments.

Significant student metaphors for teachers show continuity with the previous official metaphors (Figure 6.2): teachers are *engineers of the soul, candles, keys,* and there is a consonance with current official metaphors of teachers as *cultivators, nurturers, farmers* or *gardeners,* and *weapons.* Figure 6.3 lists common examples of metaphors from our corpus for both 'teacher' and 'learning'. This shows a number of points beyond the fact of continuity of metaphors in Chinese education.

First, the use of the same metaphors for both 'teacher' and 'learning' (e.g. *light, food and drink, friend or parent, book or pen*) surely shows recognition of the overlapping of concepts: teaching as an activity depends on the presence of learners and learning, yet most learners need teachers. This might indicate a high degree of student dependence on teachers, for example, *learning as farming* needs a *farmer* (a teacher) and *learning as construction work* needs

A teacher is. . . .	Learning is. . . .
A light: gives brightness, warmth, love, life, guidance, direction; is a source of knowledge and energy.	**Light:** brings brightness, hope, beauty, love, knowledge, guidance, direction to the future.
A candle: burns itself to enlighten others; shows devotion and self-sacrifice.	**A candle:** lets students see wisdom, hope; lights up the mind; brightens students' lives.
Food and drink: gives necessary nutrition, flavour, knowledge; helps students to grow; gives energy; is attractive, delicious and fragrant; can bring a bitter and sweet taste.	**Food and drink:** is daily nourishment for the healthy growth of body, mind and spirit; is essential for growth; the more, the better; it is delicious; can be bitter or sweet.
A friend or parent: gives care, help, encouragement, guidance; shows closeness, good communication; shares knowledge, feelings and happiness.	**A friend or parent:** for knowledge, care, frequent contact, closeness, comfort, companionship, happiness, beauty, love.
A gardener, farmer: gives care, shelter and protection; cultivates and nurtures students' growth, spreads knowledge; is hardworking; brings beauty and sacrifices for the future.	**Farming:** has growth processes for knowledge, intelligence, feeling, life; takes time, needs care and cultivation; students make hard efforts for future rewards, success, beauty and happiness.
The engineer of the soul: produces talents for the future; designs, modifies and builds up students' spirits.	**Construction work:** building up the human soul, the foundation of success, of a good life; building knowledge and a spiritual world; it needs daily effort.
A weapon: two-edged, cuts ignorance but also cuts creativity; increases feelings but hurts friends.	**A weapon:** to defeat others with knowledge; valuable; two-edged – has both positive and negative sides.
A book: a rich source of knowledge; guides generations to progress, solves problems, is full of answers.	**A book:** endless knowledge, truth, beauty, effort through hardship.
A pen: uses up its own ink to produce knowledge and record valuable things.	**A pen:** writes students' future life; needs hard work.
Water: needed for knowledge and life; vast, endless, constantly moving knowledge; has an enduring effect.	**Water:** the necessity, vastness and value of knowledge; nourishes, satisfies and purifies; source of happiness and life.
A boat: carries students to the unknown; gives hope and helps them to achieve goals.	**A boat:** drifting or goes with direction towards a goal; needs constant effort.
A bridge: to knowledge and wisdom; links students to learning, progress and success.	**A bridge:** to the world, knowledge, success, the future; links dreams and reality
A ladder: students climb to knowledge; a support for progress.	**A ladder:** to endless knowledge, wisdom, growth, progress, success, light, life.
A key: opens up minds; opens the door to knowledge, wisdom and life.	**A key:** opens the mind; opens the door to knowledge, wisdom, success, the future.

Figure 6.3 Representative metaphors for 'teacher' and 'learning' given by students

an engineer of the soul (a teacher). The identification of both 'teacher' and 'learning' as *a book* could further reinforce a 3Ts idea (teacher, text, test) but tests and exams are not mentioned frequently and the metaphors have a strong holistic quality that goes beyond a teacher or text-centred classroom.

Second, the students' explanations for their metaphors (the entailments) have far more depth of feeling than simply education as instruction, shown by the frequency of *warmth, brightness, beauty, hope, love,* and *life;* teaching and learning are not simply cognitive acts, shown by the range and high frequency of terms like *knowledge, truth, wisdom, mind, feeling, spirit* and *soul.* The tone of many of the Chinese students' metaphors is thus deeply reflective. The tone is also affective: many students show strong feeling for teachers and for learning, seen in frequent mentions of *care, closeness, comfort, sharing* and *companionship.* However, learning is not easy. It demands *constant effort, hard work* and may involve *hardship.* The roles of the teacher are broader and far more nuanced than the official metaphors might suggest. In the words of many students (Figure 6.3 and elsewhere in the data), these teacher roles in relation to students include sharing knowledge, giving enlightenment, helping progress, nurturing growth, caring, guiding, directing, supporting, advising, leading, controlling, mediating, protecting, sheltering, cleansing, purifying, understanding, entertaining, being close, giving friendship and beautifying life.

Third, the picture of teaching and learning is not uniformly positive. Although a positive view is the clearly dominant one, there are negative (but critically reflective) elements: teachers are *tigers because they may attack me at any time; a stone pressing on students' heads, which gives them a headache; a mixture of an angel and a devil; a surgeon cutting off the cancer in us, but also cutting off our creative skills.*

Learning can also be a blend of positive and negative. It is *torture in fire and ice; a doctor but also an assassin; an olive, bitter at first then sweet; a durian, it smells terrible but when you try it, it is delicious; coffee, it has bitterness and sweetness – at first it is bitter, later sweet and wonderful.* These negative and mixed critical evaluations may reflect increased student diversity with the expanding numbers (a few students struggle – they would not have been admitted to university previously) and a change from the past (students feel more open to admit negative elements or have a more socially realistic view now). Some negative elements are expressed with creativity, humour and poignancy, so perhaps these qualities are more evident now as ELT policy, for example, emphasizes creativity: *A teacher is an ancient clown, you scarcely dare laugh at it; a teacher is a rich slave owner, rich with knowledge but we are their slaves and we want to get a little spiritual food from them.* Some mixed evaluations show a change over time as students develop:

> *In primary school, the teacher is like a babysitter, caring for students; in middle school, the teacher is like a candle, giving the light of knowledge; in university, the teacher is like a road sign, giving students directions, but it is up to students to choose their way.*

A teacher is a god in primary school, all they said was right; a priest in the middle school, their words were correct but I began to have my own thinking; Satan in the university, I don't want to be seduced by him, but angels before the exams – their words are gospel, every sentence.

Fourth, on the positive side, is the students' widespread recognition of teacher devotion, suffering and sacrifice as an important part of a holistic and humane educational landscape. This is found in the entailments of many metaphors, as can be seen in the examples in Figure 6.4, but this element of teaching is rarely, if ever, mentioned in educational studies especially in the West. While teachers can readily recognise the sentiments here, the point of interest is that many students are aware of this and can articulate it in a creative variety of metaphors.

Some of these examples (Figure 6.4) are common or at least understandable elsewhere (e.g. the candle is a common metaphor for a teacher in the Middle East); others are not: calling a teacher 'an old cow' in Britain or Australia is likely to be understood as a gender-based insult because she is thought to be unpleasant, ugly or stupid.

Learning as a journey

The most frequent metaphor in the data is that 'learning' is a journey over a landscape. This overarching metaphor is richly characterised and it is realised by a huge number of expressions. An analysis of the conceptual model behind it gives insights into Chinese cultures of learning. The journey is described by different students as *endless, exciting, hard, happy, marvellous and mysterious.* It is *an expedition of exploration, an exploration in the dark; an exploration of time and space; an adventure, searching the universe,* and *seeking treasure.* These epithets are often accompanied by conditions which indicate a mindset of preparedness and a sense of the process as well as the goal: *only if you try your best can you reach your goal; you can arrive only by persisting; it needs a strong will and a healthy body to arrive; we need to be ready for any difficulty for a happy ending; only if you stick to your dreams will you be finally successful; you can enjoy beautiful scenery during the journey of learning; you should not put too much emphasis on arriving but keep an eye on the road and appreciate the landscape.*

The destination of the journey of learning is *heaven* or *happiness*. It is *a journey to paradise; a happy paradise, we can travel freely in it; a place for fair angels; the studious student's Garden of Eden; a garden in the sunshine of heaven; a journey to get happiness, to the fountainhead of happiness.* There is an interesting theme of religious symbolism here: *learning is a church, it is supposed to take you to heaven.* Some students write of happiness as both the destination and a characteristic of the journey: simply, *learning is happy travelling; learning is happiness.* The journey is also often characterised as *realising our dreams, desires* and *ideals.* The means to do this is usually *travel*

Metaphors for teachers	Entailments of metaphors
A piece of ice	Melting, running out herself to wet students' dry hearts.
Chalk	Teaching their knowledge to students but losing their youth gradually, it writes out the whole world, leaving marks of knowledge, sacrificing itself, writing down the most beautiful text even with the last bits.
A red candle	Burning itself and enlightening us, lighting my desire for knowledge, sacrificing itself to give light to others.
A falling leaf	It sacrifices itself enriching the soil, burning its own youth, living an ordinary life with a moment of magnificence; it falls to bring up the next generation by fertilising the soil.
A silkworm	It produces silk selflessly until the last minute of its life; devoting its whole life to others, it sacrifices itself but gives silk to create the most beautiful clothes for people.
An old cow	She has selfless devotion and gives great help in life, silently suffering; she won't stop until she has given out all her strength to serve society.
A bee	Selflessly working hard for others, spreading the pollen so that flowers will grow.
A gardener	He uses his own sweat to water flowers for the motherland; he pours out his blood and sweat selflessly to cultivate our growth.
An engineer	He is selfless to offer himself to enrich others.
A boatman	He sacrifices himself to help others reach their goals.

Figure 6.4 Examples of students' metaphors showing the devotion and sacrifice of teachers

along a road or to see learning as *a ladder, steps* or *a bridge* (i.e. as a medium or means to ascend upwards or cross to reach dreams): *learning is a wide road to ideals; the road to heaven; a ladder to paradise; a ladder to ideals; steps to paradise; a bridge leading us to our desires, to cross the gap between ideal and reality; a bridge between the real and your ideals.* Crucially, in modern China, the 'paradise' is strongly linked to future success. In the words of many, the journey is *the essential way to success; the highway to success; the road to success and to make dreams come true, the essential road to the peak of success; the bridge to success; the ladder to success; a bridge to success, crossing reality to your goal.*

However, this journey is not at all simple. It is 'a journey through hell to heaven'. This is reminiscent of the life journey through hell and the mountains of purgatory to a paradise beyond time and space in the most famous poem in Italian, the Divina Commedia by Dante (1265–1321) or perhaps of the difficult travels of Xuan Zang (604–664) across mountains and deserts to the west, a journey of learning to get the Buddhist scriptures from India for China (portrayed in fantasy as the Journey to the West in the Monkey stories of Wu Chengen (1506–1582). For these students, learning is *the journey from hell to heaven; a way leading to heaven but also to hell; a road with thorns, but at the end there's a paradise filled with flowers; it is a pilgrimage, searching for your true self.* Hell is briefly but graphically described: it is *torture, horror, war, a vast sea of woes; a bottomless chasm, a bottomless pit, an abyss, an endless hole, a black hole; to separate flesh from the spirit; more suffering than separation and death; a curse, poison, purgatory, hopeless and painful if you don't study, God's punishment for humans.*

In many expressions with oxymorons, the students show that for them pain and suffering are necessary stages in the journey to happiness: the journey is *full of pains with satisfaction; taking pain and sweetness together; a journey with both hardships and happiness; bitter happiness; travelling in rain and sunshine; the process is bitter, the result is sweet; no pain, no gain; no sweat, no sweet.*

Many students indicate two further conditions for success in their journey of learning. The first of these is that they should make a constant effort and show continuous determination. This is a matter of *sweat and efforts* and it seems to correspond to the selfless sacrifice and devotion of teachers (Figure 6.4). Students say they must *strive without stopping, you can be more happy because of your effort; if you want to get greater success, you should make greater efforts; if you want to make progress, you must make efforts; climbing a high mountain to reach the top, you should be more diligent than others, we just need to climb unremittingly; only if you climb ceaselessly can you arrive at the top, we should keep learning constantly, endlessly.* Such effort is said to be a marked contrast with American students, who as the necessary condition for successful learning may emphasise the need to possess talent and intelligence, rather than the need to make this sort of constant effort (Stevenson and Stigler 1992). In many sailing metaphors, this critical need for effort by Chinese students is linked to *sailing in the wind against the current* where *not to advance means dropping back*: students say they must *go ahead or fall behind; if you can't make progress you will fall behind; you will fall behind, if you don't make efforts; sailing against the tide; if you don't make progress you will rush away in the opposite direction.* This constant effort is held to be well worthwhile because these students have a strong belief in their future success, which is linked to heaven and realising their dreams. *Learning is the road to success and to make dreams come true; learning is walking on the highway to success; making an effort results in success; learning is the essential road to the peak of success.*

The second condition is the need for direction and guidance, either explicitly from a teacher or implicitly in many metaphors of a lighthouse, beacon or guiding light, which is the teacher (Figure 6.3). Thus students state the condition: *only when we find the correct direction can we reach the right destination; you need a guiding light; the hope of light, guiding the way of your head; the lighthouse that guides ships sailing in the darkness, it leads us to go forwards; our teacher, guiding our direction forward; the encouragement of a teacher, a teacher who constantly points out the way.*

In the journey of learning, students are conscious of a time dimension – a positive past and of how they are changing some of their past in the move towards a future (which is always *bright* and linked to *success*). Learning is *the road travelled by our ancestors, moving along the road on which our fore-fathers have passed*. In a favourite quotation from the seventeenth century Isaac Newton (who derived it from the twelfth century French scholar Bernard de Chartres), which students have learnt from English textbooks, learning is *standing on the shoulders of giants* or in more contemporary terms, it is *a time tunnel, through it we can enter ancient times as well as predict the future.* This past does not, however, fix the present; it is mutable:

> *Learning is the means to change our destiny, the change from the old to the new, the change to forget the past and adapt to a new life, supplementing the past with new knowledge continuously.*

> *Learning is a beautiful future, the key to making your dreams come true, a key to realising ideals, a bright lamp, illuminating our future. It can give you what you want, bring you your dream, you can gain anything that you want if you use your heart and control yourself to reach your goal.*

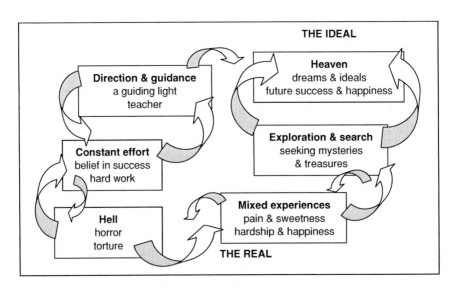

Figure 6.5 A map of Chinese students' metaphors for 'learning is a journey'

Continuity and some change in landscapes of learning

As shown, some students display awareness of continuity of the past, but more generally the landscape outlined above has geological features which reflect traditional Chinese sayings, many of which are well known, which are taught to children by modern parents and stem from the Confucian heritage (Jin and Cortazzi 2008) (see examples in Figure 6.6). These relate to values, many of which will presumably survive rapid technological developments in learning, the increased individualism, personalised and applied learning, and the need for critical and creative thinkers (the obvious changes).

More specifically, there are key passages within the Chinese classics, appearing like geological sub-strata, which underlie some features of the landscape of current cultures of learning and, surprisingly, they match some recent reforms and requirements (Figure 6.1) by giving a step-by-step process of study. The *Zhong Yong* (The Mean), as one of the Four Books of the Confucian classics, gives this sequence as part of a learning journey:

Aspects of learning	Traditional Chinese sayings
Importance	It is a waste of time to live without learning.
Making an effort	If you make enough effort, you can grind an iron pillar into a needle. . . . Personal practice with effort. . . . The master leads the student to the door, but the perfection of the learner's skill lies in the individual learner's own effort.
Make constant progress	Learning is sailing a boat against the current; not to advance is to drop back.
Diligence	Work diligently and tirelessly, learning only comes from diligence; without diligence, one ends up with an empty belly. . . . 30% talent, 70% study.
Reciprocal relations	In education, teachers and students mutually benefit.
Asking questions	Learning, learning, if you want to learn, you've got to ask.
Reflective thinking	Learning without reflecting gains nothing; thought without learning is dangerous. . . . Learning without reflecting is like eating without digesting.
Suffering setbacks	Without terrible sufferings one cannot be a superior person . . . Suffer a loss, learn a lesson . . . If rivers do not bend, the waters will not flow forward.
Future success	If you are full of learning, do not fear that fortune will not visit you.

Figure 6.6 Some traditional Chinese sayings about aspects of learning

one must learn extensively, examine carefully, think prudently, distinguish clearly and practise sincerely the good way. He should not stop learning until he has known all, neither should he stop asking until he has exhausted his questions, nor should he stop thinking until he has found all the answers, nor should he stop distinguishing until he has made the differences clear, nor should he stop acting until he has done his sincere best. If others succeed by making one ounce of effort, I will make ten times as much effort.

(Zhong Yong, transl. Fu 2006: 85)

This sequence was advocated in commentaries by a leading scholar of the Sung dynasty, Zhu Xi (1130–1200), who had them written for all to see as the basis for education in the White Deer Grotto Academy in 1180. He also wrote:

In learning we have to read for ourselves, so that the understanding we reach is personally meaningful. Nowadays, however, people read simply for the sake of the civil service examinations . . . reading must be an experience personally meaningful to the self . . . in reading we must first become intimately familiar with the text so that its words seem to come from our own mouths. We should continue to reflect on it so that its ideas seem to come from our own minds. Only then can there be real understanding.

(Cited in Gardner 1990: 17, 148, 43)

Another of the classics, the *Li Ji* (Book of Rites) gives this advice for teachers on the way (the Way or Tao) of learning:

In his teaching the superior man guides his students but does not pull them along; he urges them to go forward and does not suppress them; he opens the way, but does not take them to the place. Guiding without pulling makes the process of learning gentle; urging without suppressing makes the process of learning easy; and opening the way without leading the students to the place makes them think for themselves. Now if the process of learning is made gentle and easy and the students are encouraged to think for themselves, we may call the man a good teacher.'

(Lin 1938: 247)

While 'the guide' here plainly fits into current students' metaphors of learning, making learning 'gentle and easy' does not match the journey through 'hell' that many students still describe (though it might be a solution once there).

The journey through hell to heaven (Figure 6.5) would be recognised by many current Chinese educators though, including the eleven eminent university leaders portrayed in detail by Hayhoe (2006), who comments that all of them endorse the traditional way of the scholar, with Confucian concerns. Their careers reveal a drama of struggle and suffering, with bitter-sweet experiences, but their teaching and educational administration were driven by constant effort, devotion and inspired vision for the future. None would claim to have reached heaven, and some are reticent about hell (drawing a veil over the Cultural Revolution) but all contributed to the remarkable journey of progress of education in China and the recent changes. The institutional histories of their universities have at least some features of this journey, too. The journey of ELT (Figure 6.2) could also be characterised in large part as such a journey. The massive interest and numerical involvement in learning English is in some ways a huge success after difficulties, setbacks and constant effort by teachers and policy makers. However, the very existence of the new requirements (Figure 6.1) and recognition of newer needs shows change in progress and this demonstrates that heaven is still some distance away. This study of students' metaphors shows continuity and some change: one change is the fact that there are so many creative metaphors among Chinese students now, compared with the few in the 1990s (Cortazzi and Jin 1999).

A geological stratum underlying the current landscape shines through these metaphors. This is the sense of educational values in Chinese cultures of learning. Teachers are fundamentally sources of knowledge and guidance, energy, warmth, hope and love; they show profound care and a sense of cultivation of humanity and morality. Learners strive constantly for knowledge, knowing that this is a long process which requires constant effort; learning may be a bitter-sweet experience but there is guidance and cultivation from teachers and a strong belief in success and the value of learning now for the future. Allowing that there are exceptions to this and that the model may represent the ideal (of course not all features of this journey of learning apply to all learners), and that there are certainly a few negative elements and experiences, the model provides insights to those outside China. Insights include the features of teachers having a cleansing and purifying function and beautifying life, while showing devotion and sacrifice, while learners are hardworking because they believe this leads to success and that their dreams can be realised through struggle.

Finally, we can see the research process for investigating the landscape metaphors of learning as the five steps of study outlined in the *Zhong Yong*. First, to learn extensively we have collected a large corpus of students' metaphors of learning. Second, to examine them carefully we have translated those in Chinese, grouped all metaphors into inductively-derived categories and sub-classified them according to the entailments. Third, to think prudently about the metaphors we have related them to official metaphors and to the case study of the development of ELT in China (we have also reflected on them from photos, videos and classroom observations). Fourth, to distinguish clearly the individual expression from socially-held values we have only mapped frequently occurring metaphors whose entailments matched those of other frequent metaphors: we confirmed the categories discussed through extensive cross-checking within the data sets. Fifth, for sincere practice we have thought about how the results related to continuity and changes in education in China but also about how those outside China can learn insights by considering the Chinese changing landscapes of learning. There are many educational landscapes around the world and different journeys of learning in different cultures. Thinking about Chinese journeys with a map in our hands gives Western teachers a clear orientation to teach Chinese students in China or abroad. It gives both Chinese and Western teachers (and, interestingly, perhaps Western students) the means to reflect on their own educational practices of teaching and learning, wherever they are. In this way, we can all look at our own inner landscape so that the Chinese landscape changes us.

References

Adamson, B. (2007) 'Depoliticization in the English curriculum', in A. Feng (ed.) *Bilingual Education in China*, Clevedon: Multilingual Matters.

Berendt, E. A. (ed.) (2008) *Metaphors for Learning: Cross-cultural Perspectives*, Amsterdam: John Benjamins.

British Council (2009) *India and China ELT Today* (seminar, 21 May 2009), London: The British Council.

Buley-Meissner, M. L. (1991) 'Teachers and teacher education: a view from the People's Republic of China', *International Journal of Educational Development*, 11(1), 41–53.

Cameron, L. (2003) *Metaphor in Educational Discourse*, London: Continuum.

Cameron, L. and Low, G. (eds) (1999) *Researching and Applying Metaphor*, Cambridge: Cambridge University Press.

Cortazzi, M. and Jin, L. (1996a) 'Cultures of learning: language classrooms in China', in H. Coleman (ed.) *Society and the Language Classroom*, Cambridge: Cambridge University Press.

Cortazzi, M. and Jin, L. (1996b) 'English teaching and learning in China', *Language Teaching*, 29(2), 61–80.

Cortazzi, M. and Jin, L. (1999) 'Bridges to learning: metaphors of teaching, learning and language', in L. Cameron and Low, G. (eds) *Researching and Applying Metaphor*, Cambridge: Cambridge University Press.

Cortazzi, M. and Jin, L. (2001) 'Large classes in China: "Good" teachers and interaction', in D. A. Watkins and Biggs, J. B. (eds) *Teaching the Chinese Learner: Psychological and Pedagogical Perspectives*, CERC/ACER: Hong Kong.

Cortazzi, M. and Jin, L. (2002) 'Cultures of learning: the social construction of educational identities, in D. C. S. Li (ed.) *Discourses in Search of Members*, New York: University Press of America.

Cortazzi, M., Jin, L. and Wang, Z. (2009) 'Cultivators, cows and computers: Chinese learners' metaphors of teachers', in T. Coverdale-Jones and Rastall, P. (eds) *Internationalizing the University: The Chinese Context*, Houndmills: Palgrave-Macmillan.

Feng, A. (ed.) (2007) *Bilingual Education in China*, Clevedon: Multilingual Matters.

Fu, Y. (transl.) (2006) *A Selected Collection of the Doctrine of the Mean*, Beijing: Sinolingua.

Gardner, D. K. (1990) *Learning to be a Sage*, Berkeley: University of California Press.

Hayhoe, R. (2006) *Portraits of Influential Chinese Educators*, Hong Kong: CERC, The University of Hong Kong.

Jin, L. and Cortazzi, M. (1993) 'Cultural orientation and academic language use', in D. Graddol, Thompson, L. and Byram, M. (eds) *Language and Culture*, Clevedon: Multilingual Matters.

Jin, L. and Cortazzi, M. (1998) 'The culture the learner brings: a bridge or a barrier?', in M. Byram and Fleming, M. (eds) *Language Learning in Intercultural Perspective*, Cambridge: Cambridge University Press.

Jin, L. and Cortazzi, M. (2004) 'English language teaching in China: a bridge to the future', in W. K. Ho and Wong, R. (eds) *English Language Teaching in East Asia Today: Changing Policies and Practices*, Singapore: Eastern Universities Press.

Jin, L. and Cortazzi, M. (2006) 'Changing practices in Chinese cultures of learning', *Language, Culture and Curriculum*, 19(1), 5–20.

Jin, L. and Cortazzi, M. (2008) 'Images of teachers, learning and questioning in Chinese cultures of learning', in E. Berendt (ed.) *Metaphors for Learning, Cross-cultural Perspectives*, Amsterdam: John Benjamins.

Lakoff, G. (1987) *Women, Fire, and Dangerous Things*, Chicago, IL: University of Chicago Press.

Lakoff, G. (1993) 'The contemporary theory of metaphor', in A. Ortony (ed.) *Metaphor and Thought*, Cambridge: Cambridge University Press.

Lakoff, G. and Johnson, M. (1980) *Metaphors We Live By*, Chicago, IL: Chicago University Press.

Lam, A. S. L. (2005) *Language Education in China: Policy and Experience from 1949*, Hong Kong: Hong Kong University Press.

Li, L. (2004) *Education for 1.3 Billion*, Beijing: Foreign Language Teaching and Research Press.

Lin, Y. (transl.) (1938) *The Wisdom of Confucius*, New York: The Modern Library.

Ministry of Education (1985, 1999) *Daxue yingyu jiaoxue dagang (College English Teaching Guidelines)*, Beijing: Ministry of Education.

Ministry of Education (2001) *Curriculum Development and Teaching Requirements for Schools* (in Chinese), Beijing: Ministry of Education.

Ministry of Education (2004, 2007) *Daxue yingyu kecheng jiaoxue yaoqiu (College English Curriculum Requirements)*, Beijing: Ministry of Education/Foreign Language Teaching & Research Press.

Ross, H. (1992) 'Foreign language education as a barometer of modernisation', in R. Hayhoe (ed.) *Education and Modernisation: The Chinese Experience*, Oxford: Pergamon Press.

Spencer-Oatey, H. (ed.) (2007) *e-Learning Initiatives in China: Pedagogy, Policy and Culture*, Hong Kong: Hong Kong University Press.

Stanley, P. (2010) 'The hidden curriculum: a critical analysis of tertiary English teaching in China', in J. Ryan (ed.) *China's Higher Education Reform and Internationalisation*, London: Routledge.

Stevenson, H. W. and Stigler, J. W. (1992) *The Learning Gap: Why our Schools are Failing and what we can learn from Japanese and Chinese Education*, New York: Summit Books.

Zhao, Y. and Campbell, K. P. (1995) 'English in China', *World Englishes*, 14(3), 377–390.

7 English language teachers as moral guides in Vietnam and China: maintaining and re-traditionalising morality

Phan Le Ha, Paul McPherron and Phan Van Que

This chapter examines the role English-medium teachers play as moral guides/role models to students in Vietnam and China. While rapidly transforming, these societies are also attempting to maintain or in some cases re-introduce morality through education. The chapter draws on historical, sociocultural, and philosophical perspectives in respect of two central research questions: *how do students in Vietnam and China perceive the role of teachers as moral guide/role model? How are the moral instructions of Confucianism and local philosophies re-traditionalised through ELT classrooms?*

Recent work in English language teaching (ELT) has compelled researchers and practitioners to examine the political and moral tensions in English-language classrooms around the world (Johnston 2003, Kumaravadiveliu 2003, Edge 2006). At the same time, authors such as Phan and Phan (2006) point out that much of this work has focused on Western ethics and morality without examining the role moral instruction has in teacher identity in many non-Western societies. Ramanathan and Morgan (2007) further connect questions over values and morals to language policies and surges in globalisation around the world. This chapter picks up the above themes in ELT by examining the role English-medium teachers play as moral guides/role models to students in Vietnam and China. While rapidly transforming, these societies are also attempting to maintain or in some cases re-introduce morality through education. The chapter draws on historical, sociocultural, and philosophical perspectives in respect to two central research questions: *how do students in Vietnam and China perceive the role of teachers as moral guide/role model? How are the moral instructions of Confucianism and local philosophies re-traditionalised through ELT classrooms?* Qualitative data from journals and interviews were obtained with over 150 university students in Vietnam and over 60 university students in China.

Background

> As globalisation draws us all into greater proximity, it is essential that we nurture, prize, and support the diverse cultures and historical experiences of the countries in which The World Bank operates. We simply cannot conceive of development without cultural continuity.
>
> (Wolfensohn 1999)

> I have come to be convinced that the nation-state, as a complex modern political form, is on its last legs.
>
> (Appadurai 1996: 19)

What does it mean to ensure 'cultural continuity' in an era of economic and cultural globalisation? At the same time, what role do nation-states have in the processes of globalisation and cultural change, or is their influence really 'on its last legs'? These are just a few questions raised in the growing work on globalisation and nation-states (Anderson 1983, Appadurai 1996, 2001, Blommaert 2005, Louie 2007; Ong 2007), and recent work in English language teaching (ELT) has placed these questions about the political tensions of globalisation and 'cultural continuity' squarely into English-language classrooms around the world (Johnston 2003, Kumaravadiveliu 2003, Edge 2006). In particular, work addressing English language teaching has documented the cultural politics of English as an international language (EIL) and the ethics of ELT in multiple contexts (for example, Phillipson 1992, Pennycook 1994, 2007, Canagarajah 1999, Block and Cameron 2002, Ramanathan 2005, Edge 2006, Phan 2008).

These studies form a variety of perspectives about the role of English in cultural and economic development and, more importantly for our study, the goals and roles of teachers of English at all levels of education. Many writers propose that teachers of English should focus on student access to English as the current language of opportunity (Crystal 2003, McKay 2002), but others argue that English teachers must also make explicit the politics of English language policy and values of multilingualism in their teaching of English (Pennycook 1994, 2007, Joseph and Ramani 2006). Alternatively, we have noticed that teachers of English in countries such as Vietnam and China, similar to teachers of other subjects, are also expected to educate students to behave morally and respect and carry on local values, traditions, and national duties, which include building the nation and preparing for their futures as personal success is important to the overall future of the nation. In this way, both in and out of class, teachers are expected to be the moral guide in all settings (see Nguyen 2002, Doan 2005, Phan and Phan 2006 for work on morality in education in Vietnam; see Berthrong and Berthrong 2000, Bell and Chaibong 2003, Bell 2008 for work in China). All of the expected roles are important to help connect the local and global worlds of students and thus make their worlds more meaningful. In a globalising world, however, is the focus of these roles diminished, particularly the desire of teachers to inculcate a love of country through moral actions? While there are studies addressing the roles of teachers and students in the English classroom in divergent contexts (for instance, Chowdhury 2003, McDevitt 2004, Sakui 2004, Pham 2007), discussions of the roles of teachers as moral guides have not been made a focus in these studies, except in the work of Phan and Phan (2006). This chapter, therefore, picks up on questions of how traditions of moral education are maintained, altered, or even re-appropriated by students in the ELT classrooms of two Asian neighbouring 'nation-states', China and Vietnam.

Writers on globalisation often comment that the role of nation-states in the lives of their residents is diminishing, and Appadurai (1996, 2001) writes that the nation-state is fast being replaced by international culture flows of languages, ideas, people, and media. He admits, however, that we often still view the world in terms of nations because we do not have the conceptual or linguistic imaginations to, in effect, 'put into words' the realities of our late modernist or post-modernist times. Further, Blommaert (2005) recognises that a person's 'national identity' is much less fixed to 'a language' or 'an identity' and is instead a multiple 'repertoire of different possible identities, each of which has a particular range or scope and function' (390). At the same time, he posits that the 'state' in 'nation-state' still has a power to shape globalising surges and changes in linguistic, cultural, and political standards. Thus, in addition to picking up questions about moral education from the perspective of how it is framed by teachers and students in the ELT classroom, this chapter begins with an overview of how educational policies in Vietnam and China have instituted morality education in recent years, and the role of the 'state' in shaping the realities that teachers in China and Vietnam are responding to in their own classrooms.

Specifically, this chapter focuses on grounded data and ethnographic observations in respect to two central research questions:

1. How do students in Vietnam and China perceive the role of teachers as moral guide/role model?
2. How are the moral instructions of Confucianism and local philosophies re-traditionalised in ELT classrooms?

In analysing these research questions, we first offer a section below detailing the history of moral education in Vietnam and China and the cultural politics of English as an international language (EIL) followed by a section describing the university settings, data sources, and students in China and Vietnam in this study in depth. The data is then analysed according to the research questions. We argue that English language learning and teaching is about more than language learning and teaching, and the data presented here illustrate how English teachers and students in divergent contexts represent ideological, personal, and community struggles over language use, identity, and cultural practices. As the chapter examines the tensions over if and how students and teachers maintain or re-introduce (hence our term *re-traditionalise*) the notion of teachers as moral guides, we show that for many students of English in Vietnam and China a very strong assumption remains about the role of a teacher as a moral guide. We end the chapter, however, with a discussion of the multiple effects of this role of moral guide: facilitating students' access to English while connecting teachers and students to local know-ledges and practices but also functioning as a way to re-institute nationalist and often patriarchal values. Through placing an explicit emphasis and understanding of moral education as one part of a teacher's repertoire of 'cultural identity', we argue that teachers and students can find spaces to engage with tensions over Western-based reforms of English language policy and rework multilingualism and multiculturalism into their teaching and learning of English.

Moral education and the role of teacher as moral guide/role model

Vietnam

Moral education in Vietnam is introduced from pre-school to tertiary levels and has been made a focus in national education policy, education law, and the constitution of Vietnam (Nguyen 2002, Mayumi 2004, Doan 2005, Phan and Phan 2006). Currently, Vietnamese moral education often includes character education, civic education and socialist ideas education. It is carried out by teachers and others through multiple channels, such as schools, communities, and families. Examining the national curriculum of moral education, Doan (2005: 452) clarifies the term 'moral' in the Vietnamese context as follows:

> 'Moral' in the Vietnamese context is a broad term, relating to the prac-
> tice, manners or conduct of human beings in relation to each other. Moral
> education is also associated with standards of behaviour justified by
> people as right and proper, and is to be conducted willingly without the
> interference of law. Moral education is also understood as perspectives,
> viewpoints and behaviour of people in such social relations as self in
> relation to other persons, groups and organisations.

Nguyen (2002) conflates moral education with ethics education and discusses visions of Vietnam on ethics and civic education, pointing out that 'the Vietnamese government and educators always consider that ethic and civic education is an important part of curriculum in the Vietnamese school – from pre-school to the higher education institutions' (3). She quotes President Ho Chi Minh's saying that 'talent without morality is useless' [co tai ma khong co duc cung vo dung] to argue for the significant role of ethics and civic education in all aspects of the education system (3). According to Nguyen

(2002: 4), the following three pillars serve as the basis for civic education in contemporary Vietnam:

1. The concept of Vietnamese leadership on ethics and civic education in the socialist ideology.
2. The national tradition on ethics-morality that is based upon a two millennia history.
3. The common ideas on citizen's rights and duties in the Republic which rooted from the Enlightenment.

These pillars are incorporated in both the subjects entitled 'Moral Education' or 'Civic Education' and other subjects in school curriculum. They are simultaneously manifested in all forms of activities taken by schools, families, communities and organisations to help students absorb and practise embedded moral values and citizen's duties. These pillars are reflected in a number of common Vietnamese phrases that imply the role of morality in the society, for instance, 'morality first, knowledge second', 'Hong – Chuyen' (red mind and expertise, meaning socialist ideology, values and expertise), 'talent and virtue', and 'intellect and morality' (Doan 2005: 451).

While Doan (2005) offers a detailed overview of moral education in the entire Vietnamese educational system, she expresses a critical stance towards moral education in Vietnam, which she sees more as political education especially from secondary and high school levels onwards. However critical, it is clear in her arguments that moral education is crucial in forming citizens with both morality and knowledge, especially as Vietnam is undergoing modernisation processes. Quoting Nguyen (2005) and Duong (2000), Doan (2005) pours out her concern that due to the lack of proper and effective methods of moral education and the over-emphasis on political and legal education in the educational system, social problems increase while morality decreases among young people (also a common lament in contemporary China, see Yu 2008). As such, 'the objectives of education are not easily achieved, as expected in the Education Law [of Vietnam]' (459). Both Duong (2000) and Nguyen (2004) (cited in Doan 2005: 462) contend that 'the values of traditional morality are still held in high esteem by the public and are expected to have an increasing role in the formal education'. Moreover, as seen in Rydstrom (2001), many leaders, policy makers, pedagogues and educators in Vietnam have made it explicit that moral education is crucial for the production of children's good morality and nation building. All these points urge the need to understand how demonstrating morality and moral education is conducted by educators and how teachers have been viewed as moral guides, moral educators and role models in the society since its infancy (Duong 2002, Phan 2008).

In terms of talking about Vietnam in the context of opening its door to the world, English language education plays a very important role, particularly after the collapse of the former Soviet Union accompanied by the refusal of people to learn Russian and the increasing popularity of English in the country since the late 1980s (Phan 2008). But what are the relationships between English language education and moral education in Vietnam? Does it mean that the teaching of this international language and its assumed underlying Western values that may challenge traditional values goes against general concepts of morality and behaviour expected in Vietnamese classrooms? Is it possible that teachers of English still perform their moral guide role? To respond to these concerns, Phan and Phan (2006) found that within the domain of English language teaching in Vietnam, teachers of English themselves are not only aware of their role as moral guide but also proactively acquire this role as part of their professional development and growth. Documenting the role of morality in education in Vietnam from historical, sociocultural, philosophical, educational and empirical perspectives, these authors (also authors of this chapter) reveal a strong emphasis on moral education and the teacher as moral guide which has been perceived, expected and practised in Vietnamese society since ancient Vietnam.

As seen in Doan (2005) and Nguyen (2002), together with receiving moral education through formal education in Vietnam, students and young people there learn and appreciate traditional moral values through other channels, such as through the family and religious and community education. In the process of modernising Vietnam, young people are seen as the driving force and therefore equipping them with morality and an awareness of citizen's duties is considered essential. Learning English is part of this modernising process in Vietnam today and English language education is also seen as contributing to educating students morally (Phan 2008). While there are very few studies on the moral guide role of English language teachers, studies on what students expect from teachers of English and their perceptions of these teachers' roles within and beyond the domain of English language teaching seem missing in the literature. Similarly, it can be instructive to offer some comparisons between students in China and Vietnam who are responding to similar historical and philosophical traditions.

China

> The Master said, 'How would I dare to consider myself a sage (*sheng*) or an authoritative person (*ren*)? What can be said about me is simply that I continue my studies without respite and instruct others without growing weary'. Gongxi Hua remarked, 'It is precisely this commitment that we students are unable to learn'.
>
> (The Analects of Confucius, 7.34, Ames and Rosemont, trans. 1998)

Similar to Vietnam, the Chinese Communist Party (CCP) has used moral education in recent years to instill socialist values and a love of country in the educational curriculum, but the party has always sought, at least in official policy, to deny ancient traditions such as Confucianism; and somewhat differently from Vietnam, the recent introductions of moral education in China that have been overtly tied to Confucian traditions and beliefs in some ways go against official state policies and Communist doctrine. While the term 'Confucianism' has typically grouped together multiple strands of thought and writings,[1] Reed (1995) writes that the role of education to cultivate the proper values and virtues in society has been a unifying belief in Confucianism throughout its long history. Berthrong and Berthrong (2000) go as far as to write that this focus on maintaining moral harmony in the world through education and the study of The Analects even helped to unify the Chinese empire at various times in China's 5,000 year history. They note that Confucius set an example by advocating education for all levels of society, and he was willing to teach anyone who was willing to learn and interested in becoming a moral person. Of utmost importance for Confucius was that education should help students work toward becoming *ren* or moral citizenship through the practice of rituals, filial piety, and benevolence.

The cultivation of *ren* has always been fundamental to Confucian education but difficult to translate into English. Ames and Rosemont (1998) write that the term *ren*, which they translate as 'authoritative person', is not just one characteristic or concept but closer to 'human becoming' because it signifies 'the cognitive, aesthetic, moral, and religious sensibilities' or 'field of selves' a moral person acquires throughout life (49). In discussing the role of teachers as moral role models in China, Jin and Cortazzi (1998) translate *ren* as 'humanity' or 'love', and they write that all teachers in the Chinese educational context need to practice this *ren* with their students. In fact, modeling of virtuous behaviour is a common theme in both Confucian and Chinese histories. Reed (1995) writes that:

> Culture heroes, role models and moral exemplars are one means through which the continuity of Chinese culture has been expressed over the centuries. The incorruptible scholar/official, the chaste widow, the loyal servant, were universally recognized literary and historical types who served as standards for behaviour and as conduits for transmitting the most cherished values and ideals of the Chinese culture. (99)

From these definitions, the concept of *ren* can be understood as a continual process of personal cultivation and demonstration of caring for others and the world, and not a fixed product determined by natural or cultural constraints. Despite his entreaties that he is not *ren*, Confucius may be modelling *ren* himself by simply working 'without respite' and 'without growing weary' for the good of his students.

Scollon (1999) points out that both Confucian and Socratic discourses on education place an emphasis on moral education and becoming *ren*, but she notes that each philosophy has a different view of morality and how to teach it. For Socrates, a teacher had the role of a midwife in that the teacher does not give 'birth' to the great ideas or morals that students should learn, but 'his role in relationship to the youth is to lead him to the truth by means of questioning' (19). Since forming arguments and responding to intense questioning was the primary way to uncover 'truths' and 'morals', it follows that teachers would want all students to participate in classroom discussions and learn the correct way to form an argument. In comparison, she argues that for Confucians, education is not based on uncovering truth; rather, teaching should focus on imparting wisdom in order for students to learn to practise morally correct actions. She writes:

> The main difference between Socrates and Confucius is the former was interested in truth and universal definitions, his method centering on following out the consequences of a hypothesis, whereas the latter was more concerned about action. One learns in order to gain wisdom so that one may act appropriately. (17)

Scollon (1999) summarises the Socratic and Confucian discourses on education as sharing a desire to teach moral education, but their different foci on universal truths versus correct actions and 'performance' of virtues leads to two different interaction frameworks in the classroom.

Recent education policy in China, however, has revealed some tensions in the Confucian role of morality in the classroom and the desire of teachers to lead students towards the wisdom of how to act appropriately. Specifically, the Education Ministry in the 1990s – through curriculum and teacher education projects – placed emphasis on incorporating Western-based teaching methodologies, such as Communicative Language Teaching (CLT) and Task-based Language Teaching (TBLT) methods (Savignon 1983, 2001, Brumfit 1984, Ellis 2003, Nunan 2005). Further, Jin and Cortazzi (2002) write that these reforms are aimed at imitating Western-based teaching methods instead of a Confucian system that is seen as not emphasising creativity.

> Following the emphasis in the 1980s and 90s on the development of quantity in education, the late 1990s saw a change of direction towards 'quality education' in schools at the national level. This includes reforming and simplifying the curriculum, lessening homework loads and developing more rounded education; recognizing class work in addition to the end-of-term examinations for assessment; and emphasizing creativity, imagination, thinking and independent study skills . . . To break away from rote learning, it is currently emphasised that at least a third of class time should be devoted to learners' active participation. A shift from the 'teacher as the main performer' to the 'teacher as a conductor or director' is advocated. (57)

In recent years, administrators and language policies in China typically invoke this 'teacher as conductor' model of teaching similar to CLT and TBLT methods, but questions remain about how student-centered classrooms would incorporate moral roles for teachers in English language classrooms.

For example, the handbook for *College English Curriculum Requirements* (2006), published by the Chinese educational ministry, draws on the discourse of teachers as facilitators with no mention of teachers as moral guides for students. In fact, it explicitly cautions against a 'teacher-centered pattern of language teaching' (23), and the handbook notes that:

> the objective of College English is to develop students' ability to use English in an all-around way, especially in listening and speaking, so that . . . they will be able to enhance their ability to study independently and improve their cultural quality so as to meet the needs of China's social development and international exchanges. (7)

Thus, learning English through Western-based methods that emphasise individuality not only help to improve speaking skills but also allow students access to an undefined 'cultural quality'. Jin and Cortazzi (2002), however, write that these new models of teaching and learning may be very popular, but it is unclear how established *Chinese cultures of learning* in which moral education is a key dimension will be incorporated and how students will respond to these new teaching models. They quote, for example, a student who does not want to talk during classes, 'No questions can be allowed when the teacher is talking to the class, so we should ask during break. We should not interrupt the teacher's thought. This is a kind of respect' (67).

At the same time that moral education has been ignored or at least set aside by recent English curriculum changes in China, there has been a large 'renaissance' of Confucianism in popular and academic writing in many parts of China. One of the most well known phenomena is the extraordinary popularity of Yu Dan's lecture series on state television 'Yu Dan Insights into the Analects' and her best-selling 2006 book *Professor Yu Dan Explains the Analects of Confucius*, a self-help book that has sold over ten million copies worldwide. As Bell (2008) writes, many academics, both inside and outside China, are sceptical of the simplicity of Yu's writing, but it is noteworthy that so many Chinese feel comforted by re-reading and learning about Confucian morals and values. In academic writing, authors such as and Kang (2006) have articulated political reforms and policies based on Confucian moral principles. Based on his analysis of the terms 'rejuvenate' and 'renaissance', Kang (2006) feels that Chinese leaders, while not openly advocating a Confucian political agenda, also desire a return to traditional Confucian values:

> Jiang Zemin put forward 'the great renaissance of the Chinese nation'. Please remember that it was 'rejuvenate China' in the Deng Xiaoping

era. 'Rejuvenate' gives the feeling of starting all over again, suggesting that we were no good in the past, and that we are starting to strive for brilliance and glory today. But 'renaissance' is completely different. It is in itself a positive evaluation of history, meaning that one recognizes a great past and acknowledges a decline. But it also means more a return to prominence, a rising once again to renewed greatness. It is a great change from 'rejuvenate' to 'renaissance', and by no means useless wordplay. In fact, the different wording reflects a revolutionary change in the attitude of the CCP toward traditional Chinese culture. (85)

As a counterpoint to the drive to re-traditionalise Confucianism in the PRC, Wong and Chiu (2005) also argue that much of the current discourse on morality and Confucius, particularly in their analysis of Chinese political leaders in Hong Kong from 1997 to 2004, ignores Confucian ideals such as reflection on proper conduct and the importance of challenging immoral leaders. Instead, they argue that the recent Chinese emphasis on Confucius only defines morality in terms of being a loyal Chinese citizen, developing a sense of responsibility to state and city, and obtaining a set of survival skills to combat a relativistic world (19). Wong and Chiu (2005) argue that Confucius did not value unconditional respect for teachers, but Chinese leaders are more interested in control and maintenance of power than correct actions and democracy.

In light of the above discussions, it is clear that morality still plays a key role in the educational, political, and cultural landscapes in Vietnam and China, but there are some clear tensions in both countries between the maintenance of state order, the drive to internationalise, and the desire to preserve traditional values such as through moral education in schools. The following data sections will expand on these tensions and further explore how the moral instructions of traditional values including Confucianism and local philosophies are re-traditionalised through ELT classrooms in Vietnam and China.

The study

This chapter is based on a study conducted with over 150 university students at one university in northern Vietnam, and over 60 students at one university in China, named here China Southern University (CSU). The students at both universities were either English education majors or preparing for English-language careers by taking advanced academic English at university and were in their early 20s. The 150 students in Vietnam were in their third and final years at university and came from different parts of Central and Northern Vietnam, while the 60 students in China were mostly from the southern province of Guangdong and in their first through fourth years at university. They were asked to write journal entries based on several guided questions during semester one of their third and final years, and the researchers followed up this journal writing with later interviews with the students and teachers over the course of a semester-long class. The guided questions were '*In your opinions, what makes/constitutes a good teacher of English? What do you expect to learn from a good teacher of English? Write about lessons which have interested you; and write about teachers of English who have inspired, motivated and interested you.*' For a more detailed summary of the data sources, see McPherron (2008, 2009).

CSU was founded in 1981 and there are approximately 7,000 undergraduate students at the university. All students take an English entrance exam to place them into classes and must complete English courses to a specific level depending on the requirement of individual academic departments. Requiring English language classes is part of the university's mission to reform the educational system of China and align itself with Western models of education. One author of this paper was an instructor at this university when the student journals were collected, and he maintains continued contact with many of the students in the study through email correspondence and visits to the university.

The university in Vietnam is a comprehensive university, and English is one of the majors the university offers to its students. The university has trained many English language graduates and in this way helps serve Vietnam's ambition to integrate itself with the region and other parts of the world. Teachers of English at this university are all Vietnamese.

How do students of English in Vietnam and China perceive the role of teachers as moral guide/role model?

A strong connection between teacher as moral guide/role model and Vietnamese and Chinese identities

In all the journals written by the 150 students in Vietnam and almost all the 60 students in China, the message 'teacher as moral guide/role model' appeared very explicitly. For example, some Vietnamese students who majored in English and wanted to be teachers of English after graduation wrote:

> I think it's part of Vietnamese culture that teachers educate students both academically and morally. When we talk about teachers, we talk about their role as moral guide.

> For me, being a teacher does not only mean teaching students about knowledge. Teaching morality to students is very important too.

> A good teacher of English is also like a good teacher of other subjects. He/she also needs to educate students academically and morally.

> Producing students with both knowledge and morality is the most important quality of teachers, regardless of what subject they teach.

Other Vietnamese students stated that they would not want to be teachers of English but expressed a strong concern on the matter of *teacher as moral guide* with a particular reference to the influence of English and pop culture in contemporary Vietnam. For instance:

> Nowadays some young people do not respect their teachers and adults. They copy the life style of Western people in movies and are ignorant of the social values and norms expected by the Vietnamese society. They mix English with Vietnamese in their speaking. It's ridiculous. I really think teachers of English need to guide students how to behave.
>
> I want to become a proud Vietnamese who can speak English well, not a Vietnamese who doesn't speak well either language. If I was a teacher of English, I would definitely share this opinion with my students. I don't think my teachers of English so far are aware of this issue. It's a matter of orientation for young people while their characteristics are still being formed. That's why we need good teachers.

These students also referred to Vietnamese sayings which emphasise the moral aspect of being a teacher in the society. These sayings include '*a teacher is an engineer of the soul*', '*teachers set good [moral] examples for students*', and '*respect teachers, respect morality*'.

Data obtained from the students in China further confirmed the view of the role of teachers as moral guide, as shown below:

> The professional knowledge is not the most important thing, the virtue is. The virtue is also the most important thing to a monk. After the virtue, professional knowledge is the most important thing to a teacher.
>
> (Joseph, a third year Chinese student in international business)

> What kind of teacher you are speaks louder than what you teach and how you teach. What I mean here is that a teacher's behaviours and personalities are more important than his or her career success. . . . A teacher is allowed to make mistakes. Even a good teacher is not necessary to be a sage.
>
> (Echo, a 3rd year student in English)

In the same way, Julie, a 2nd year English major, drew on another famous Chinese adage, *yan chuan shen jiao* [Teach by personal example as well as verbal instruction] and wrote:

> That is to say, the teachers should teach the students both by saying and acting. It seems to me more persuading than saying. For instance, it takes little effect for a teacher spends seven hours on talking about the advantage of blood donation rather than have an attempt by himself.

Other students, such as Joyce, a 2nd year English major, described a good teacher as someone who 'sets himself as a hardworking image, and encourage us to learn more'. Students in journals and interviews mentioned that all teachers, both foreign and local can be moral role models and, as Joyce wrote, all teachers should teach 'good qualities such as hard-working, goodness, critical towards our study, and life, and so on'. Joyce interestingly commented on the how the position of teachers as moral role models is mostly a social construction. She wrote, 'The old saying, *wei ren shi biao* [a teacher culti- vates people's knowledge and good actions] has existed in Chinese people's mind for thousands of years, it is a truth in many people's mind'. This truth may be an historical construction, but one that many students at CSU appeared grounded in and united by.

As part of being moral examples in the classroom, some students at CSU noted that teachers – both foreign and Chinese – should offer criticism of poor student work and behaviour. For example, Windy, a 3rd year student majoring in English, voiced a desire for teachers to criticise her English since they have more knowledge of English than students. She wrote that a good teacher should have 'professional knowledge, excellent English skills and critical thinking', and she felt that CSU English teachers – in particular the foreign teachers – were too easy in these respects (see Stanley 2010 for a further discussion of this).

> [ELD] teachers just take English classes too easily. Their easy-going style makes Chinese students think they can be lazy or do work not seriously. Playing games, watching movies and other entertainment are good for students in some situations. To tell the truth, I'm not an excellent or smart student. As a result, I will hope my teacher help me improve my English skills. Also, I'm a little lazy and too proud sometimes. So I expect my teacher make some comments on my work directly, even negative. I think many Chinese would be affected by their teachers' activities.

In interviews, many of the senior students stated that CSU teachers did not prepare them for important exams such as the CET 4 and CET 6. Windy described Chinese students as too 'lazy' to study on their own, especially to speak on their own, similar to local teachers who mentioned the need to 'take special care' with Chinese students who expect teachers to encourage them through explicit correction and evaluation. In a way, the students and teachers offered a negative depiction of Chinese students who are used to being 'force-fed' knowledge through traditional teaching methods, but the students interviewed, however, did not advocate an alternative or Western- style 'facilitator' in the classroom; rather, they demanded a relaxed atmo- sphere as well as the explicit guidance and expertise of teachers. In fact, many students described effective teachers they have had who have taken a central position in classrooms in order to get the attention of students and allow students to feel that they are acquiring important knowledge.

The data obtained from the students in Vietnam and China suggest that being a teacher in these two countries is coupled with demonstrating morality.

Also, almost all the student participants perceived teacher as moral guide/ role model as being part of Vietnamese and Chinese identities. In other words, they tended to claim that being Vietnamese and Chinese teachers, regardless of what subject they teach, equalled enacting the moral guide/role model role. This is what is happening in English language classrooms in both Vietnam and China.

Varied degrees of resistance and ambivalence to the teacher as moral guide/role model

However strong the sentiment was to view teachers as moral guides/role models in Vietnam and China, some of the student participants expressed varied degrees of resistance and ambivalence to this role of teachers, taking into consideration the demands of globalisation and different values they put on the teaching profession.

> I don't totally agree with 'English teacher should be moral role for their students' . . . For teachers, it's not necessary to be a good model, but I think *at least they should be responsible for their jobs* [our emphasis]. Instead of misleading students, just teach them to build up the ability for judging what's right or wrong, to be honest even though you aren't a perfect model.
>
> (Jay, a 2nd year Art School student from Macau)

> I don't think the English teachers should be moral role models. Teaching is simply a kind of occupation. Teachers are responsible to what they teach to students, besides which everybody has his own life. Teachers are human beings, as the same we are. However, *it doesn't mean they can do whatever they want, such as illegal or immoral behaviors* [our emphasis]. What I stress is a life that belongs to yourself, but not lived for others.
>
> (Mitchell, a 2nd year student in English from Guangzhou)

Serena, a 2nd year Journalism major, specifically pointed out that the moral role model view of teaching does not work in a globalising world.

> I am not going to say it [teachers as moral role models] is an outdated criterion, but I think this criterion is unfitting for today's teachers. In the past of China, the teachers were not expected to teach maths, science, foreign language, etc. Those teachers were great thinkers. They lived with the students and taught them morals or political strategies. In that case, the teachers would have greater influence on the students. However, today, the students should be diversified to adapt to the changing world. *The global economy requires diversifications not just moral disseminator* [our emphasis]. In addition, some English teachers are from foreign countries. They may show much respect for freedom. They may have different acknowledgments about morals. So I don't think it is a good idea to judge a good English teacher by 'wei ren shi biao'.

A number of Vietnamese student participants reported that many teachers of English in Vietnam nowadays tended to devote more to their outside earning jobs than their teaching at universities. They felt that these teachers, therefore, did not pay attention to their students' performance. However, the students also felt sympathy for their teachers who had to earn extra money to keep up with a modern society's pressures. They wrote:

> I understand that our teachers of English need to live well first. They don't have much time these days. But so what, they have families, children going to school. If they *teach us well* [our emphasis], that should be enough. I won't complain.
>
> Well, teachers of English and students of English like us, we all have multi jobs at the same time. It's too easy earning extra with English. So who cares if students are late for class or don't even attend? But I must admit there are teachers who are very strict and would give you a hard time if you don't behave. You may dislike them 'cause they're harsh *but I think they care for you* [our emphasis]. Teachers are not all the same. Neither are we. Not all of us respect teachers and work hard.
>
> Teacher as moral guide? A classic saying but kind of lost its meaning these days. We learn many things from our teachers, not just morality. So if teachers inspire us with their confidence, knowledgeability and dynamics, then that is ok. But of course you still like *decent ones*, [our emphasis] don't you?

Although these students acknowledged that they did not demand their teachers of English to be moral guides or role models, a sense of teacher as moral guide/role model is still implied in their responses to varied extents. They still expected or at least wanted their teachers to be 'decent', 'responsible for their jobs', 'teach well', 'care' for them, equip them with other knowledge 'not just [being a] moral disseminator' and not to conduct 'immoral behaviours'.

How are the moral instructions of Confucianism and local philosophies re-traditionalised through ELT classrooms?

Continuation of teachers as modelling good behaviour and promoting idealised social cultural values

As discussed earlier in this chapter, both Vietnam and China promote their social cultural values and ideologies through their moral education embedded in their curricula. In the English language classroom, these values and ideologies are also incorporated and practised in teaching and learning tasks as well as in extra curricula activities. Good teachers are often portrayed as a model for young generations to look up to and become inspired, as is shown below.

Irene, a teacher at China Southern University since 1983, embodies characteristics of the teacher as role model. During the spring semester of 2007, a small group of teachers and students participated in a group called the 'Digital Storytelling Club'. As part of the group, participants wrote narratives of specific events in their lives and the lessons they had learned. The group members then created short movies of their narratives with music, pictures, and drawings. For her digital story, Irene shared how she became a teacher and how she views her position and relationship with students in the classroom. It is particularly interesting how she frames her story of becoming a teacher as one of over-coming struggles. She never overtly instructs students to work hard or be diligent in studying, but through her story a message about the correct way to gain wisdom surfaces.

> Teaching English always bring fun to me. I love to see those adorable young students staring at me, questioning me, and laughing with me. Xiao Ru, one of my favorite students now is a wonderful English teacher in New Zealand. Yun Qian once he wrote a lovely poem made me thrilled and excited for one month. Jing Xuen, a gifted and talented art student gave me a portrait of me, drawn by himself. Students always show their shining potentials in my classroom. *One of my strong points is I can always ignite their sparks into big flames.* As a language educator I have met many distinguished language professors, and I wrote many academic papers and text books. My students love of my books, make me feel proud of myself. And I also feel so proud of my students.

Members of the Digital Story group showed the video presentations to the entire campus at a large screening at the end of the semester, and one author of this chapter also showed them to students in his academic writing classes. In Irene's story, students at the campus presentation commented on her ability to overcome adversity and her deep respect for academic work and professors. Just as Confucius did, Irene is modelling for students her tirelessness in studying and teaching, and students can take her example as a spark to ignite their own love of learning English and acquiring knowledge. This respect for learning was echoed in class discussions of Irene's story and in many student journals discussing Irene as a model teacher.

The student participants in Vietnam applaud teachers who are able to transfer values promoted in the classroom into activities in society and reify social cultural values through their teaching of English. They saw these teachers as their role models. For example, some of them wrote:

> My favourite teacher of English was able to transfer her love for our culture to us. She did not only design many activities to help us appreciate our culture but also encouraged us to form discussion groups beyond classroom activities to explore our culture further while practising our English.

In her teaching of reading and writing, she often gives us texts on beautiful minds, and then asks us to collect anecdotes on people with good behaviours and qualities to be used as topics for our writing and reading lessons. I find myself live better and want to do good things for others. I've volunteered to teach English to poor children.

Many of us come from poor families in rural Vietnam and she has been helping us a lot. She looks for part-time jobs for us, spending her own time teaching us English after class, and helps build up our confidence in using English. We're about to graduate now and we again want to help our poor students. We want to do something like forming a club offering free English lessons to students with difficulties. She's our lifetime model. She has taught us so much more than the English language itself.

These student participants made a very important point in relation to the teacher as moral role in carrying values and passing them on to younger generations. The subsequent section addresses this point further.

How does a teacher as moral guide/role model connect students' local and global worlds?

Localising global concerns and globalising local concerns

In Vietnam, we noticed that teachers do not only teach in order to bring the values that are promoted in class into the local community but also actively invoke an image of a caring community within the classroom. This is evident in the data obtained from the student participants. Several student participants in Vietnam mentioned activities their teachers conducted in speaking skill lessons that tackled both local and global concerns. For example, students were asked to discuss potential cultural and national identity issues when Vietnam becomes a member of WTO and engages more actively with globalisation processes. They reported that this activity enabled them to think of Vietnamese cultural national identity more seriously and thoughtfully. They, at the same time, expressed their opinions on how to enrich cultural identity without losing it. This seems to be a global concern, not just among Vietnamese, given the pressing tendency of globalisation and regionalisation (Appadurai 1996).

Classrooms as imagined and real communities: the global and the local in student–teacher relationships

Teachers and students create new identities and engage in 'imagined' communities in the English classroom. The global and the local seem to mingle and enable a third space – perhaps an imagined space – for teacher-student relationships to operate. For example, Wendy – a Chinese teacher of English – reported that in her English classroom she maintained a parental relationship with students through the use of the expression 'I love you'. In an interview, she explained how this phrase was used in her classroom.

> For Chinese people, especially they will take responsibility. I will take special care with them [her students]. If I see them and they do something wrong, I will tell them. Because I am a mother, I will see my student as the way I will treat my child. If my child has the same problem, I will treat them the same way. Many of my students call me 'Mother'.

Pat, another Chinese teacher of English at CSU, also described students who would call her 'mother' and even tell her that they loved her. Similar to Wendy, Pat noted that she would rarely use *teng* [love fondly] or *ai* [love] with friends or family members when speaking Mandarin, but she freely uses phrases such as 'I love you' with students in English. Both Wendy and Pat felt that they could more easily express an emotional connection with students in English than they were comfortable expressing in Mandarin Chinese.

The depiction of Chinese teachers as parents is often used as a metaphor for the traditional teaching styles that the reform movements aim to replace (College English Curriculum Requirements 2004, Hulbert 2007), but Wendy and the other teachers go further to actually take up familial terms in English and allow their students to call them 'mother', a communicative practice that seems rare in North American contexts and to our knowledge has not been described in the literature on English teaching in China. In creating new meanings in English while also performing traditional care-giving roles, the teachers and students at CSU evoke what Kramsch (2006) describes as the 'different worlds' and inbetween identities of language learners. She notes that these new meanings and imagined communities are inherent to language learning, cultural contact, and what she (in Kramsch 2007) calls the 'communicative trust' between teachers and students that is apparent in language classrooms.

Qin He Li

As a final note on the expectations of morality education and teacher–student relationships in China and Vietnam, two CSU students, Sam and Echo, and one CSU English teacher, Iris, summarised a notion that was common in many of the interviews and journals that we analysed on the topic of morality education and teacher identity. In discussing the translation of the term 亲和力 *qin he li*, the group raised aspects of what an 'effective' teacher is in the English classroom, a definition that incorporates aspects of many roles and discourses found in the student and teacher narratives presented throughout this chapter.

1. S: 我觉得，这个问题，就是要善于引导学生去讲，就是善于沟通，亲和力要强 (I think, this question, [a teacher] is good at conducting students to speak/talk. That is [teacher] should be good at communication, and *qin he li*).
2. L: 这个亲和力 (this *qin he li*) I don't know how to translate.
3. E: Easy-going 亲和力 (*qin he li*). A charm with the students.
4. L: The teacher should easily dominate the class, lead the class, lead the whole students to do what he or she expect them to do. The teacher is very nice and knowledgeable. The teacher is the model or is the facilitator.
5. E: Want to follow. Students want to follow the teacher. Oh, my teacher is so wonderful.

Qin he li cannot be just broken down compositionally into its individual character meanings, and as implied from the discussion, understandings of *qin he li* appear to be context and situation dependent. It can be noted, however, that alone as an adjective *qin* 亲 can mean 'close' or 'intimate' or as the noun 'parent' or 'relation' and is used in terms such as *qin'ai* 'dear', as a formal letter greeting, and *qinqi* 'relative' (*Oxford English–Chinese Pocket Dictionary* 2005). In the same way, *li* 力 stands for 'power' or 'strength' alone as a noun, and is used in two-character terms such as *nengli* 'ability' and *liqi* 'physical ability' or 'energy' (*Oxford English–Chinese Pocket Dictionary* 2005). Also, *he* 和 is a conjunction meaning 'and' or 'together' (*Oxford English–Chinese Pocket Dictionary*, 2005). Taken together, Iris's final statement in 4. appears to be a common definition of *qin he li* as it incorporates a teacher who 'easily dominates the class', 'is very nice and knowledgeable', and 'is the model or is the facilitator', a description that incorporates many of the roles of teaching at CSU discussed in this chapter, and perhaps could be translated simply as 'caring but authoritative'.

Qin he li carries the social and cultural values, expectations and emotional attachments encoded into many Vietnamese sayings and proverbs about teachers. These include 'Without teachers, one can't do anything', 'He who teaches you one word is a teacher, he who teaches you half a word is also a teacher', 'If one wants to cross the water, build a bridge. If one wants his child to be educated, respect/love the teacher', 'The first day of the Tet [Lunar New Year] holiday celebrates the father, the second day the mother, the third day the teacher', 'A teacher is like a fond mother', 'Like teacher, like student', 'Respect teachers, respect morality', 'Rice father, clothes mother, knowledge teacher', 'Teaching is the most noble profession among other noble professions', and 'A teacher is an engineer of the soul' (Breach 2004, 2005, Phan and Phan 2006).

The broad description of *qin he li*, as shown above, however, sets a high standard for English teachers in China or Vietnam since – as Echo mentioned above – students will just 'want to follow' a good teacher, implying that good teaching may somehow just come naturally to the most effective teachers.

Good teaching seems to embody moral and/or manners teaching to varied degrees; and good teachers tend to be those who are also seen as role models and/or moral guides, though there may be different ways to define this role in contemporary Vietnam and China, as indicated in the data.

Conclusion and implications

Writing about the inherent incompleteness in all language and policy research, Canagarajah (2005) writes, 'rather than treating them [unresolved tensions] as a problem for policy formation, we should think of tensions as opening up more complex orientations to language in education (LIE)' (195). In the same way, we began this chapter with the goal of investigating tensions in the multiple interpretations of 'cultural continuity', morality education, and English as an international language in China and Vietnam. In this way, the chapter analysed the descriptions of teachers in English classrooms at Chinese and Vietnamese universities. We found that despite broad education reform of pedagogy and curriculum in both China and Vietnam, teachers and students in both countries are not unanimously abandoning the roles that teachers have traditionally taken in educational settings (Cortazzi and Jin 2002, 2006, Jin and Cortazzi 2002, Nguyen 2002, Doan 2005), nor are they rejecting the expectations of spoken proficiency and student individualism articulated in discourses of education reform and internationalisation. Instead, in articulating Chinese and Vietnamese educational traditions while indexing international norms, the teacher–student relationships illustrate what Bauman (2005) calls the multiple *identifications* available to teachers in the globalising age. He writes:

> Perhaps instead of talking about identities, inherited or acquired, it would be more in keeping with the realities of the globalizing world to speak of identification, a never-ending, always incomplete, unfinished and open-ended activity in which we all, by necessity or by choice, are engaged.
>
> (Bauman 2005: 453)

This notion of *identification* as an unfinished process describes well the divergent descriptions and images of teaching in the present chapter.

As a way to conclude this chapter, we want to further explore some of these identifications in relation to implications for English classrooms and teacher training.

English language classrooms

In analysing the above data, it is clear that teachers and students in China and Vietnam are interpreting English and language pedagogy in creative ways, but it is equally important to note that new English language curricula in

China and Vietnam are dominated by communicative language teaching (CLT) notions of teachers as facilitators, often ignoring or explicitly eliminating the role of teachers as moral guides. While the teachers in Vietnam and China predominantly assume parental and moral guide roles, it will be interesting to document the changing role of teachers in both countries as a younger generation that has learned English through increasing exchanges and contact with international communities. Anecdotally, we have noticed that younger teachers in both countries appear much more eager to embrace new teaching methods such as CLT, marking a potential generational shift in English teachers and their roles inside and outside the classroom. At the same time, even these younger teachers still recognise the importance of teachers as moral guides, and we argue that this concept will remain a strong aspect of educational culture in Vietnam and China for years to come. In fact, it is primarily foreign teachers and researchers, such as the researchers of the studies reported here, who openly worry about the cultural dominance of English as an international language and its effect on teaching roles, revealing an underlying belief by Vietnamese and Chinese teachers that globalisation and English learning may not have the totalising effects on their cultures as some predict. Regardless, it will be interesting to continue longitudinal studies of the changes in teaching roles in China and Vietnam as their economies continue to grow and more young teachers are trained explicitly in the CLT approach.

In addition, we are tempted to label the multiple roads and traditions that the teachers and students draw on in English language classrooms as *hybrid*, but the analysis presented in the chapter moves away from labelling any one practice, utterance, or position as simply representative of *hybridity*. In this way, we have pointed out students and teachers do not just have multiple identities, but what Bauman (2005) calls multiple *identifications*. The students and teachers in Vietnam and China adopt so many discourses, ideas, and affiliations that the term identity – even if defined as multiple and contested – connotes a coherence that does not exist in any student or teacher, and the use of a term such as identification draws attention to the unfinished work of all identity processes in English language classrooms. This does not imply that the term identity should be replaced with identification; rather, the process of identification is part of the larger theoretical construct of identity in ELT (Norton 2000, Lin 2007). In their invocation of 'our China' or 'our Vietnam' and a common tradition, students and teachers reveal the power of a common collective identity and it is important to continue examining identity as the term people use to 'label' themselves and their groups, but we must also continue to examine identification as the process of defining these larger cover terms. In short, moral education needs to be understood more broadly, incorporating both local and global concerns about educating citizens, representing the global and the local connections made by Vietnamese and Chinese teachers and students.

Teacher education

In terms of teacher education, it is clear that the teacher as moral guide/ role model needs to be considered in teacher training curriculum and made explicit in TESOL teacher training courses in Vietnam, China, and through-out the world. Further, as mentioned above, the focus should not just be on how teachers are maintaining traditions but how through their new *identifications* they are re-traditionalising and re-creating local and global cultures. In this way, teacher education students in China, Vietnam, and elsewhere should be encouraged to explore breakdowns and changes in tra-ditional and reform practices. Today, the field of ELT for many practising teachers is oversaturated with new methods and theories on language and teaching. Instead of focusing on theories of language – be they structural or functional – and teaching methods – be they text-based, communicative, or social semiotic – teacher education materials and classes should incorporate more ethnographic studies based on actual teaching and learning contexts. These studies should not be considered as periphery applications and exam-ples of a theory or macro-strategy, but as the core reading and discussion for a course. Is this possible? In the university M.A. TESOL programmes where we work, this shift has already occurred with positive results. Responding to the generalised and de-contextualised classrooms in most TESOL methods books, instructors put together reading packets for ELT methods classes that focus on ethnographies and action research studies, and future teachers discuss in detail the appropriations of teaching methods and English intelligibility standards around the globe. In these re-imagined teacher-preparation classrooms, novice teachers look for themes and prac-tices across settings, but more importantly, they notice the unique tensions and heterogeneity of learners and teachers in each context. They examine these ethnographies in terms of their own conceptions and assumptions about learning and the cultural backgrounds of students, a process that Watson-Gegeo (2004) calls the *limit experiences* of all teaching contexts. The emphasis here is on the break-down of personal, local, and global spaces and meanings as a way to show teachers that local appropriation should be expected.

In training teachers this way, a common theoretical vocabulary is not ignored, but the focus is simply on adapting theories to local contexts, not changing local contexts to fit a theory such as communicative competence. Kumaravadivelu's (2003, 2006) writing about post-methodology offers a good starting point and vocabulary for novice teachers as an introduction to this divide between global theories and local insights and cultural practices such as the enduring role of teachers as role models in China and Vietnam explored in this chapter. In adopting an alternative post-method framework in education, teacher education programmes can reinforce that teaching is not only about the choices and experiences of individual students and teachers in independent classrooms; rather, teaching is part of ongoing inter-national, national, and local dialogues over cultural continuity, globalisation, and cultural flows – dialogues that continue to shape the role of teachers as role models in different ways in China and Vietnam.

Note

1 In fact, Confucian scholars have pointed out that Confucianism and Confucian writers have not always expressed a unified system of beliefs or doctrine of philosophy (Bell and Chaibong 2003). They often cite the adoption of Daoist cosmology and Legalist examinations in the Han dynasty and recent re-traditionalising efforts as examples of how Confucianism has always been transforming and open to internal and external debate.

References

Ames, R. T. and Rosemont, H. (Trans.) (1998) *The Analects of Confucius*, New York: Random House.

Anderson, B. (1983/2006) *Imagined Communities: Reflections on the Origins and Spread of Nationalism* (new edn), New York: Verso.

Appadurai, A. (1996) *Modernity at Large: Cultural Dimensions of Globalisation*, Minneapolis: University of Minnesota Press.

Appadurai, A. (2001) 'Grassroots globalisation and the research imagination', in A. Appadurai (ed.), *Globalisation*, Durham, NC: Duke University Press.

Bauman, Z. (2005) 'Identity in the globalizing world', in S. Shapiro and D. Purpel (eds) *Critical Social Issues in American Education: Democracy and Meaning in a Globalizing World*, Mahwah, NJ: Lawrence Erlbaum.

Bell, D. (2008) *China's new Confucianism: Politics and Everyday Life in a Changing Society*, Princeton: Princeton University Press.

Bell, D. and Chaibong, H. (eds) (2003) *Confucianism for the Modern World*, Cambridge: Cambridge University Press.

Berthrong, J. and Berthrong, E. N. (2000) *Confucianism: A Short Introduction*, New York: One World Publications.

Block, D. and Cameron, D. (eds) (2002) *Globalisation and Language Teaching*, New York: Routledge.

Blommaert, J. (2005) 'Situating language rights: English in and Swahili in Tanzania revisited', *Journal of Sociolinguistics*, 9, 390–417.

Breach, D. (2004) 'What makes a good teacher?', *Teacher's Edition*, 16, 30–37.

Breach, D. (2005) 'What makes a good teacher?' (Part II), *Teacher's Edition*, 17, 28–35.

Brumfit, C. (1984) *Communicative Methodology in Language Teaching: The Roles of Fluency and Accuracy*, Cambridge: Cambridge University Press.

Canagarajah, S. (1999) 'Safe houses in the contact zone: coping strategies', *TESOL Quarterly*, 33(3), 349–70.

Canagarjah, S. (2005) 'Accommodating tensions in language-in-education policies: an afterward', in A. L. Lin and P. Martin, P. (eds), *Decolonisation, Globalisation: Language-in-education Policy and Practice*, Clevedon: Multilingual Matters.

Chowdhury, R. (2003) 'International TESOL teacher training and EFL contexts: the cultural disillusionment factor', *Australian Journal of Education*, 47(3), 283–302.

College English Curriculum Requirements (2004) Beijing: Ministry of Education Press.

Cortazzi, M. and Jin, L. (2002) 'Cultures of learning: the social construction of educational identities', in D. Li (ed.), *Discourses in Search of Members*, Lanham: University Press of America.

Cortazzi, M. and Jin, L. (2006) 'Changing practices in Chinese cultures of learning', *Language, Culture, and Curriculum*, 19(1), 5–20.

Crystal, D. (2003) *English as a global language*, Cambridge: Cambridge University Press.

Dan, Y. (2006) *Professor Dan explains the Analects of Confucius*, Beijing, Zhonghua Book Company.

Doan, D. H. (2005) 'Moral education or political education in the Vietnamese educational system?', *Journal of Moral Education*, 34(4), 451–463.

Duong, T. T. (2000) Suy nghi ve van hoa va Giao duc Viet Nam. TP HCM: NXB Tre.

Duong, T. T. (2002) Suy nghi ve van hoa giao duc Vietnam. TP HCM: NXB Tre.

Edge, J. (2006) *(Re)locating TESOL in an Age of Empire*, New York: Palgrave.

Ellis, R. (2003) *Task-based Language Learning and Teaching*, Oxford: Oxford University Press.

Hulburt, A. (20 April 2007) 'Re-education', *The New York Times*. Online. Available HTTP: <http://www.nytimes.com> (accessed 23 March 2008).

Jin, L. and Cortazzi, M. (1998) 'The culture the learner brings: a bridge or a barrier?', in M. Byram and M. Fleming (eds) *Language Learning in Intercultural Perspective, Approaches Through Drama and Ethnography*, Cambridge: Cambridge University Press.

Jin, L. and Cortazzi, M. (2002) 'English language teaching in China: a bridge to the future', *Asia Pacific Journal*, 22(2), 53–64.

Johnston, B. (2003) 'Values in English language teaching', Mahwah, NJ: L. Erlbaum Associates.

Joseph, M. and Ramani, E. (2006) 'English in the world does not mean English everywhere: the case for multilingualism in the ELT/ESL profession', in R. Rubdy and Q. Jiang (eds) *Political Confucianism*, Beijing: SDX Joint Publishing.

Kang, X. (2006) 'Confucianization: a future in the tradition', *Social research*, 73(1), 77–120.

Kramsch, C. (2006) 'The multilingual subject', *International Journal of Applied Linguistics*, 16(1), 97–110.

Kramsch, K. (2007) 'The uses of communicative competence in a global world', in J. Liu (ed.) *English Language Teaching in China: New Approaches, Perspectives, and Standards*, London: Continuum.

Kumaravadivelu, B. (2003) *Beyond Methods: Macrostrategies for Language Teaching*, New Haven: Yale University Press.

Kumaravadivelu, B. (2006) *Understanding Language Teaching: From Method to Postmethod*, New York: Routledge.

Lin, A. (ed.) (2007) *Problematizing Identity: Everyday Struggles in Language, Culture, and Education*, Mahwah, NJ: Erlbaum.

Louie, A. (2007) *Chineseness Across Borders: Renegotiating Chinese Identities in China and the United States*, Durham, NC: Duke University Press.

Mayumi, D. (2004) 'An analysis on moral education curriculum in Vietnam', *Bulletin of the Graduate School of Education*, Hiroshima University. Part 3, Education and human science, 52(20040328), 115–122.

McDevitt, B. (2004) 'Negotiating the syllabus: a win-win situation', *ELT Journal*, 58(1), 3–9.

McKay, S. L. (2002) *Teaching English as an International Language: Rethinking Goals and Approaches*. Oxford: Oxford University Press.

McPherron, P. (2008) *Internationalizing Teaching, Localizing English: Language Teaching Reforms Through a South Chinese University*, unpublished dissertation, University of California, Davis.

McPherron, P. (2009) '"My name is Money": name choices and global identifications at a South-Chinese university', *Asia Pacific Journal of Education*, 29(4), 521–536.

Nguyen, P. A. (2004) 'Pursuing success in present-day Vietnam – young graduates in Hanoi', in D. McCargo (ed.) *Rethinking Vietnam*, London: Routledge, pp. 165–176.

Nguyen, T. O. (2005, April 21) Bai hoc lam nguoi bi bo quen [First lessons for human beings have been neglected], Tuoi Tre Newspaper, p. 10.

Nguyen, T. M. L. (2002) *Civic Education in Vietnam – The Present Context*. Online. Available HTTP: <http:03%20Civic%20Education%20in%20Vietn%20Nam%20-%20Dr%20Nguyen%20Thi%20My%20Loc.doc> (accessed 19 October 2007).

Norton, B. (2000) *Identity and Language Learning*, New York: Pearson.

Nunan, D. (2005) *Task-based Language Teaching*, Oxford: Oxford University Press.

Ong, A. (1999) *Flexible Citizenship: The Cultural Logics of Transnationality*, Durham, NC: Duke University Press.

Oxford English–Chinese pocket dictionary (2005) Oxford: Oxford University Press.

Pennycook, A. (1994) *A Cultural Politics of English as an International Language*, London: Longman.

Pennycook, A. (2007) 'The myth of English as an international language', in S. Makoni and A. Pennycook (eds) *Disinventing and Reconstituting Languages*, Buffalo: Multilingual Matters.

Pham, H. H. (2007) 'Communicative language teaching: unity within diversity', *ELT Journal*, 61(3), 193–201.

Phan, L. H. (2008) *Teaching English as an International Language: Identity, Resistance and Negotiation*, Clevedon, UK: Multilingual Matters.

Phan, L. H. and Phan, V. Q. (2006) 'Vietnamese educational morality and the discursive construction of English language teacher identity', *Journal of Multilingual Discourses*, 1(2), 136–151.

Phillipson, R. (1992) *Linguistic Imperialism*, Oxford: Oxford University Press.

Ramanathan, V. (2005) *The English-Vernacular Divide*, Buffalo: Multilingual Matters.

Ramanthan, V. and Morgan, M. (2007) 'TESOL and policy enactments: perspectives from policy', *TESOL Quarterly*, 41(3), 447–463.

Reed, G. G. (1995) 'Moral/political education in the People's Republic of China: learning through role models', *Journal of Moral Education*, 24(2), 99–111.

Rydstrom, H. (2001) '"Like a white piece of paper". Embodiment and the moral upbringing of Vietnamese children', *ETHNOS*, 66(3), 394–413.

Sakui, K. (2004) 'Wearing two pairs of shoes: language teaching in Japan', *ELT Journal*, 58(2), 155–163.

Savignon, S. (1983) *Communicative Competence: Theory and Classroom Practice*, Reading, MA: Addison-Wesley.

Savignon, S. (2001) 'Communicative language teaching', in M. Celce-Murcia (ed.) *Teaching English as a Second or Foreign Language* (3rd edn), Boston: Heinle and Heinle.

Scollon, S. (1999) 'Not to waste words or students: Confucian and Socratic discourse in the tertiary classroom', in E. Henkel (ed.), *Culture in Second Language Teaching and Learning*, Cambridge: Cambridge University Press, pp. 13–27.

Watson-Gegeo, K. (2004) 'A different world: embodied experience and linguistic relativity on the epistemological path to somewhere', *Anthropology of Consciousness*, 15(2), 1–23.

Wolfensohn, J. D. (1999, October) 'Culture and sustainable development: a framework for action', Paper presented at the *Redesigning Pedagogy: Research, Policy, Practice Culture Counts: A Conference on Financing, Resources and the Economics of Culture in Sustainable Development*, Florence, Italy 4–7 October 1999.

Wong, V. and Chiu, S. (2005) 'Towards a Confucian notion of youth development in Hong Kong', *International Journal of Sociology and Social Policy*, 25(10/11), 14–36.

Yu, T. L. (2008) 'The revival of Confucianism in Chinese schools: a historical–political review', *Asia Pacific Journal of Education*, 28(2), 113–129.

Part IV

Reform and internationalisation in the disciplines

8 Ten years of curriculum reform in China: a soft knowledge perspective

Wee Tiong Seah

This chapter examines the Chinese mathematics curriculum reform. The approach adopted reflects the socio-culturally situatedness of curriculum reform, examining the cultural and pedagogical values underpinning professional practice. It will interrogate what appear to be valued by reform policies and initiatives, how these reflect, enrich or contradict local pedagogical and societal cultures, and what these mean for the successful execution of the intended curriculum in schools. It argues that the explicit articulation of values inherent in the reform process, and the subsequent negotiation of value differences and conflicts that surface, can bring about a culturally relevant and empowering reform.

Introduction

China operates the largest school Mathematics education system in the world, with more than 11 million teachers teaching more than 109 million, 60 million and 43 million students in primary, junior high and senior high schools, respectively (China Ministry of Education 2007a, 2007b) across the most populous country in the world. In China, as in many if not all other nations around the world, the quality of school Mathematics education – and the crucial relationship with the country's economic development – is of prime interest to all levels of governance. Given the country's stake in the global economy, and in consideration of the increasing numbers of Chinese who work and live overseas, the ongoing improvement and development of China's school Mathematics education standard should be of interest to political, business and education stakeholders outside China as well.

China has excelled in its school Mathematics education, and this continued excellence is dialectically related to the country's economic development (ICME11 Chinese delegation 2008; see also Kelly 2009). In the light of China and East Asian students' consistently high performance in international comparative studies (see Mullis, Martin and Foy 2008; OECD 2004), educators and researchers in the 'West' have for some time been trying to make sense of how their local school Mathematics curriculum might adopt or adapt some of China's pedagogical ideas. These efforts have been supported by the findings of cross-cultural research such as Cai (2007), Leung (2001) and Ma (1999). The publication of the compilation *How Chinese Learn Mathematics: Perspectives from Insiders* in 2004 (Fan, Wong, Cai and Li 2004) further highlights the global academic interest in the Chinese Mathematics education system.

Yet, China's latest (Mathematics) curriculum reform exercise has only in recent years been rolled out to all levels of primary and secondary schooling. How best can the ideals of this reform programme be realised such that students' high performance in Mathematics is maintained? Indeed, how do practitioners and other stakeholders regard the pedagogical potentials of these reform objectives? What does this mean for the maintenance or further stimulation of excellence in school Mathematics education in China? In optimising Chinese students' access to resources in – and entry to – foreign universities and research centres, as well as to the practices of the world business and economy activities, to what extent does the Chinese Mathematics reform feel the pressure to adopt so-called international 'best practice' in Mathematics pedagogy?

This chapter is concerned with evaluating the Chinese Mathematics curriculum reform in the context of the maintenance of – or further improvement to – the Mathematical performance and learning of Chinese students. This can certainly be approached through a cognition-based perspective, drawing upon established models of education or curriculum theories, as well as reference to the experiences of other education systems. For example, one might go about doing this with the perspective of numeracy, assessing the various components of the reform curriculum against the ideals encapsulated in numeracy initiatives. The approach to be adopted in this chapter, however, will reflect the socio-culturally situatedness of curriculum reform. In particular, key features in the implementation of the reform curriculum will be considered by examining the cultural and pedagogical values underpinning practice. It will interrogate what appears to be valued by reform policies and initiatives, how these reflect, enrich or contradict local pedagogical and societal cultures, and what these mean for the successful execution of the intended curriculum in schools and classrooms. The distinction between valuing as a form of 'soft' learning, and cognitive and affective processing as 'hard' learning will be made. To do this, the wider context of academic interest in China's Mathematics education system is first offered below. A brief account of the history of school Mathematics education in China follows, as a means of situating the discussion. Various challenges to the meaningful implementation of the current curriculum reform at the societal, institutional and personal levels will be identified. Suggestions for resolving these through adopting the socio-culturally based perspective will be argued for. In particular, the discussion will exemplify how the explicit articulation of values operating in the various facets of the curriculum reform, and the subsequent negotiation of value differences and conflicts that surface, can bring about a culturally relevant and empowering reform, one which promises to further consolidate student excellence in the discipline while being responsive to emergent trends of thinking and acting in the wider society, and one which is an expression of an educational culture that brings in 'Western' best practice without sacrificing the essence of local norms and practices.

Interest in the Chinese Mathematics education system

Over the last few decades, the Chinese education system has attracted an unprecedented amount of attention from educators and politicians around the world. Not only are teacher education universities in the coastal cities (such as East China Normal University in Shanghai) receiving an increasing number of visiting scholars from Western countries, institutions inland (such as Southwest University in Chongqing), which normally have few English-speaking staff members, are also host to increasing numbers of such scholars. This phenomenon may be attributed to a few factors, one of which is China's impressive economic development since *gaige kaifang* (opening to the world) in 1978, and the potential leverage the nation exerts on the world economy following the global financial and economic crises in the late 2000s. Given that the quality of a nation's formal school education impacts on the knowledge, skills and dispositions of its workforce, and how workforce quality is in turn a variable of economic strength, this aspect of China's hard power (Nye 1990) draws attention to the features of its education system.

Another major factor for the increased interest in China's school Mathematics education programmes is possibly the consistent phenomenon in international comparative studies such as the *Trends in International Mathematics and Science Study* (TIMSS) and the *Programme for International Student Assessment* (PISA) of East Asian nations emerging as top performers at both primary and secondary school levels (Mullis, Martin and Foy 2008, OECD 2004). Nations performing well across these studies have attracted much attention, given that TIMSS assesses student Mathematical knowledge whereas PISA examines the extent to which students are able to apply this Mathematical knowledge to novel problem-solving situations. The association of such nations as Singapore, Hong Kong, Korea and Taiwan with Confucian Heritage Cultures (CHCs) (Wong 2008) has in turn reflected the Chinese roots of most of the populations within these East Asian nations. This commonality amongst the top performing East Asian nations has then directed attention to the Chinese civilisation with its long history of valuing academic *excellence*.

Another factor comes about through the increased number of ethnic Chinese immigrants settling in Western countries such as the United States, Canada and Australia, and the apparent higher (Mathematics) achievement of their children in the local school systems and in Mathematics competitions. For example, for many years now, the number of ethnic Chinese students performing at the top level of the Victorian Certificate of Education

(VCE) examinations (effectively the university entry examinations for students in the State of Victoria, Australia) has been way above the demographic proportion of ethnic Chinese there. The same can be observed in the composition of many national International Mathematics Olympiad teams. In 2007, for example, the fifth-placed United States team of six competitors was made up of three ethnic Chinese members, who also won the two gold medals for their team. The team from multicultural Singapore, on the other hand, was made up of entirely ethnic Chinese members.

All these have created the perception in the Western world of a different, 'other' Mathematics curriculum in East Asia, but in China particularly. An understanding of the nature of this difference is important for those in Mathematics education administration and research, and for those outside these spheres of the profession as well. For the former, an informed unpacking of those aspects of China's Mathematics education system which foster – and other aspects which constrain – the realisation of intended objectives would provide useful reflective ideas. What appear to be the causes of success in one culture need not have the same effect when applied in another culture, what with the interaction between these perceived factors of success with local pedagogical norms and community practices. Indeed, the seduction of the 'exotic' can sometimes prompt education systems to adopt initiatives which are unnecessarily costly and perhaps even inconsequential. As for the other stakeholders, it is in their interest that knowledge informed by culturally-sensitive perspectives serves to promote greater understandings between nations amongst their citizens, business leaders and politicians.

The current school Mathematics curriculum reform in China is part of the national curriculum reform, *kecheng gaige*, which was introduced to schools in the early 2000s. By 2005, all beginning students in China's elementary and junior secondary schools were expected to follow the new curriculum (UNESCO 2007; see also the chapters in Part 1 of this volume). By 2010, the senior secondary reform curriculum is expected to be implemented in all schools across the country. As the curriculum reform approaches full implementation across all levels and all schools, this might be an ideal time to explore the extent to which aspects of the reform curriculum are being successfully implemented in schools, and to identify and understand the challenges, as a means of stimulating further reflection and discussion for finetuning the trajectory of the reform exercise.

Acknowledging the role of soft learning

An adoption of cognitive and/or affective perspectives only in reviewing the Mathematics curriculum reform in China (and elsewhere) runs the risk of robbing us of a more holistic understanding of what has worked and what has not. Many cognition-based education models originated in the 'West' and any argument that these can be applied to *any* learning environment should be challenged. For example, the direct importation of Singapore

Mathematics textbooks to some 140 schools across the USA in the late 1990s is a case in point (Chenoweth 2000, Gowen 2001), even though these text-books were already being published in the English language. For example, there were issues relating to the use of units of measurement which are different across Singapore/Britain and the USA (Chenoweth 2000), and the contexts of many of the word problems in the textbooks were alien to American students. There is culturally-based knowledge which underlies cognitively-based pedagogical considerations such as the ways in which Mathematical concepts are introduced, and exercise problems laid out, in the Singapore textbooks. Mathematical content organisation in Singapore textbooks also assumes a level of teacher content knowledge amongst Singapore teachers which is not paralleled in America (Chenoweth 2000). Furthermore, an affective approach only would be equally unsustainable, since the level of affect need not relate to student understanding or performance. For example, below average self-efficacy means were reported by both high-performing countries such as Finland, the Netherlands, and Korea, and lower per-forming nations like Brazil and Thailand in PISA 2003 (Thomson *et al.* 2004, Figure 7.12: 187). At the same time, high-performing Asian students (from Japan, Korea, Hong Kong, and Macau) reported the four lowest Mathematics self-concept scores amongst the nations surveyed.

Thus, according to Huang (2004), 'although many theoretical systems for discussing educational objectives . . . have been introduced into China, their direct application in educational practice is handicapped by cultural traditions' (104). There appears to be a need to *complement* approaches to the analysis of curricula with a recognition that meaning- and decision-making draw upon culturally-based values as much as they do cognitively- and affectively-based knowledge. What is advocated here is that even greater insight might be gained if, instead of viewing values underpinning perspectives, deci-sions and actions as being separate from cognitive and affective functionings, we regard the socio-culturally based values as underpinning the cognitive and affective functionings that in turn mould perspectives, decisions and actions. That is to say, the rationalising and feeling experiences in making sense of and making decisions about phenomena are by nature culturally-situated. This kind of cultural knowing which 'sits behind' what the mind and heart are learning has been conceptualised as 'soft' learning (Seah 2009), as opposed to 'hard' learning with the mind and heart which are comparatively more tangible and observable. According to Seah, while hard learning might refer to the part of learning experience which draws upon an individual's mental processing and affective response to attain varying levels of awareness and understanding, soft learning refers to the part of the learning process which draws on the individual's experience and internalisations within the socio-cultural environment(s) he/she functions or has functioned. In particular, soft learning facilitates sense-making through such socio-cultural factors as socio-economic status; language and discourse; race and ethnicity; gender; as well as attitudes, beliefs and values.

An example might be the (hard) learning of number and computation expected of school students in many nations. Yet, the extent to which notions of number, counting and arithmetic operations are effectively acquired and understood is regulated by the soft learning which would have taken place concurrently in the minds and hearts of students. The student who has been raised in a typical 'Western' family will likely take it for granted that knowledge relating to the cognition of adding, subtracting, multiplying and dividing is an important life-skill. However, in a traditional indigenous community in Australia, say, the soft learning which is activated amongst students is likely to be different; counting activities, for example, have never been seen as important as one's ability to visualise spatially one's environment in the featureless landscape around him/her (see, for example, Kearins 1981). What then are the implications and issues of implementing such a Mathematics curriculum in communities where spatial sense and geometrical skills are more valued than number sense?

How one thinks/reasons and how one feels are guided intuitively by one's 'culture code' (Rapaille 2006). Accordingly, a good way to review China's (Mathematics) curriculum reform over the past decade or so might be to explicate the values (as a manifestation of soft knowledge) that are encapsulated in and embraced by the Chinese culture. To better achieve this, it would first be necessary to relate to the long history of Mathematics education in China, in the context of the 5,000 years of history of the Chinese culture, as well as more contemporary realities of Mathematics education and schooling in the Chinese society.

Mathematics education in China

Mathematics education in China has had a long history. Arithmetic was one of the six classical arts that were already being taught in ancient China more than 2,000 years ago (Li 2008, Yao 2000). Mathematics has traditionally played an important role in the imperial courts throughout many dynasties in China. This, together with imperial China's valuing of government officials candidates' *performance* in the imperial examinations (which developed over the period 400–900 AD), had led to a societal valuing of *Mathematical performance* as a reflection of a family's success, prestige and power. Details of these and other aspects of the important roles which Mathematics historically and currently plays in different levels of the Chinese society are available elsewhere (see, for example, ICME11 Chinese delegation 2008). What follows is an abbreviated account of the history of Mathematics education in China, with the aim of explicating the values that are encapsulated in and embraced by the Chinese culture, as a means of better understanding the soft knowledge relevant to this discussion.

'Western' Mathematics was introduced into China in about 1600 (Li 2008) through the Christian schools that were run by foreign missionaries. 'In 1607, the first 6 volumes of Euclid's *Elements* were translated into Chinese by the

Chinese mathematician Xu Guangqi and the Italian Jesuit Priest Matteo Ricci' (Li 2008: 127). However, it was not until after imperial rule ended with the 1911 Revolution that 'Western' Mathematics was taught across almost all elementary schools throughout China (Zhang 2005).

The establishment of the People's Republic of China in 1949 stimulated an overhaul of China's education system to one which was based on the Soviet Union's. The primary Mathematics curriculum in China at that time was characterised by content which was condensed and focused, with a valuing of *logic* and *deduction* (Zhang 2005). In the 1960s, a finetuning of the Soviet Union-based primary Mathematics curriculum led to a new valuing of *practicability* and *applications*. The emphasis of the Mathematics education system became one of learning basic knowledge and basic skills (Zhang 2005). The 1966–1976 Cultural Revolution had an impact on the development of Mathematics education in China as well. In line with the prevailing doctrine of the country, Mathematics education emphasised applications to particular areas, namely, the labour and manufacturing sectors (Zhang 2005).

Zhang (2005) observed that pedagogical exchange between the Chinese and their counterparts in the 'West' after 1976 had led to the introduction into China's curriculum of such pedagogical ideas as problem-solving, standardised assessment, and Bloom's taxonomy of educational objectives. The move in the 1990s to strengthen China through further developing technology and education had led to the valuing of *ability training* (Zhang 2005). At the same time, this was also a period which saw the 1992 Mathematics curriculum reinforcing China's valuing of the 'two basics' (*shuang ji*) (that is, basic knowledge and skills) and 'three abilities' (that is, computation, logical thinking and spatial visualisation) in the pre-Cultural Revolution years (Wong, Han and Lee 2004). Indeed, there is ample evidence 'on the ground' today that Mathematics education in China still values very highly the role of *foundational knowledge and skills* (see also ICME11 Chinese delegation 2008).

Thus, for more than a hundred years now, the Mathematics discipline that is taught in schools has been 'Western' Mathematics similar to the Mathematics that was being taught in Europe or in the United States. On the other hand, traditional Chinese notions of how this 'Western' Mathematics is expected to be taught effectively to students (and which includes the ways in which the intended curriculum was to be written) had been infused with Russian and other Western pedagogical ideas, as well as other ideologies.

It was located within this reality that one of the most significant and comprehensive curriculum reforms in the nation began in 1999. The primary school section of this reform began its trialling process in 2001, and by 2005 all beginning students in China's primary and junior secondary schools were placed in the new curriculum (UNESCO 2007; see also the chapters in Part 1 of this volume for an expanded discussion of this process). This comprehensive reform is characterised by a content which is essentially Westernised in its conception and articulation. The reform signalled the country's intended move away from an education system whereby teachers impart knowledge to students, to one which emphasises the development of lifelong learning abilities (Huang 2004), the importance of education bridging what is learnt in schools with students' experience in society, and the importance of students assuming greater initiative and autonomy in their own learning (Wang 2005). A more encompassing view of what constitutes assessment and a pedagogical emphasis on harnessing learning technologies (Zhang 2005) were also developed. In essence, the traditional valuing of *yingshi jiaoyu* (examination-oriented education 应试教育) was to give way to a reform discourse which emphasises *suzhi jiaoyu* (quality education 素质教育).

In the Chinese language, however, the term *suzhi* in *suzhi jiaoyu* takes on different meanings depending on whether it is being used as a noun or adjective. *Suzhi* (quality) is a noun in the current reform rhetoric, rather than an adjective describing the quality expected of school education. Thus, there are indicators within this latest Mathematics curriculum reform of an institutional emphasis on attending to particular groups of individuals according to their needs and capabilities (instead of providing a common education experience for all students). For example, a feature of this curriculum reform exercise had been the replacement of a unified syllabus and unified textbooks with a set of unified curriculum statements (ICME11 Chinese delegation 2008), thus laying the way for the curriculum to be realised through different textbooks (*yi gang duo ben*). Interestingly, local provinces' valuing of *efficiency* (e.g. in collating and comparing student scores of local examinations) has often meant that the same textbooks are being selected in these communities, thus putting in jeopardy the intention for *ying cai shi jiao* (因材施教, teaching according to students' capabilities). At the same time, the approval for Shanghai to structure its own school Mathematics curriculum and examinations in 1997 (Wong, Han and Lee 2004) not only represents the Chinese central government's acknowledgement of the coastal city's capacity and resources, but it might also be regarded as a test-case of customising curriculum innovation according to the unique resources and needs of different provinces/cities in the future.

Although 'this process of curriculum reform is mainly inspired by Western experiences, with inputs coming from a series of study-tours to developed countries that took place prior to the reform' (UNESCO 2007: 6–7), the Chinese government also desires a school curriculum which supports the development of a harmonious society with Chinese socialism features. Thus, the curriculum reform is intended to 'enable, through education, new advanced cultures and concepts to spread in schools and society at large, to build among the Chinese people a co-operative and constructive partnership of democracy, equality, dialogue, consultation and mutual understanding' (Wang 2005). There is official interest in maintaining a sense of balance between adopting foreign cultures and local experience in the structuring of pedagogical experiences for students. Thus, socio-cultural and political factors (and the values underlying these) are at work both at the intended, policy level and the implemented, articulation level.

In this context, the next sections will highlight issues related to the introduction of the Mathematics curriculum reform in China, these being high-stakes assessment, decentralisation of curriculum planning, the perceived 'Western' basis of the reform pedagogy, information and computer technology, rigour of reform Mathematics, and teacher professional development. The discussion will draw on understandings of the relevant soft learning, including the values that are emphasised traditionally in the Chinese Mathematics education system, as well as the values that underlie innovative pedagogical ideas.

High-stakes assessment

Examinations have traditionally occupied an important place in the Chinese (Mathematics) education system. An important factor in this discussion is the likelihood that examination performance will continue to play an important role in a child's education in China and, in particular, in determining the next phase of his/her formal learning journey. Practically, academic performance in the university entrance examinations has been crucial in a student's tertiary entrance process, especially with regards to prestigious universities in Beijing and other major cities. Not only is this emphasis on examinations performance a result of limited university places for the large number of senior secondary school graduates, but it is also shaped by a marketplace which is not absorbing all the university graduates every year. According to Villa (2009), 'China will turn out 6.11 million college graduates this year [2009] who will join one million unemployed graduates from 2008 who are still looking for work'. Thus, as long as academic performance in high-stakes university entrance examinations has a bearing on a student's future career prospects, it will be relatively more difficult for parents and educators to accept new ways of teaching and learning, unless these pedagogical initiatives promise to optimise the examinations performance of their respective children and students.

As alluded to above, this phenomenon reflects the Chinese culture's valuing of academic *performance* in enhancing one's future quality of life. The imperial China's system of selecting officials through the examinations system has translated to a cultural valuing of examinations *performance* as a measure of personal and family success, prestige and wealth. China's one-child policy in the last few decades has only reinforced this cultural value further (see Wang 2010 on the impact of this phenomenon on the parental pressures on Chinese students). Previous reform attempts to de-emphasise *performance* as an indicator of successful Mathematics learning have largely failed, while the examination-oriented 'regular system' has proven remarkably resilient, bouncing back with renewed vigour after each assault. In their actions, China's educators remained committed to preserving examination-defined quality and left to their own devices, the features of the regular system with its links back to the imperial examination system would inevitably re-emerge (Dello-Iacovo 2009: 2).

The importance placed by the wider society on examinations performance has meant that many teachers and schools 'teach to the test'. Anecdotal feedback from academics and teachers in China reveal that after all, a teacher's performance and career prospects are often tied to the performance of his/her students in the high-stakes examinations, and schools with excellent student performance likewise receive more funding. Yet, in Shanghai, for example, the low proportion of Mathematics tertiary entrance examinations items that assess student applications of Mathematical concepts (despite a curriculum which promotes the place of Mathematics in one's world) has meant that schools and their teachers do not devote as much revision time on applications-type problems. This demonstrates the need for (high stakes) examinations to reflect reform curriculum objectives, especially in cultures such as China where there is a socio-cultural perception that examinations performance is a measure of teacher/school effectiveness.

In other words, reform policies run the risk of being embraced at a tokenistic level if the society continues to value student *performance* in high-stakes assessments. Indeed, many members within the Mathematics education community in China believe that 'the "exam-oriented education" has become the biggest obstacle for the development of Mathematics education in China. . . . [and it] not only impedes China's Mathematics education but also undermines China's future competitiveness' (ICME11 Chinese delegation 2008: 44). Given China's population, there may indeed be few alternative models for an examination-oriented education for a key school subject such as Mathematics. However, there might also be opportunities for the Chinese cultural valuing of *examinations* and *performance* to be capitalised upon in ways which promote the pedagogical approaches encapsulated in the reform curriculum. This certainly calls for new and creative ways of assessing student learning and assessing for teacher learning as well. Although 'the evaluation method has not yet correspond [sic] to the curriculum reform' (ICME11 Chinese delegation 2008: 33), charting new directions for the different modes of assessment, including the high-stakes university entrance examinations, does appear to be the next task to embark on in the rolling out of the reform curriculum (the chapter by Kang and Liu in this volume discusses some emerging initiatives to develop other forms of assessment of student work and achievement such as through the use of student portfolios).

Most significantly, the views expressed by the Chinese Mathematics education community above indicate an awareness that reforms in curriculum and pedagogical practice should be contextualised in a notion of Mathematical performance which is in itself fluid across time and space. That is to say, if the curriculum reform exercise is to be understood as supporting and maintaining student performance, then the idea of performance should take on different meanings in different periods of Chinese history, in line with changes in the social, political and economic landscapes within the nation, and in the global situation without. The barrier, however, appears to be deep-rooted cultural valuing of *performance* as defined and dictated by the educational authorities. After all, throughout China's history, the imperial court – and, to a great extent, the government too – has recruited the best brains through highly competitive selection processes, processes which are unlikely to change much in time given their efficiency in enabling the identification of capable officials. As such, performance in high-stakes assessment practices is likely to continue to dominate students' lives, and lead to their valuing of this aspect of learning and working in the rest of their professional and personal lives.

The decentralisation of curriculum planning

A feature of the current (Mathematics) curriculum has been a tripartite education administration model. Under this organisation model, curriculum planning and the assessment of its delivery is not just the sole responsibility of the central government; the different provincial governments and school leadership teams are also expected to play active roles. As has been witnessed in other education systems (e.g. Switzerland), this organisational model not only improves the efficiency of the education service, but a greater level of direct participation by local education authorities can allow for a more effective cultural customisation of the (Mathematics) curriculum for multicultural societies such as China. With the structuring of proper guidelines, this can be an efficient model without threatening the need to maintain a unified national curriculum. Decentralisation, however, should not be an excuse for reduced central government funding (directly or otherwise). The implications of such a development would be undesirable, both for the success of the reform and for the maintenance of social harmony within the Chinese society (see Dello-Iacovo 2009), thereby eclipsing any educational benefits associated with decentralised curriculum planning.

In the area of school Mathematics education, the possibility of more customised lesson delivery afforded by the decentralised organisational model presents opportunities for the socio-cultural nature of Mathematical knowledge to be introduced more explicitly to students in a nation which has a diverse range of cultures. China's 55 ethnic minorities, which constitute about 9.4 per cent of the country's population, are spread out across some 64.3 per cent of land in China. A greater integration of ethnoMathematics (D'Ambrosio 1985) in the school Mathematics curriculum will not only help to realise the reform curriculum's aims of relating what is taught at school with what is experienced outside school, but it can also unlock for students the valuing of such convictions as *progress* (see Bishop 1988). According to D'Ambrosio (1985), ethnoMathematics refers to 'the Mathematics which is practised among identifiable cultural groups, such as national-tribal societies, labor groups, children of a certain age bracket, professional classes, and so on' (45). The valuing of local, ethnic Mathematical practices in a culturally-sensitive Mathematics curriculum can instil students' pride in their own cultural heritage, while promoting harmony through mutual respect and under-standing of associated norms and practices. From another perspective, a school Mathematics curriculum that is enriched with ethnoMathematics can thus motivate more students in its learning, thus contributing to the addressing of the worrying observation that Mathematics is the weakest subject amongst the ethnic minorities in China. In this way, the cultural responsiveness associated with a Mathematics curriculum that has direct input from local governments and school leadership teams can have a positive impact on student affect, engagement and what Clarkson, Bishop and Seah (2010) call 'Mathematical well-being'.

Concern over the basis of the reform pedagogy

At the level of implementing the curriculum reform, what are immediately obvious to educators, parents and their children would be the changes made to the content, and how this content is taught in the classroom. Much of the association of the 'Western' pedagogical ideas with the reform curriculum relates to the very ways in which school Mathematics would be taught and learnt in the classrooms. At this level, there is concern over the pedagogical ideas underlying the reform curriculum, that is, reform ideas of how school Mathematics might be optimally taught and learnt are not necessarily perceived to be workable at the community and home levels. Much of this concern is rooted in the valuing of traditional cultures. For example, if students are expected to take more initiative in the learning process, to what extent will teachers be prepared for students to pose 'what if' or 'why' questions during lessons? How will teachers respond to solution approaches which might not appear to be as efficient as the one which they themselves have introduced to the students? Wong, Han and Lee (2004) expressed such types of concerns more academically, cautioning that 'more discussions and investigations should be made on how Mathematics should be learned' (56).

It was evident, for example, in my several observations of primary school Mathematics lessons in Shanghai, Shangyu and Suzhou in 2008 that teachers value student *precision* in Mathematical speech. Teachers would often be observed modelling the use of Mathematical vocabulary of new concepts taught, and getting their students to recite these. In a Grade 1 class in inner suburban Shanghai, the teacher in a cluster lesson study class went beyond chorus recitation of the teen numbers, to providing her students with the opportunity to then name the numbers in the correct order to a peer, followed by individual recitations. In fact, it was interesting to find a guest speaker delivering an academic talk at Beijing University calling upon his audience to repeat selected keywords and key phrases after him! While this teaching/lecturing practice might not be in conflict with the objectives of the Mathematics reform curriculum, questions might still be raised in terms of student perceptions of the extent to which their own Mathematical experiences (and ways of vocalising these) are legitimised.

Anecdotal evidence suggests that for many teachers and educators, the recognition of Chinese students' excellent performance in international Mathematics studies and in international Mathematics Olympiads has actually reinforced pedagogical practices that have served them well and which have propelled them to the best performance. Thus, as another example, there is the ongoing valuing of the *two basics* in the Chinese society. While there may still be good reasons to emphasise student mastery of basic knowledge and skill, the different demands of a quickly-changing world do call for a different set of lifeskills amongst people. Indeed, the valuing of *two basics* alone can present a barrier to the inculcation of Mathematical innovation and creativity amongst Chinese students, a barrier to expose students to Mathematical problems that are meaningfully grounded in their respective environments (ICME11 Chinese delegation 2008), and indeed, a barrier to facilitate a rounded development amongst students. This phenomenon can be compounded by a cultural valuing of *transfer of experience/wisdom* which is in some ways related to a deficit-theory perspective. Thus, while student creativity will play a role in fulfilling the reform curriculum's aim of fostering inquiry learning, any difficulty in fostering student thinking 'outside the box' cannot be attributed to 'lack of intelligence. The greatest impediment is cultural. As an Asian society, we tend to be paternalistic' (Ngiam 2009). This cultural value can also be potentially articulated in teachers' pedagogical practice, which can run counter to reform pedagogies promoting the valuing of *student-centredness*.

The gradual weakening of the *de facto* global leadership of the United States of America has also played a role in boosting a sense of academic nationalism within China. In the shadow of the unpopular wars America engaged in and of the role its financial institutions played in initiating the global economic crisis in the 2000s, there is a slide in the appeal of America's soft power (see Nye 1990). At the same time, there has also been a global desire for a multipolar world order, associated with a greater sense of nationalism in individual nations. Thus, there can be a growing perception in the Chinese society (and elsewhere) that 'the West is not necessarily best'.

In the area of Mathematics education, parents and teachers have been aware of the continuing relatively weaker performance of students in Western nations in international comparative tests such as the *Trends in International Mathematics and Science Study* [TIMSS] and the *Programme for International Student Assessment* [PISA]. They would no doubt be aware too that East Asian cultures have consistently been occupying top spots in such tests (e.g. Mullis, Martin and Foy 2008, OECD 2004). In this sense, then, that the conceptualisation of the current Mathematics reform curriculum has been based on Western pedagogical frameworks can be a source of potential resistance in its implementation. Institutional-level emphases that the reform seeks to draw upon the essence of (Mathematics) education practices and beliefs from both the East and the West will continue to play an important role against such perceptions. Credibility can be increased by demonstrating the continuing Mathematical performance of students in Singapore, South Korea and Japan despite these countries modelling their own Mathematics education reforms after Western discourse in the recent past.

Integration of information and computer technology in Mathematics education

One aspect of the concerns over the pedagogies promoted in the curriculum reform arises from its stipulation for the integration of computer technology into Mathematics teaching. The aim is to 'help students better understand the nature of Mathematics' (ICME11 Chinese delegation 2008: 41). This expression is different from corresponding aims in many Western nations' Mathematics education curriculum statements. Whereas ICT is harnessed in 'Western' developed nations as a tool for reducing the chores involved with computations, to check computed results, and/or to explore inherent patterns (see, for example, VCAA 2005), there is in the Chinese curriculum a metacognitive component to student use of learning technologies as they learn and 'do' Mathematics.

Given the challenges posed by China's size, and given the shortage of needed funding in many schools (especially those located away from the coastal cities), the need for student and teacher access to the technological tools is a real issue. In Shanghai, the locally-made Casio calculators that have been approved for use in the college entrance examinations since 2000 sell for about 150 yuan. This is an affordable price, given that Shanghai residents' average disposable income was 6,795 yuan in the first three-month period of 2007. Over the years, thus, China has no doubt achieved great strides in equipping classrooms and students with a range of hardware and software. This achievement is crucial not just from the pedagogical perspective, since any community (mis-)perception of inequitable distribution of (ICT) resources amongst schools might affect wider societal sentiment.

Access to ICT resources, be it real or perceived, might be seen in the community as an aspect of social inequity. This is certainly an undesirable social scenario which the education system can avoid. However, even with available access, the barrier against greater harnessing and integration of learning technologies in school Mathematics education still exists. In China, reasons accounting for this 'might be that teachers seldom have time to learn how to use relevant ICT tools due to their heavy teaching load. . . . [and] that teachers feel it is more troublesome and time-consuming to use ICT' (ICME11 Chinese delegation 2008: 41). Thus, although more creative means of upskilling teachers may improve ICT integration to some extent, the real issue in China (and indeed, in many places elsewhere) appears to be one of establishing a professional culture which values *technology* in pedagogical practice.

Rigour of Mathematics in the reform curriculum

As is similarly evidenced elsewhere in the world, a reform curriculum which aims to achieve 'Mathematics for all' or numeracy/Mathematical literacy will inevitably draw concerns from the academic, educational and general communities that the standard and rigour of Mathematics being taught in schools will be compromised (Wong, Han and Lee 2004). It is as if the Mathematics content of a curriculum that is designed for all students is necessarily so non-technical that it does not qualify as Mathematics anymore in the eyes of career mathematicians. This is no less different in China; a meeting of senior Mathematics education researchers, as well as other stakeholders from the political and academic publishing sectors, in late 2008 had identified as the main concern facing school Mathematics education the falling standard of student command of the discipline. At the same time, there have been many teacher educators who identify as the main problem facing Mathematics education the weaker Mathematical knowledge that is possessed by the younger teachers.

On the other hand, Mathematics Olympiad competitions are being taught in more and more schools in China, and increasing numbers of students are participating in such events. Much like the tuition sessions and after-school lessons which are very much a part of the daily lives of many students in China, Mathematics Olympiad coaching has become a commodity that is valued by parents. Does this development reflect a shifting education climate in China which now values student performance in Mathematics Olympiads as a marker of success or intelligence? If this is so, this presents another aspect to societal concern over the rigour of reform Mathematics as perceived by the society.

Sustained and meaningful professional development

It is reasonable to argue that student performance is supported by effective teachers, and that the maintenance of this achievement calls for teachers' participation in regular professional up-skilling opportunities. Teacher in-service professional development in China has often, though not exclusively, involved experienced teachers and local educators sharing their professional knowledge and skills with classroom teachers, and often providing 'demonstration' lessons. However, the reform curriculum implications for changes to classroom practices would necessitate corresponding changes in teacher pedagogical experiences, beliefs and values, all of which are not likely to be met by professional sharings of what had been mastered proficiently in classrooms elsewhere. Enacting the reform curriculum also requires the classroom teacher to employ a diverse range of teaching methods (ICME11 Chinese delegation 2008); this may not be an easy task to be facilitated by classroom teachers who had been functioning in an essentially unified curriculum up to the recent past. As a result, 'in many cases, teachers are simply continuing to teach as before' (Dello-Iacovo 2009: 5).

An associated barrier to the curriculum reform process is the teachers' continued reliance on the textbooks at the expense of other pedagogical resources (Huang 2004). This has implications towards realising the reform's aims of catering for student individual difference and of encouraging students to be more active participants (Huang 2004), especially when a teacher regards the content in the textbook – and how these are arranged within it – as representing *the* curriculum.

It appears that what teachers feel to be heavy teaching loads might impact on opportunities and/or the quality of professional development experiences (ICME11 Chinese delegation 2008). This might be tackled in two ways, that is, through generating more teachers to make a difference to teacher teaching loads, and by more creative designing of more flexible professional development deliveries.

It will not be easy to train enough teachers to generate the supply required to lead to reduction of teacher workloads, not to mention the corresponding developments elsewhere that is needed to support this (e.g. the expansion of school infrastructure). On the other hand, it is relatively easier to stimulate more flexible delivery of professional development. One aspect here is the role played by teacher professional journals of Mathematics education in China in promoting teacher change. That most articles in the more than 30 different teacher professional journals of Mathematics education are written by class-room teachers has meant that the knowledge and skills needed to promote useful teacher change is contingent on more contributing teacher-writers sharing innovative teaching experiences. There is also the issue of access; one of the earliest and most popular journals, *Shu xue jiao xue*, has seen its circulation decline from a peak of 40,000 copies per issue to some 20,000 copies currently, in a country which has more than 20,000 secondary schools alone.

As is the case with the other factors discussed here, there are pockets of success stories across China. An excellent example is the establishment of several *Xuexi yu fazhan gongtongti* (学习与发展共同体), that is, Learning and Development Communities [LDCs] in Beijing, Inner Mongolia and several other areas across China over the last few years (see Ryan, Kang, Mitchell and Erickson 2009; also see Chapters 1 to 3 in this volume). This initiative has been developed by Dr Changyun Kang of Beijing Normal University in collaboration with school leaders and teacher researchers in collaboration with researchers in Canada and Australia, and its conception has been informed by the experiences of the established Professional Learning Communities in Canada and of the Project for the Enhancement of Effective Learning in Australia.

The success of the LDCs has demonstrated what is possible when several enabling factors are present. One of these would be the active involvement of Mathematics education researchers – they brought with them to the teacher participants of the LDCs novel and innovative pedagogical ideas that are aligned with the reform, they were able to model these ideas, and in so doing, they affected what the teacher participants valued about best practice in the school Mathematics classroom. Indeed, these researchers can complement existing action research activities undertaken by the widespread teacher research networks called *yanjiuzu*. Thus, it is worth exploring the possibilities for real change in professional practice through collaboration of Mathematics education researchers from Chinese universities and centres and of the curriculum writers of the reform curriculum with existing teacher research networks. Perhaps, too, this is an area where Mandarin-speaking Mathematics education researchers in other countries might support China's Mathematics curriculum reform, such as through the provision of workshops at the school district levels.

The role of values

The discussion thus far has attempted to unpack the issues relating to the current reform of the Mathematics curriculum in China from the perspective of the soft learning underlying what stakeholders think and feel. In particular, this discussion highlights the role that socio-culturally-based values plays in affecting the perceptions, meaning-making and decisions experienced by the stakeholders at all levels. By its own nature, values as part of soft learning are extremely internalised within cultural groups and amongst their members. In China's case, the situation is likely to be further exacerbated by its geographical features, where some far-flung communities may still function as they have been over the last few hundred years (Kelly 2009). What appears to be highly valued, and thus highly influential in facilitating the interpretation and implementation of the curriculum reform, is rooted in the academic nationalism that China is experiencing. This has led to a valuing of, say, the *two basics* which threatens the development of student creativity as advocated in the reform curriculum. Also, as another example, the society's valuing of *performance* (not just in schools, but in the arena of international comparative studies) accounts for the continual emphasis on *high-stakes assessment*, which in turn impedes the realisation of some of the reform ideals. Similarly, the valuing in the Chinese society of *rigour* in Mathematics can pose a barrier to a reform curriculum which promotes *Mathematics for all*. It is logical to argue, then, that a better understanding and harnessing of relevant values underlying this phenomenon will enable more meaningful engagement with the issues presented above.

The value differences and dissonance associated with these issues extend beyond pedagogical approaches to a much more deep-seated factor, which is the ways in which the nature of Mathematics itself is valued. That the reform curriculum advocates for the learning of Mathematics to be related to students' life experiences (Wang 2005) is but just one example in which the initiative is being perceived by some as eroding the rigour of the discipline, given its alignment with the 'Mathematics for all' catchphrase. While public and academic debates over numeracy as a poor cousin of Mathematics rage on in many nations around the world, what is rather unique in China is a sense that the practices of its teachers and educators value *rigour* that is inherent in the discipline. This potentially adds another layer of obstacles to the successful implementation of the reform goals for Mathematics education across China.

The academic nationalism which appears to be much valued today might reflect the Chinese sense of pride in being *yan huang zi sun* (炎黄子孙, a term which refers to the ethnic Chinese as descendents of a long line of proud history, but has assumed a nationalistic connotation since the later period of the Qing dynasty). The painful lessons of exploitations of the Chinese by Western powers in China's history are not lost in the Chinese psyche, and these have often been the context of high-ratings movies and drama serials even today. Thus, it is hard to imagine the Chinese population adopting wholesale Western pedagogical practices. China's success in hosting the Olympics Games in 2008 and its relative political and economic strengths that are emerging in the current global climate will only serve to deepen the valuing of national and racial *pride* amongst its population in general, and amongst stakeholders in Mathematics education in particular.

By design or otherwise, and definitely partly due to its long history, the different facets of Chinese society (such as economic, financial, and governance) are used to navigating through different political, economic, financial and/or educational frameworks at the same time (Kelly 2009). That is to say, the Chinese are generally used to confronting values that are different and/or in conflict in productive ways. In this context, top-down attempts at instituting behavioural change or even value change will likely prove futile. What is perhaps needed to facilitate more effective and productive Mathematics curriculum reform in China, instead, is to build on the reform's model of decentralised curriculum planning, and acknowledge that as different stakeholders come together, their responses to the inevitable situations of value differences are contextualised in the prevailing sociocultural conditions. Seah's (2005) research with immigrant Mathematics teachers on their socialisation experiences in Australian schools, for example, has mapped five different approaches that people tend to take in such circumstances. These are adapted for the current discussion in Table 8.1.

It is evident from Table 8.1 that the status quo, assimilation and accommodation responses make up a continuum representing the extent to which what are valued in the current and reform curricula are espoused differently. The amalgamation and appropriation responses, however, represent another category, in that they are both culturally productive; in both these responses, the introduction of new initiatives and the accompanying soft learning have resulted in real and sustained changes to current practices and norms. When either amalgamation or appropriation takes hold, the particular aspect of school Mathematics education can be considered to have 'moved on'. What differentiates the two is the extent to which elements of the current and

Table 8.1 Responses to perceived value differences in the implementation of
Mathematics curriculum reform (adapted from Seah 2005)

Response	Assumption	Practice
Status quo	The culture of the current curriculum and what it values should be espoused.	I continue to facilitate the learning of Mathematics in the same way as I have been doing.
Assimilation	The reform curriculum should influence the surface characteristics of my facilitation of Mathematics learning.	I include cultural contexts of the reform curriculum in my practice, such as in the way the students are seated in class.
Accommodation	The culture of the reform curriculum and what it values should be espoused.	The reform curriculum is embedded in the way I facilitate Mathematics learning.
Amalgamation	The essence of what is valued in the current curriculum and the reform curriculum should be drawn upon.	I facilitate Mathematics learning in ways which reflect a synthesis of what is best in both the current and reform curricula.
Appropriation	What is valued in the current and reform curricula should interact to inform Mathematics education.	I facilitate Mathematics learning in ways which reflect an adaptation of the reform curriculum and the current curriculum to each other.

reform curricula might be separated in practice and in form. In some ways, this is similar to the distinction between mixtures (corresponding to amalgamation) and compounds (corresponding to appropriation) in Chemistry.

Table 8.1, then, suggests that a more efficient strategy of facilitating the uptake of the reform recommendations is to empower stakeholders' negotiation of value differences. This may capitalise on existing values (such as that of *assessment*, as was suggested earlier in this chapter), but may also assist teachers and other stakeholders to tease out the values that are inherent in the forms of pedagogical practices that have come together. That is to say it may be helpful for the design of professional development activities to focus even more on what is valued in the various recommendations of the reform curriculum, rather than the forms which these might take. Thus, professional development programmes provide the scaffolding to support participant consideration of the relevance and desirability of, say, *student-centred* pedagogy with their colleagues. That this valuing is necessarily expressed through arranging students in group seating or other identified classroom practices should be challenged, so that stakeholders' valuing of issues such as – and subsequent concern for the lack of – *space* can be dealt with as a separate issue.

Facilitating stakeholders to unpack underlying values will also assist them in engaging in sense-making processes that focus attention beyond the policy rhetoric. For example, the current curriculum reform reflects governmental

aims of realising *suzhi jiaoyu* (quality education), but differential cultural interpretations of what it means for a learner and citizen to cultivate sufficient
suzhi (that is, quality) exist. While some may infer that the reform curriculum
aims to mould students into citizens who are cognitively skilled, ethically
moral, and spiritually nationalistic, this view may not be shared across the
country, and may even be at odds with Western conceptions of what is a
quality education. This last point is evident in Hulbert's (2007) observation
that while for Asian parents 'the emphasis is on practice and mastery . . .
American parents, busy enrolling their young kids in arty extras, are likely
to stress self-expression and creativity' (5).

Concluding remarks

Stakeholders' reactions to the Mathematics curriculum reform in China
are often concerned with maintaining the excellent achievement of Chinese
students in Mathematics. Insofar that elements of the Chinese curriculum
reform suggest the adoption of 'Western' pedagogies (such as the fostering
of student *creativity*, the promotion of '*Mathematics for all*', and the harnessing of *information and communication technology*), there are signs from
its Mathematics education (research) community that Westernisation should
not be at the expense of local traditions of teaching and learning Mathematics
in schools. Reflecting the Chinese traditional concept of achieving yin-yang
balance, the ICME11 Chinese delegation (2008) concluded its national
presentation to the Mathematics education research community in the
following way:

> The East and West civilizations have their own unique charm. We
> hope to improve our mutual understanding and learn from each other
> through extensive communication, and eventually achieving a balance
> between the two civilizations. (46)

Drawing upon the essence of two cultures is consistent with the amalgamation, or even the appropriation, approach mentioned above. In fostering the
generation of new cultures, these approaches represent powerful processes,
and near-future efforts to further implement the reform curriculum in
schools throughout China may benefit from an approach targeted at critical examination of the soft learning embedded in the reform statements in
general, and of the professional, national and personal values that are in interaction in particular.

A mediating factor here has been that in a society such as China's, the
traditional societal valuing of *respect for elders* (which is also reflected in
Confucian teachings) lends much credibility and adds another layer of
authority to the societal concern that the reform curriculum threatens
Chinese students' peak performance in Mathematics. The (professional and
academic) opinions and views – and experiences – of the elder members of

the society and of groups in the society are often highly respected. The extent to which curriculum reform initiatives are implemented in school districts and in individual schools can thus be influenced by the professional and academic stances of the elder members within.

Similarly, the enduring nature of cultural norms and traditions should not be overlooked by the Mathematics education research community in China. As observed by Zhao (2009):

> Chinese scholars in the 19th century wanted China to learn from Britain. Later, Japan became the model. Such efforts to modernise never got on the right track because the Chinese tried to use Western learning for practical purposes while keeping Chinese learning for essence. (A15)

This phenomenon appears to be still very much alive. 'In general, the *suzhi jiaoyu* education reformers have attempted to learn from and borrow from Western educational methodologies without committing themselves to the conceptual bases which underpin them' (Dello-Iacovo 2009). At its best, this phenomenon represents the assimilation approach to the negotiation of value differences. The knowledge, skills and values that are acquired exist at a superficial level, and may not have been internalised. In such a context, it might be argued that students will not only be unable to learn what is presented superficially, but they may be able to discern what is actually valued (or not) beyond what is visible and explicit in the classroom practice.

The culturally productive approaches of amalgamation and appropriation appear to be embraced officially. The articulation of this intention into professional development programmes across cities and provinces might benefit from an approach targeted at critical examinations of the soft learning embedded in the reform statements in general, and of the professional, national and personal values that are interacting with one another in particular. What this discussion has attempted to achieve is to expose some of the issues that might impede sustained implementation of the reform, as well as the culturally-based values that underlie these. Explicit mindfulness of these by all stakeholders at the national, provincial, school and classroom levels as they participate in the reform rollout will be the next crucial factor determining the extent to which the intended reform is expressed in the Mathematics that is taught in schools, and the extent to which China's school Mathematics education continues to contribute to the nurturing of numerate citizens who are also well-prepared to participate on the world stage.

After a decade of (Mathematics) curriculum reform in China, the world (including China) presently finds itself in economic meltdown. In a country where social inequality is very high, where in 2004 the top 20 per cent of the Chinese population were enjoying a combined income that was 11.4 times that of the lowest 20 per cent (Ho 2009), the urgency for Mathematics education to espouse a valuing of *Mathematics for all* in its role as a societal leveller is very real indeed. In the words of China expert Wing Thye Woo,

China's 'earliest [economic] reforms led to providing more jobs, which reduced poverty significantly. But now . . . what the poor need most now is help with building their human capital through education . . . initiatives' (Ho 2009). The Mathematics reform curriculum has the potential of enhancing this huge source of human capital in China; our understanding and harnessing of the relevant soft learning in general, and values in particular, at this crucial time of reviewing and actualising the reform initiatives would empower the nation to realise this potential.

References

Bishop, A. J. (1988) *Mathematical Enculturation: A Cultural Perspective on Mathematics Education*, Dordrecht, The Netherlands: Kluwer Academic Publishers.

Brooks, D. (2008) 'The behavioural revolution', *The New York Times*, 28 October 2008, A31.

Cai, J. (2007) 'What is effective Mathematics teaching? A study of teachers from Australia, mainland China, Hong Kong SAR, and the United States', *ZDM The International Journal on Mathematics Education*, 39, 265–270.

Chenoweth, K. (2000) 'Singapore math doesn't add up without backing', *Washington Post*, 17 February 2000, M1.

China Ministry of Education. (5 January 2007a, 2009) 'Number of enrolment of schools of all types and level providing formal programmes'. Online. Available HTTP: <http://www.moe.gov.cn/edoas/website18/56/info33456.htm> (accessed 28 February 2009).

China Ministry of Education. (2007b, 2009 January 5) 'Number of schools by level & type and their fulltime teachers'. Online. Available HTTP: <http://www.moe.gov.cn/edoas/website18/79/info33479.htm> (accessed 28 February 2009).

Clarkson, P., Bishop, A. and Seah, W. T. (2010) 'Mathematics education and student values: the cultivation of mathematical well-being,' in T. Lovat and Toomey, R. (eds), *International Handbook on Values Education and Student Well-being*, New York: Spinger, pp. 111–136.

D'Ambrosio, U. (1985) 'EthnoMathematics and its place in the history and pedagogy of Mathematics', *For the Learning of Mathematics*, 5(1), 44–48.

Dello-Iacovo, B. (2009) 'Curriculum reform and "quality education" in China: an overview', *International Journal of Educational Development*, 29(3), 241–249.

Fan, L., Wong, N. Y., Cai, J. and Li, S. (eds) (2004) *How Chinese learn Mathematics: Perspectives from Insiders*, Singapore: World Scientific.

Gowen, A. (2001) 'East meets West in math classes: 4 schools import curriculum from Singapore', *Washington Post*, 18 October 2001, T14.

Ho, A. (26 February 2009) 'Can China grow itself out of trouble?', *The Straits Times*.

Huang, F. (2004) 'Curriculum reform in contemporary China: seven goals and six strategies', *Journal of Curriculum Studies*, 36(1), 101–115.

Hulbert, A. (1 April 2007). 'Re-education', *The New York Times Magazine*, 1–10.

ICME11 Chinese delegation (2008) 'Mathematics education in China: tradition and reality: China national presentation at ICME-11', In East China Normal University, *Mathematics Education in China: Tradition and Reality: China National Presentation at ICME-11* (1–48), Shanghai, China: East China Normal University.

Kelly, D. (2009, February) '*Reform wrong footed: what the global crisis reveals about China's patchwork governance*'. Speech presented at Monash University, Victoria, Australia.

Kearins, J. M. (1981) 'Visual spatial memory in Australian Aboriginal children of desert regions', *Cognitive Psychology*, 13, 434–460.

Leung, F. K. S. (2001) 'Teachers' attitudes towards Mathematics teaching in Beijing, Hong Kong and London', *Shuxue Tongbao*, 8, 2–4.

Li, J. (2008) 'Curriculum development in China: perspectives from curriculum design and implementation', in Z. Usiskin and E. Willmore (eds), *Mathematics Curriculum in Pacific Rim Countries: China, Japan, Korea, and Singapore (Proceedings of a conference)* (127–140), Charlotte, NC: Information Age Publishing.

Ma, L. (1999) *Knowing and Teaching Elementary Mathematics: Teachers' Understanding of Fundamental Mathematics in China and the United States*, Mahwah, NJ: Lawrence Erlbaum Associates.

Mullis, I. V. S., Martin, M. O. and Foy, P. (2008) *TIMSS 2007 International Mathematics report: Findings from IEA's Trends in International Mathematics and Science Study at the Fourth and Eighth Grades*, Chestnut Hill, MA: TIMSS & PIRLS International Study Center, Boston College.

Ngiam, T. D. (2009) 'Fostering the freedom to think', *The Straits Times*, 10 February 2009, A18.

Nye, J. S. (1990) *Bound to Lead: The Changing Nature of American Power*, NY: Basic Books.

Organisation for Economic Co-operation and Development [OECD] (2004) *Learning for Tomorrow's World: First Results from PISA 2003*, Paris, France: Organisation for Economic Co-operation and Development.

Rapaille, C. (2006) *The Culture Code: An Ingenious Way to Understand Why People Around the World Live and Buy as They do*, NY: Broadway.

Ryan, J., Kang, C. Y., Mitchell, I. and Erickson, G. (2009) 'Cross-cultural research collaboration in the context of China's basic education reform', *Asia Pacific Journal of Education*, 29(4), 427–441.

Seah, W. T. (2005) 'Negotiating about perceived value differences in Mathematics teaching: the case of immigrant teachers in Australia', in H. Chick and J. L. Vincent (eds), *Proceedings of the 29th conference of the International Group for the Psychology of Mathematics Education* (Vol. 4: 145–152), Melbourne: PME.

Seah, W. T. (2008, November) '*Researching Mathematics education in different cultures*', Paper presented at the Conference of the Development of Mathematics Education for Chinese Ethnic Minorities, Chongqing, China.

Thomson, S., Cresswell, J. and de Bortoli, L. D. (2004) *Facing the Future: A Focus on Mathematical Literacy among Australian 15-year-old Students in PISA 2003*, Victoria, Australia: Australian Council for Educational Research.

United Nations Educational Scientific and Cultural Organization [UNESCO]. (2007) *China-Europe Exchange on Curriculum Reform*, unpublished manuscript, Geneva, Switzerland.

Victorian Curriculum and Assessment Authority [VCAA] (2005) *Discipline-based Learning Strand: Mathematics*, East Melbourne, Victoria: Victorian Curriculum and Assessment Authority.

Villa, A. (2009) 'China targets graduate unemployment', *BizChinaUpdate*, 16 February 2009.

Wang, J. (2005) 'Curriculum reform of elementary education in China'. Online. Available HTTP: <http://www.chinese-embassy.org.uk/eng/zt/Features/t214562.htm> (accessed 12 November 2008).

Wang, S. H. (2010) 'Chinese students studying abroad: the role of parents' investment in their children's education', in J. Ryan (ed.) *China's Higher Education Reform and Internationalisation*, London: Routledge.

Wong, N. Y. (2008) 'Confucian heritage culture learner's phenomenon: from "exploring the middle zone" to "constructing a bridge"', *ZDM Mathematics Education*, 40, 973–981.

Wong, N. Y., Han, J. and Lee, P. Y. (2004) 'The Mathematics curriculum: toward globalization or Westernization?', in L. Fan, N. Y. Wong, J. Cai and S. Li (eds), *How Chinese Learn Mathematics: Perspectives from Insiders*, Singapore: World Scientific.

Yao, X. (2000) *An Introduction to Confucianism*, Cambridge, UK: Cambridge University Press.

Zhang, L. (2005) 'A review of China's elementary Mathematics education. *International Journal for Mathematics Teaching and Learning*'. Online. Available HTTP: <http://www.cimt.plymouth.ac.uk/journal/zhang.pdf> (accessed 27 January 2009).

Zhao, L. (2009) 'China's S'pore dream', *The Straits Times, 6 February 2009*, A15.

9 Multidimensional citizenship education and an internationalised curriculum in a time of reform: is this the future trajectory for schools in China and Australia in the twenty-first century?

Libby Tudball

Educators across the world are now considering how policies and programmes in schools can ensure that students develop the knowledge, skills and capacities required in a globalised world. There is a need for internationalisation of curriculum and multidimensional approaches so students can engage with change in their own contexts, be adaptable and productive citizens and workers within a global cultural and market economy and able to respond to common environmental, social, and economic global concerns. This chapter explores and compares how China and Australia are developing citizenship education and possible future trajectories for the twenty-first century that increase international-mindedness.

Global contexts for reform

Educators internationally are being challenged by a range of complex questions in relation to necessary reform and possible future trajectories for education. A growing focus globally is on the development of citizenship education (CE) in schools, to ensure that students are able to understand and engage with twenty-first century concerns and realities. Citizenship education aims to develop in students the knowledge, skills and capacities to empower them to be active and informed participants in their own communities and in the wider world. Grossman (2002) recognised that:

> We are living through a transformation that is rearranging the politics and economics of the past century. The problem with present educational systems is that they have not, by and large, adjusted to the new historical realities, that, for better or worse, have resulted from processes of globalisation. . . . Certain changes must take place in the content, the methods and in the social context of education, if schools are to become more effective agents of citizen education in a global age'. (36)

Kalantzis and Cope (2008) agree that social, cultural and technological change in particular 'are throwing into question the relevance and appropriateness of heritage education' (xvi), or old ways of teaching and learning emphasising basic skills, teacher talk, textbooks and didactic strategies in school education. They also suggest a need for content and learning that is 'more engaging, more effective and more appropriate to our contemporary times, and our imaginable near futures' (xvii). In spite of their very different political contexts, in both China and Australia many educators have recognised imperatives to reconsider the ways in which education policies, programmes and practices can encourage students to develop the knowledge required to live and work in an increasingly globalised and interdependent world (Lee and Leung 2006, Kennedy 2001, Tudball 2005). A decade ago, the multinational Citizenship Education Policy Study (CEPS) (Cogan 2000) found that in order to meet the challenges of the twenty-first century, we need a more comprehensive vision of citizenship, namely 'multidimensional citizenship', that requires citizens to address a series of interconnected dimensions of thought, belief and action including *personal, social, spatial,* and *temporal* dimensions, and a focus on content that includes *civic knowledge, values* and *environmental education*. The report recommended that this should become the central priority of citizenship education policy. In this chapter it is argued that ten years on, this notion of citizenship education still has currency as a model that should guide future trajectories in education reform. Citizenship education is an important focus in China as the nation state grows and develops in new directions as a global power in the twenty-first century.

Students need the knowledge and skills to be adaptable and productive citizens and workers within their own local contexts, and the global cultural and market economy (Christie and Sidhu 2002, Chen and Reid 2002, Heyward 2002, Matthews 2002, Lee 2006), but in addition, they need to know how to respond to common environmental, social, ethical and political concerns. Young people in China, Australia and elsewhere are now frequently exposed to personal pressures previous generations did not face, including increasing family breakdown, and social and moral concerns often fuelled by negative multi-media models. In addition, high levels of local, national and international mobility are challenging young peoples' notions of identity, as well as their personal and social connections and wellbeing. These pressures are currently being exacerbated by global financial crises, rampant consumerism, and the strains that accompany a fast-paced, technology-driven world. The impact of technological change: mobile phones, computer games, Facebook, MySpace, Twittering, and the decline in traditional occupations, means that education reform must be constructed for youth living in social and occupational spaces very different from those of previous generations. At the same time, young people need to be readied to face major ecological challenges and the questions of sustainability and climate change. There is therefore a need to offer students opportunities to be engaged in learning that will empower them to take positive action for their own futures. Critical questions should focus on how students can develop diverse citizenship knowledge, skills, and values, and concern and actions for the betterment of common humanity. In considering the implications of the re-emphasis on Confucian philosophy in schools in East Asia, Tu (2000) asked:

> Can our society endure and prosper without developing a basic sense of duty and responsibility? Should our pluralistic society deliberately cultivate shared values and a common ground for human understanding for the sake of unity? As we become acutely aware of our earth's vulnerability, and increasingly wary of social disintegration, what direction must we take for the sake of our survival? (215–216)

Students in Beijing, Xian, Sydney, or anywhere across the world cannot now avoid being caught up in global webs that will impact on their lives and future work in our interdependent world. Increasing global flows of people, ideas, and the impact of accessible communication technologies have added further fuel to calls for internationalisation of education, and the need for educators to decide how curriculum models, and teaching and learning pedagogies, can develop a sense of both local and global citizenship amongst students. These realities create a need for educators to consider what models for citizenship will lead to effective learning in CE that move beyond the models of the past. In this chapter, the main focus for discussion is the evolution and future development of citizenship education in China, but brief illustrative comparisons are made with developments in Australia and other contexts. The model of multidimensional citizenship (Cogan 2000) is used as a framework that can assist in curriculum reform and has the potential to shift thinking about curriculum and to encompass more holistic processes and content.

Background to reform of citizenship education in China

China has a long history of inclusion of what can be described as 'citizenship education' in schools that has shifted according to contemporary political priorities. Liu (2004) argues that the closest terms to describe citizenship education in China would include 'political education, ideological education and moral education' (see the chapter by Phan *et al.* in this volume for a fuller discussion of the role of moral education in China). Frequently the three terms have a 'three-in-one in connotation, and can be used interchangeably' (Liu 1998: 120). Liu maintains that these concepts are so interrelated, that they merge variably into ideopolitical education (*sixiang zhengzhi jiaoyu*) and ideomoral education (*sixiang pinde jiaoyu*). It is only in the past few years that the term civic education has also been more commonly used (Liu 2004). Zhao and Fairbrother (2010) argue that 'throughout the Maoist era (1949–76), Chinese education served twin purposes: to cultivate scientific and technological talent as an impetus for national rejuvenation and as a mechanism for political indoctrination' (1), but 'unsurprisingly, ideological-political education played an essential function. Once Deng Xiaoping came to power in 1978, China embarked on top-down reforms dissolving the original central economic planning system and pursuing a market model' (1). Zhao and Fairbrother (2010) drawing on Mok (1997) comment on the enormous changes in the past thirty years and note that:

> Chinese society has witnessed a struggle for the relaxation of strict political control and authoritarian party rule, and an eagerness to build a democratic civil society, especially from the intellectuals and grassroots. Ideological shifts and social transitions opened the door in turn to educational reforms, such as curriculum reforms and the decentralization of educational policy and school financing and administration (1)

Chen and Reid's (2002) work provides important documentation of the progress of reform in CE in China. They argue that until the mid 1980s, 'Citizenship education implementation in schools remained unchanged, owing to some lasting effects of the Cultural Revolution on people's political literacy' (61). They note that, 'Citizenship Education expressed in Communist terms was to educate youngsters to become heirs to the cause of proletarian revolution' (61). Further, their view is that: 'China accomplished its social transition and established its own concept of socialist citizenship, which emphasized loyalty rather than initiative, obligations rather than rights, commitments rather than freedom, and community rather than individualism' (62).

At the Central Military Commission (1982), the late leader, Deng Xiao Ping said that:

> All people of the nation should be brought up as good citizens with self-discipline and a sense of responsibility, with knowledge and skills, with good mental and physical health and motivated by the noble ideals of socialism.
> (Selections from Deng Xiaoping II: 408, in Chen and Reid 2002)

In 1986, the Central Party Committee approved and issued an important document titled: *A Resolution on the Guidance of the Socialist Enrichment of Spiritual Civilisation.* In it, Chen and Reid (2002) noted, 'the question of Citizenship Education was once again brought forward, but with the emphasis on awareness and consciousness of a citizen's rights and responsibilities' (63). An *Experimental Teaching Outline for the Course of Ideological and Political Education in Secondary Schools* was issued by the Chinese Ministry of Education (MOE), in which the aim of Citizenship Education was made explicit and divided into three levels:

1. to equip students with a basic knowledge of contemporary politics, the economy, social morality and the legal system,
2. to nurture in them good character, good behaviour and fine discipline,
3. to encourage them to realise their role, function and responsibilities as good citizens' (Educational Science Press 1984).

A *Citizen Manual* was published in 1988, including chapters on topics such as Democracy, the Legal System, Obligations, Rights, Social Morality, Discipline, Public Order, Foreign Affairs and Criminal Justice (Chen and Reid 2002: 64). This handbook was endorsed by the Central Party Committee and informed the development of teaching materials in schools.

Recent developments in citizenship education in China

Since the early 1990s, the Chinese government has promoted 'socialist modernisation', the 'promotion of spiritual civilisation' and 'the development of moral and cultured citizens' (Chen and Reid 2002: 64). At the same time, many other nations in the world including the UK and Australia have argued for a re-emphasis on values education, to encourage young people to explore their own beliefs and the core beliefs held by their communities and nations, and this has commonly been connected to citizenship education initiatives. At present in China, citizenship education is implemented mainly as 'Ideological and Moral Education' in primary schools and as 'Ideological and Political Education' in secondary schools, but Chen and Reid (2002) note that it has been absorbed into education in other ways:

1. Through cross-curricular themes.
2. Through activities organised by the Youth League and the Students' Union.
3. With 'three-in-one' (schools, families and communities) co-operation.
4. Through symbolic events like commemoration days, the national flag, the national anthem and the national emblem, etc. (65)

In other parts of the world, each of these aspects of citizenship education is also common. In Australia, the local and national focus of citizenship education continues, but there is increasing emphasis on global dimensions. In the UK, as an interdisciplinary theme, global education has developed strong links with citizenship education, and there have been a number of calls for 'global citizenship' education (Marshall 2005). In Australia, many schools have developed cross-curricular themes such as studies of rights and responsibilities that may include curriculum content drawing on history, politics, and legal studies. Also in Australia, engagement of students in clubs such as Amnesty International, in student action teams to solve school-based issues such as truancy, and in environmental 'green groups', are seen as strategies that ensure student involvement in authentic and purposeful citizenship activities. National parent organisations recognise the vital role of the partnership between teachers, schools, students and families in citizenship activities (Dejaeghere and Tudball 2007).

In the past decade, Chinese school leaders and policy makers on the mainland in both regional areas and in key metropolises, including for example, Shanghai and Hong Kong, have seen citizenship education as a key element of education reform (Chen and Reid 2002, Lee and Leung 2006). In Hong Kong, the 1996 *Guidelines on Civic Education in Schools* stated the need for students to learn more about concepts of global citizenship, the global village, human rights, and global responsibilities (Education Department 1996: 37). The Hong Kong junior secondary Civic Education syllabus (1998) suggested such topics as a world of diversity, global citizenship, and other basic issues (e.g. life and dignity, equality, and freedom) to be taught in schools (Curriculum Development Council, 1998: 17–20). In more recent curriculum reforms, various newly developed curriculum documents invariably mention the need to cultivate global awareness. For example, in Hong Kong in the reform blueprint document *Learning for Life, Learning through Life* (2000), global economic changes and the move to the knowledge economy were noted:

> Hong Kong is also facing tremendous challenges posed by a globalized economy. Politically, reunification with China and democratization has changed the ways Hong Kong people think and live. Our social structure is fast evolving, and there is an urgent need to alleviate the disparity of wealth. The society is adapting its culture and mainframe to these changes. The rapid development of information technology has opened up new domains in all aspects of our lives and creating new challenges. (Hong Kong Education Commission 2000:3)

In addition, the cultivation of global awareness was suggested in 'A Message from the Chairman of the Curriculum Development Council' (Curriculum Development Council 1998) which says:

> To cope with the challenges of the 21st century, education in Hong Kong must keep abreast of the global trends, and students have to empower themselves to learn beyond the confines of the classroom. The school curriculum, apart from helping students to acquire the necessary knowledge, should also help the younger generation to develop a global outlook, to learn how to learn and to master lifelong skills that can be used outside schools (in Lee and Leung 2006).

In Shanghai, similar efforts in developing global citizenship education can also be found. A report published by the Shanghai Education Research Institute in 2002 argued that Shanghai students need the talents of 'four haves': have ideals, have morals, have discipline and have culture [education] to encourage a strong sense of justice, a specialisation complemented by diverse abilities, and globally versatile knowledge and skills (Lee and Leung 2006: 71). The report says, 'Education has to face modernisation, face the world and face the future'. 'Facing the world' can only be realised by developing a global perspective that comprises five elements: global awareness (e.g. understanding interdependence, the globe as one world, peaceful development, environmental protection, international justice, etc.), global knowledge (e.g. world geography, world history, current international issues, lingua franca, international trade, etc.), global skills (e.g. global values, including empathy, human rights, respect for life, justice and peace, etc.), and global behaviour (e.g. participating in action that promotes world justice) (Ministry of Education 2001: 1, in Lee and Leung 2006: 71).

In order to achieve these goals, across China, educators have re-stated the importance of implementing citizenship education in schools, with a particular emphasis on the more public aspects of 'morality'. Chen and Reid (2002) agree that Citizenship Education developments in China have emphasised:

> promoting the spiritual and moral development of young people, and preparing them to be moral citizens with self-discipline and a sense of responsibility, with knowledge, good mental and physical health and motivated by the noble ideals of socialism (73).

Why multidimensional citizenship education?

The emphases on CE discussed in the previous section necessitate reform of curriculum content and approaches. At the same time that interest in CE was burgeoning in China, Australia and elsewhere, Cogan and Derricott's (2000) publication *Citizenship for the 21st Century: an International Perspective on Education* reported the findings of the major multinational *Citizenship Education Policy Study* (CEPS). This project involved 182 policy experts from nine nations in the spheres of politics and government, business, industry and labour, science and technology, health and education, and cultural and academic fields to determine (a) emerging global trends; (b) the perceived impact of these trends on the changing character of citizenship over the next 25 years; and (c) the implications of these changes for educational policy. The CEPS Study identified seven 'increasingly significant challenges' to life on the planet requiring continuing attention over the next 25 years:

- The economic gap among countries and between people within countries will widen significantly.
- Information technologies will dramatically reduce the privacy of individuals.
- The inequalities between those who have access to information technologies and those who do not will increase dramatically.
- Conflict of interest between developing and developed nations will increase due to environmental deterioration.

- The cost of obtaining adequate water will rise dramatically due to population growth and environmental deterioration.
- Deforestation will dramatically affect diversity of life, air, soil, and water quality.
- In developing countries population growth will result in a dramatic increase in the percentage of people, especially children, living in poverty.

(Cogan and Derricott 2000: 9)

It is imperative that the school curriculum provides students with opportunities to understand these issues and to develop ways to take positive action to respond realistically to these concerns as part of citizenship education. In Australia for example, since 2005, active involvement of schools in the international 'Make Poverty History' campaign has meant that students are making a tangible difference through fund raising and service learning. There has also been an increasing interest in sustainability education so that students develop realistic views, but are also able to act responsibly about personal and environmental concerns.

The key recommendations to emerge from the CEPS study concluded that the *multidimensional citizenship* model should become the central priority of citizenship education policy and pointed to the need for curriculum reform. However, while the model does not utilise traditional disciplines as the key way of framing curriculum, it is implicit that discipline based knowledge is still important. Commonly recognised titles for subjects, geography and history for instance, are not the focus of the model, rather the concept promotes the broader notions of 'spatial' and 'temporal' understanding. The need for spatial knowledge recognises the increasing mobility of people, and the notion that local, national or regional spaces where people live and work do need to be considered as crucial elements in the ways that people construct their identity and sense of citizenship.

The use of the term 'temporal dimensions' instead of 'history' as a curriculum organiser recognises that students need knowledge and understanding of the past, present and future. Frequently, the latter two dimensions have been under-emphasised in school curriculum.

The multidimensional citizenship model also recognises the need for school education in CE to include values, civic knowledge and studies of the environment. Based on their findings, the CEPS researchers concluded that only an education that incorporates these dimensions in a rich, complex and coherent vision of citizenship will equip people to respond effectively to the challenges and demands of the twenty-first century (Grossman 2002). In order to develop *multidimensional citizenship*, the CEPS report suggested a number of implementation recommendations including focusing upon the school as a model of this concept, strengthening the links between the school and the larger community within which it exists, development of the school as an environmental model, and a more authentic curriculum for learners (Cogan and Derricott 2000: 151–170). While it is not difficult to be convinced of an educational justification for the model, there are challenges in introducing *multidimensional citizenship* into schools and curriculum, since teachers need to be prepared in its theory and practice, and able to develop programmes within classrooms and wider school and community activities that encompass all aspects (Grossman 2002). Cogan and Derricott (2000) agreed that:

> Students must see their teachers as living examples of what they are professing, as people who are personally involved in their communities, working on projects of a civic or public nature, knowledgeable about developments in other parts of the nation and the world, able to debate key civic and public issues with other colleagues in the school as well as those in the community at large, aware of the historical antecedents of these issues so that they have a context for their discourse, and possessing a vision of what might be done to resolve or at least improve the situation. (177–178)

As Figure 9.1 shows, the multidimensional model offers a very different way of reforming curriculum, to see learning as more connected and authentic.

In Australia, the education policy document, The *Melbourne Declaration on the Educational Goals for Young Australians for the C21st* (MCEETYA 2008) was developed to inform the development of national education priorities, and has synergy with the multidimensional citizenship education model. It states that all students should become:

- Successful learners
- Confident and creative individuals
- Active and informed citizens: who can make sense of their world, act with moral and ethical integrity, appreciate Australia's social, linguistic and religious diversity, and have an understanding of Australia's government, history and culture
- Be committed to values of democracy, equity and justice, and participate in civic life
- Relate and communicate across cultures, especially Asia
- Work for the common good in sustaining and improving natural and social environments
- Be responsible local and global citizens

These goals have synergy with goals for CE being defined in China, and they necessitate multidimensional approaches to curriculum development. However, in recent years considerable debate has continued in Australia amongst education stakeholders who see the discipline-based approach to national curriculum development currently underway as being an outdated way to frame curriculum, and not consistent with the goals stated above. It seems that in Australia, as in many other parts of the world, despite the rhetoric

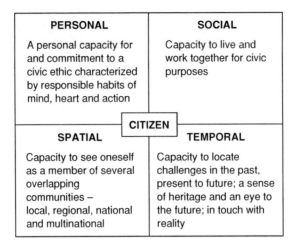

A MULTIDIMENSIONAL MODEL OF CITIZENSHIP EDUCATION
Dimensions of Citizenship

PERSONAL	SOCIAL
A personal capacity for and commitment to a civic ethic characterized by responsible habits of mind, heart and action	Capacity to live and work together for civic purposes

CITIZEN

SPATIAL	TEMPORAL
Capacity to see oneself as a member of several overlapping communities – local, regional, national and multinational	Capacity to locate challenges in the past, present to future; a sense of heritage and an eye to the future; in touch with reality

Contents of a Multidimensional Citizenship Education

CIVIC EDUCATION	VALUES EDUCATION	ENVIRONMENTAL EDUCATION
The building of a knowledge base for civic beliefs and skills for civic participation	The acquisition of dispositions and predilections that provide the foundation for civic attitudes and beliefs	The process of developing understanding, skills and values consistent with the notion of sustainable development

Figure 9.1 Key features of multidimensional citizenship education

about the need for reform outlined above, it is difficult to actually achieve curriculum reform. Many challenges remain before policy makers and schools will be able to implement a more integrated approach to curriculum development that takes current and future civic and global realities into account.

Personal, social and moral education

In both Australia and China many educators share the view that the personal dimensions of education are of critical concern, and there has been a re-emphasis on the need for personal and social learning, values and moral education (Lee and Leung 2006, Daedeghere and Tudball 2007). Students should have opportunities to form opinions on questions including: Who am I? Where do I belong? What connections matter to me? Do I have nation state loyalty? What does that mean? Does it matter? What is citizenship? How do I relate to my social groupings/peers? What issues am I concerned about? How can I relate to and understand young people who are different and the same as me, here and in the wider world? How can I think about and make a difference in my world? Debating these questions adopts a view of CE as being linked to student wellbeing, social connectedness, and community belonging. It requires a whole school approach to CE, that Lee and Leung (2006) argue is still limited in China, and in Australia is still only developed through pockets of exemplary practice, but not across all schools (Erebus Consulting 2003). In future education reform, and at a time when young people are facing challenges at the local, national and global levels, developing personal dimensions is critical.

Grossman (2002) argues that:

> in the domain of citizenship or civic behaviour, it is especially important to develop a coherent moral dialogue between the world and ourselves. The *personal dimension* of citizenship thus emphasizes the development of a personal capacity for and commitment to a civic ethic characterized by individually and socially responsible habits of mind, heart, and action. In the educational context this would suggest developing students' capacity to examine their 'basic beliefs' and their translation into the public realm. (4)

In China, the 'back to tradition' movement has been seen as an antidote to moral decline. Luan (1994; cited in Tu 2000) and his colleagues developed a list of twelve core virtues thought to be distinctively Chinese, traditional and Confucian. Yu (2008) noted that:

> instead of using original Confucian definitions of virtues such as *jen* (benevolence), *yi* (righteousness) and *li* (courtesy), they paraphrased their chosen virtues in present day language, such as love and respect for parents, respect for teachers, hard work and honesty. (114)

Text books developed around these traditional, yet redefined virtues and values in personal and social learning were circulated across China in the early 1990s, in the 'back to tradition' crusade. Zhan (1994) argued that with a strong social orientation and high moral ideals, Confucianism has much to offer contemporary educators worldwide as they struggle to battle against the trends of extreme materialism and individualism. However, Zhan (1994) argued that these movements have also generated controversy, since the back to the tradition campaigns are not seen as authentically and purposively connected to current realities and future orientations.

In both China and Australia, these 'back to tradition' movements have been contested. Lu and Gao (2004) critiqued the prescriptive top-down values and moral education programmes. They argued that the timetabled subject 'moral education' taught as a separate subject in schools, and largely isolated from the children's lives had become a moralisation memorisation process, which was 'torture for children' (497) and was politically controlled. It is interesting to note Yu's (2008) view that Confucianism has a fundamental focus on searching for goodness in human beings, relationships, order, ethics, propriety and respect, and his view is that the central government (re?)adopted Confucian values in 1994 in the name of traditional Chinese values. Yu (2008) argued that while the CCP denied the spiritual components of Confucianism, the government encouraged its use as a moral philosophy.

Yu (2008) notes that 'the "back to tradition" movement is still going strong in China' (125), for instance, one version alone of the *New Three-Character Classic* based on Confucian teachings has sold 40 million copies throughout China. He concludes that 'although recent national curriculum reforms call for more creative and critical thinking in the classroom to prepare youngsters for a more modern and global future, cultural heritage and traditional morality is still an emphasis in education policy' (126).

In Australia, the then Minister for Education (Nelson 2002) launched programmes to encourage emphasis on the promotion of core traditional values and personal learning across the nation. All schools were required to prominently place a poster proclaiming that *care* and *compassion for self and others, respect, responsibility, honesty* and *trustworthiness, freedom* and *pursuing and protecting the common good* ('a *fair go*') should be 'Values Goals' for all Australian schools. The subsequent Australian government reversed this policy and encouraged the development of school based values programmes, where local communities involve children, teachers and parents in discussions about what they value, and how they can effectively develop personal and social learning. The then Prime Minister Kevin Rudd decreed that schools need no longer display the Values posters. Yet, personal learning is still seen as a core curriculum area for schools and is implicit in the national curriculum goals.

It seems then, that there are strong arguments that the inclusion of the personal and social dimensions in CE should continue. Grossman (2002) agreed that students must:

> be able to work and interact with other people in a variety of settings and contexts, engage in public debate and discussion, participate in public life, deal with the problems and issues that face them, in ways that at the same time equip them to deal respectfully with people whose ideas and values differ from their own. . . . When we talk of the social dimension of citizenship, we refer to the broader notion of citizen participation within the context of a 'civil society.' The *social dimension* suggests that educational programmes should include opportunities for students to connect with and engage in their communities in processes that include deliberation, community service, and social action. (4–5)

Including spatial dimensions of citizenship education

The *spatial dimension* of the model also recognises contemporary realities of the flows and movements of people, and the impact of spatial concepts on peoples' identities; where they live and work, where they move in and out, from and to, in both real and now increasingly virtual communities that dominate young peoples' lives. Citizens of the twenty-first century often see themselves as members of several overlapping communities; local, regional, national, and international. The movement of people and ideas across nations and boundaries is now unprecedented in world history. However, Grossman (2002) notes that:

> at the same time people's sense of identity is and will remain rooted in the local and the personal, sometimes consistent with and other times in conflict with nation and culture. The *spatial dimension* tries to deal with this characteristic dimension, albeit contradictory, of modern life in which citizenship must be seen as being multi-level, from local to global. (6)

Including the temporal dimension

Most school curricula across the world includes an emphasis on the study of history and there is strong recognition of the importance of students' developing an understanding of their past. However, including *temporal dimensions* in citizenship education means that young people should learn from history as well as through the inclusion of contemporary and futures perspectives in curriculum. The National Centre for History Education (NCHE) in Australia recognised the need for wider dimensions, as the following extract shows:

Perspectives: the continent, the region and the world

> Located in the Asia-Pacific region, with a distinct and enduring Indigenous culture and settled largely by Europeans, Australia is a unique nation. As globalisation intensifies, Australians' lives and Australia's interests are increasingly connected to the whole world. These connections create powerful and complex challenges. Young Australians need to investigate these regional and global connections and the challenges they create through studying history.

Similarly, in China, young people need opportunities to study the history of their own nation as well as their connections with the region and the world. The NCHE (2009) also stressed the fact that students need to see links between the past, present and future through studying developments in other societies including the growth of freedom and democracy and changing identity. The *temporal dimension* also requires that current challenges be located in the context of both the past and the future, so that purely short-term solutions to problems can be avoided wherever possible. The CEPS study recommended that students have opportunities to study major world issues. Kennedy (2001) agreed that young people must be able to tackle social realities and civic 'megatrends' that impact on their lives now and in the future.

Future trajectories in teacher education

The CEPS study suggests introducing *multidimensional citizenship* into teacher education through preparation of teachers in five broad areas:

1. Cultivation of a global/cross-cultural outlook
2. Emphasis on the development of a critical perspective
3. Emphasis on democratic pedagogies
4. Improved community collaborations
5. Application of information technologies

Specifically, the CEPS researchers recommend that professional development programmes for teachers be based upon and model the application of the following:

- Deliberation-based curriculum and pedagogy
- Information and media based curriculum and pedagogy
- Multiple uses of technology for teaching, learning and researching
- Focus upon environmental issues and problems of a global nature which have local manifestations
- A globally-oriented curriculum, which uses examples, readings, illustrative pedagogical activities, etc., from other parts of the world
- Democratic decision-making processes and values
- The development of co-operative, collaborative working relationships, and
- Practice in the application of one's learning in the wider community

(Cogan and Derricott 2000: 177)

This list of key applications to successfully implement the model of *multidimensional citizenship* creates many challenges for teacher education, and a strong need for reform at the higher education level. It assumes that student teachers will be able to explore the use of information and communication technologies, learn how to model democratic classroom practices, and how to include local and global dimensions of teaching and learning that is connected to real life experience.

Development of Citizenship Education: learning from case studies of Shanghai and Hong Kong

Lee and Leung's (2006) study of teachers' views on CE in Hong Kong and Shanghai provides valuable insights into the way in which educators in these two Chinese cities are struggling with various aspects of multidimensional CE through their attempts to increase global citizenship. Lee and Leung (2006) found that: 'teaching diverse values constitutes the highest priority for global citizenship' (73) and that 'in both Hong Kong and Shanghai, over 90 per cent of the school teachers participating in the study agree that global citizenship education needs to be strengthened' (73). However, educators in both cities consider topics related to global citizenship as difficult to teach. In general, more than half of the Hong Kong educators feel that the following topics are difficult or very difficult for them, namely, 'international politics' (77.1 per cent), 'global economic issues' (71.5 per cent), 'sustainable development' (61 per cent), 'war and ethnic conflicts' (59.8 per cent) and 'global popular culture' (53 per cent). This data provides further evidence of the need for further reform in citizenship education related to global understanding. In addition, Lee and Leung (2006) noted that a majority of Hong Kong educators feel that:

> 'international politics' and 'global economic issues' are difficult or very difficult to teach . . . Hong Kong students are more concerned with local rather than global issues. The lack of interest in global issues would thus make the teaching of these topics difficult, as compared to the Shanghai counterparts. . . . However, only a minute proportion, ranging between 2.8% and 8.4% in Hong Kong and between 4.2% and 7.2% in Shanghai, of respondents indicated they have not taught these topics before. (78)

Lee and Leung's (2006) research in these two cities demonstrates that educators are attempting to implement global citizenship education but that there is insufficient teacher training, insufficient time for teaching and preparation, and a lack of teaching resources. Clearly, a strong emphasis on a multidimensional approach in teacher education programmes has the potential to help in this process. Leung and Lee (2006) asked teachers why they feel it is difficult to implement global citizenship education. About 88 per cent and 87 per cent of their Hong Kong and Shanghai respondents, respectively, felt they have not had sufficient pre-service or on-the-job training and, respectively, 90.8 per cent and 82.8 per cent of them felt they 'do not have sufficient understanding of the issues' (78). Regarding the curriculum, 92.2 per cent and 83.7 per cent of their respective Hong Kong and Shanghai respondents felt they 'do not have sufficient time to teach global citizenship issues' (78). They are equally concerned by the fact that global citizenship education is outside the syllabus (81.8 per cent in Hong Kong and 77.8 per cent in Shanghai), and that they 'do not have adequate teaching materials' (73.8 per cent in Hong Kong and 86.1 per cent in Shanghai). About two-thirds of them feel it is difficult to link the topics to students' everyday experience and encourage students to take action (Lee and Leung 2006: 79).

The future of citizenship education

The multidimensional citizenship education concept presents the view that curriculum in this area must be constructed to provide students with purposeful, relevant learning experiences that will build the knowledge, skills and attitudes they will need in their future lives. Citizenship education needs to reach beyond political concerns and current affairs even though these are important elements in well constructed programmes. Students require civic knowledge of government systems and legal processes, but the broader emphases on developing students' personal and social capacities are vital. Many teachers still do not fully understand what citizenship education can encompass and do not recognise that for CE to empower young people to be active participants in their own local and global communities they need classroom programmes, whole school events and activities, student participation in democratic action and decision making, and authentic learning that is connected to community issues. In China and Australia, and in many other global education contexts, further education reform in CE is still necessary.

In this chapter it has been argued that the multidimensional model can assist school leaders in thinking about key areas that should frame curriculum. The model encourages educators to think outside traditional frames and to consider the complex issues that young people will face in the future. In their research Lee and Leung (2006) noted that teachers in Shanghai and Hong Kong do suggest detailed curriculum content that is firmly multidimensional in its scope as Figure 9.2 shows.

Conclusion

Citizenship education is a critical aspect of school education that is connected to diverse content areas. Young people need to clarify their sense of identity, they need to know their rights and responsibilities as citizens, and how the law and government impact on their lives. They should understand what are core and accepted values in their communities. Students require opportunities while still at school for active citizenship participation so that in their adult life they can continue to be active and informed citizens. Chinese educators today are preparing young people to face a very different world and the pace of change is rapid. At the same time, Australian educators continue to struggle with similar questions about how best to prepare students for a changing world. Central to this is the recognition that Australian youth must be able to engage with Asia and the world, and develop the capacities to be active local and global citizens, just as many Chinese students now move more freely throughout the world.

This chapter has raised common questions that educators need to consider as they plan education trajectories for the twenty-first century. How well are we meeting education challenges, what models of curriculum and what

Themes	Topics may include for example:
History and culture	Traditions, cultures, religions, beliefs; global culture and major philosophies; impact of global culture on local culture
Political development	Political systems of different countries; features of international politics, development and causes; hegemony
Economic development	Overview of global economic development; international trade; operation and impact of trans-national companies; impact of economic globalisation
Poverty and socio-economic development	Uneven distribution of wealth in the world and its causes; food and hunger; poverty alleviation; developing countries
War and peace	Cultural, religious, ethnic and racial conflicts; world peace and international order; impact of war; Middle East conflicts; terrorism
Environment	Global environmental pollution; ecological development; natural resources and environmental protection; sustainable development
International community	International organisations; pros and cons of globalisation in different countries
Hong Kong/China's relationship with the world	Role of Hong Kong/China in global development; role of China in international affairs
Citizenship knowledge and values	Citizen's rights and responsibilities; relationship between the individual and the state; relationship between the individual and the world; equality and justice; respect, appreciation and acceptance of different cultures; co-operation and interdependence; empathy
Citizenship skills	Analytic and critical thinking
Curriculum design and implementation	Definition and content of global citizenship education

Figure 9.2 Global citizenship topics suggested by Hong Kong and Shanghai educators (adapted from Lee and Leung 2006: 75; see original for full list of topics)

priorities for education reform must be addressed? How can we prepare young people to be knowledge workers, and at the same time, ethical and compassionate citizens? This chapter considered responses to these complex and important questions. The application of the model for multidimensional citizenship education first developed by Cogan (2000) at the Hong Kong

Institute of Education Centre for Citizenship (now The Centre for Governance and Citizenship), has been discussed as one response to framing and reforming curriculum. This model encourages a rethinking of school curriculum that has been influential in the development of citizenship education in Hong Kong and beyond. There is no doubt that future trajectories in CE for schools in China and Australia will require multidimensional approaches as the twenty-first century unfolds and the curriculum will need to address common concerns across nations. The challenge in defining future directions will be for educators to conserve and cherish traditions in their own local and national communities that in many instances have their roots dating back thousands of years, and at the same time, respond to the inevitable challenges of new issues and concerns as they unfold. It will be critical for school educators to encourage their students to be critical thinkers, adaptable and ethical citizens who can respond positively to change. Noted thinkers in the field of CE, Lee and Kennedy (2006) remind us of the challenges of CE in Asian communities where:

> Distinctive Asian concerns focus on young people enmeshed in rich cultural traditions and diverse political systems confronted by globalized economies accompanied by liberalized values. It seems clear that as the Asian countries . . . face the challenges of globalization, they draw on national conditions and circumstances to create a citizenship education that seeks to anchor young people in traditional values. At the same time we have seen that schools, teachers and students can make a difference. Macro policy contexts may seek to develop an all embracing view of how future citizens should be prepared but local values in particular schools with particular teachers cannot be ignored. It is this interplay between the macro and the local that will determine the outcomes of citizenship education in Asian countries in the future. (6)

Acknowledgements

The author would like to acknowledge the scholarship of the following researchers whose work has informed the development of this chapter. Full reference to their work appears below:

Chen and Reid's (2002) work in documenting the development of citizenship education in China; David Grossman who was a member of the North American research team in the CEPS project and of the writing team who produced the book, *Citizenship for the 21st Century: An International Perspective on Education* (Cogan and Derricott 2000); and the work of Wing On Lee, Sai Wing Leung, Kerry Kennedy, Zhao and Gregory P. Fairbrother at the Hong Kong Institute of Education, whose research is continuing to add to knowledge of CE in China. I am grateful to be able to learn from their scholarly work.

References

Chen, Y. and Reid, I. (2002) 'Citizenship education in Chinese schools', *Research in Education*, May 2002.

Christie, P. and Sidhu, R. (2002) 'Responding to globalisation: refugees and the challenges facing Australian schools', *Mots Pluriels*, 21 May, 2002. Online. Available HTTP: <http://www.arts.uwa.edu.au/MotsPluriels/MP2102pcrs.html> (accessed 28 October 2008).

Cogan, J. (2000) 'Citizenship education for the 21st century: setting the context', in J. Cogan and R. Derricott (eds) *Citizenship for the 21st Century*, New York: Kogan Page.

Cogan, J. and Derricott, R. (eds) (2000) *Citizenship for the 21st Century: An International Perspective on Education* (rev edn), London: Kogan Pag.

Curriculum Development Council (2001) *Guidelines on Civic Education in Schools*, Hong Kong: Education Department.

Dejaeghere, J. and Tudball, L. (2007) 'Looking back, looking forward: critical citizenship as a way ahead for civics and citizenship education in Australia', *Citizenship Teaching and Learning*, 3(2).

Education Department (1996) *Guidelines on Civic Education in Schools, Hong Kong: Education Department*, Hong Kong: Education Department.

Educational Science Press (1984) *Records of Great Events in the People's Republic of China*, 1949–82, Beijing.

Erebus Consulting Group (2003) *Evaluation of the Discovering Democracy Program, Executive Summary: Conclusions*. Online. Available HTTP: http://www.dest.gov.au/schools/Publications/2004/discovering_democracy/conclusions.htm (accessed 25 October 2004).

Grossman, D. (2002) 'Multidimensional citizenship and teacher education', *Pacific-Asian Education*, 14(2), 36–45.

Grossman, D. (2004) 'Teacher perceptions of future citizens in Hong Kong and Guangzhou', in W. O. Lee, David. L. Grossman, Kerry J. Kennedy and Gregory P. Fairbrother (eds) *Citizenship Education in Asia and the Pacific: Concepts and Issues*, Hong Kong: Comparative Education Research Centre, The University of Hong Kong/Kluwer Academic Press.

Heyward, M. (2002) 'From international to intercultural: redefining the international school for a globalized world', *Journal of Research in International Education*, 1(1), 9–32.

Hong Kong Education Commission (2000) *Learning for Life, Learning through Life*, 3, Hong Kong Education Commission.

Kalantzis, M. and Cope, B. (2008) *New Learning Elements of a Science of Education*, Port Melbourne, Victoria: Cambridge University Press.

Kennedy, K. J. (2001) 'Civics education for the "techno" generation: what should we expect young people to know and be able to do as citizens?', *ETHOS* 7–12(8), 8–10.

Lee, M. (2006) 'Going global: conceptualisation of the "Other" and interpretation of cross-cultural experience in an all-white, rural learning environment', *Ethnography and Education*, 1(2) 197–213.

Lee, W. O. and Kennedy, K. J. (2006) Citizenship education in Asia: diversity, tradition and challenges for new times, *Citizenship Teaching and Learning*, 2(2): 3–7.

Lee, W. O. and Leung, S. W. (2006) 'Global citizenship education in Hong Kong and Shanghai secondary schools: ideals, realities and expectations', *Citizenship Teaching and Learning*, 2(2) December 2006.

Liu, M. (1998) Theory and practice of the issues-centred approach, *Journal of National Hualien Teachers College*, 8: 173–200.

Liu, M. (2004) 'A society in transition: the paradigm shift of civic education in Taiwan', in W. O. Lee, D. L. Grossman, K. J. Kennedy and G. F. Fairbrother (eds), *Citizenship Education in Asia and the Pacific: Concepts and Issues*, Hong Kong: University of Hong Kong Comparative Education Research Centre/Kluwer Academic Publishers.

Lu, J. and Gao, D. S. (2004) 'New direction in the moral education curriculum in Chinese primary schools', *Journal of Moral Education*, 33(4), 495–510.

MCEETYA (2008) *Melbourne Declaration on Educational Goals for Young Australians*, December 2008, Canberra: Ministerial Council for Education, Employment, Training and Youth Affairs.

Marshall, H. (2005) 'Developing the global gaze in citizenship education: exploring the perspectives of global education NGO workers in England', *International Journal of Citizenship and Teacher Education*, 1(2) December 2005. Online. Available: HTTP: <http://www.citized.info> (accessed 4 September 2008)

Matthews, J. (2002) 'International education and internationalisation are not the same as globalisation: emerging issues for secondary schools', *Journal of Studies in International Education*, 6(4) 360–390.

Mok, K. H. (1997) 'Marketisation or quasi-marketisation: educational development in post-Mao China', *International Review of Education*, 4(5–6), 1–21.

National Centre for History Education (NCHE) *History Links*. Online. Available HTTP: <http://hyperhistory.org/> (accessed 25 November 2009).

Nelson, B. (2002) *About Discovering Democracy: Introduction – Ministerial Statement.* Online. Available HTTP: <http://www.curriculum.edu.au/democracy/aboutdd.htm> (accessed 8 August 2002).

Tu, W. M. (2000) 'Implications of the rise of "Confucian" East Asia', *Daedalus*, 129(1), 195–218.

Tudball, L. (2005) 'Grappling with internationalisation of the curriculum at the secondary school level: issues and tensions for educators', *Australian Journal of Education*, 49(1), 10–27.

Yu, T. L. (2008) 'The revival of Confucianism in Chinese schools: a historical-political review', *Asia Pacific Journal of Education*, 28(2), 113–129.

Zhan, W. C. (1994) 'Key issues about education in Chinese traditional virtues', in J. Chen, C. Luan and W. Zhan (eds) *A Collection of Papers on the Study of Education in Traditional Chinese Moral Virtues*, Changchun, China: Jilin Culture and History Press.

Zhao, Z. Z. and Fairbrother, G. P. (2010) 'Pedagogies of cultural integration in Chinese citizenship education', in Kerry J. Kennedy, David L. Grossman and W. O. Lee (eds), *Citizenship Pedagogies in Asia and the Pacific*, Hong Kong: Comparative Education Research Centre, the University of Hong Kong and Dordrecht, Netherlands: Springer.

Part V

Mutual learning and adaptation

10 Mutual learning and adaptation between China and the West through learning each other's language

Jiewen Zhong

Western countries are now embracing the need to learn Chinese and whereas 'English fever' took hold in China several years ago, 'Chinese fever' is now growing in Western countries. This chapter argues that learning another language and engaging with another culture also leads to a greater understanding of one's own language and culture and offers a new way of thinking about the world in more globalised contexts. It also shows that for those wanting to engage more successfully with China, it is necessary to gain linguistic and cultural knowledge as a foundation for this engagement.

Introduction

The theme explored in this chapter is mutual learning and adaptation between China and the West in this globalised and globalising era. It explores the possibility for transfer of learning between learning the Chinese language and learning the English language, in the contemporary context of rapid increases in English and Chinese foreign language learning in the West and in the East. The chapter begins with a description of China's foreign language curriculum reform and contemporary practice. It then argues that the positive outcomes of China's foreign language teaching can provide some useful examples for the promotion of foreign language learning in Western countries. The most significant feature of this chapter is that it explores the issues from a specific perspective – morphological awareness, lending theoretical and practical evidence to promote foreign language teaching reform in Western countries. The analysis provided in this chapter demonstrates that learning a second language not only increases a person's knowledge and understanding of the context of the target language, but can also help to enhance understanding of one's own language and culture and provides a platform for mutual understanding and adaptation between cultures.

China's foreign language teaching reform

China's foreign language education dates back to 1862 (Zhang 2000). However, foreign language teaching has never been emphasised to the extent that it is today. Previously, foreign language teaching mainly served political purposes.

In the early decades following the establishment of the People's Republic of China, when the country had a close relationship with the Soviet Union, Russian was the most important and popular foreign language in China. The last few decades have seen a major shift of emphasis to English teaching and learning in China, following the reform and opening-up policy introduced in 1979. In order to build a strong country which can have its voice heard in the world, Chinese policy makers realised that the Chinese people should be armed with the global language – English, to be able to understand and learn from other countries; at the same time, China could make itself known to the world. For the past thirty years, English language learning has become hugely popular and English teaching has undergone major reform ranging from curriculum design, syllabus and textbooks to teaching approaches and assessment.

In terms of teaching approaches, the traditional method of teaching was dominated by what is known as the grammar–translation method, which emphasised grammar and structure, and methodical translation exercises. Students taught in this method turned out to be incapable of speaking and understanding English (Ng and Tang 1997), commonly described as being 'deaf and dumb' in English. The first efforts to adopt Communicative Language Teaching (CLT) in China were made by Li Xiaoju and her associates in 1979, who compiled a series of Communicative English textbooks for Chinese learners (Yu 2001). As Li (1984: 2) maintains, the ultimate purpose of language learning is to communicate, as language is the most important medium of communication. However, the introduction of new ideas and new teaching approaches is not easily accepted. Although Li and her associates introduced CLT in 1979, substantial progress in teaching practice was not made until the early 1990s, when the Chinese Government State Education Development Commission (SEDC) set a new foreign language teaching syllabus which emphasised communication as the main aim.

Since that time, great progress has been made in English teaching practice in China and this has significantly improved the English language proficiency of Chinese learners. The benefits of mastering an international language are clear, such as more frequent and effective economic, technological and cultural exchanges.

I would argue that learning a distinctive foreign language also helps Chinese learners gain a deeper understanding of their own language and culture. For instance, a native Chinese speaker does not distinguish the concept of a morpheme and a word until s/he learns English. The fact that learning a distant language promotes the understanding of one's own language gives additional support to the importance of foreign language teaching and learning. The foreign language also provides a medium for the learning of the cultures and contexts of the target language.

Exporting Chinese language to the world

The Chinese Government has realised that importing English into the country is not enough to establish itself on the world stage. In a significant marker of China's attempts to increase its influence in the world, exporting the Chinese language to other countries has now become another important national strategy. The Chinese Government is making efforts to promote the Chinese language worldwide, including sending Chinese language teachers abroad; providing a large number of scholarships for overseas students to come to China to study Chinese; holding Chinese competency competitions; and assisting in the establishment of Confucius Institutes in more than eighty countries around the world.

On the other hand, with the rapid economic development of China, the country has caught the attention of people in the West. Increasing numbers of Westerners are keen to learn more about China and its five thousand year long history and culture, and the promise of a sparkling future in the twenty-first century. To truly understand a country, its people and its culture, learning its language is an important first step. Thus, the learning of Chinese is gaining huge and increasing popularity among Westerners (BBC 2006, Xinhua 2008), and the numbers of foreigners going to China each year to learn Chinese now exceeds the numbers of Chinese students leaving China each year to study overseas. In 2008, 225,000 foreign students went to China to study, whereas 180,000 Chinese students left for overseas study that year (Xinhua 2008). Moreover, the huge potential market in China is attracting increasing numbers of foreign businesses and investment. Foreign governments and businesses that want a share in this market understand that they need to be better equipped with the language spoken in the target market. In political terms, China is a rising power, exerting increasing influence on world affairs. In order to deal with this power effectively, it is important to understand its thinking and culture, which are manifested in its language. Therefore, policy makers and educationalists have started to introduce and increase the provision of Mandarin Chinese into foreign language curricula.

In this chapter, I focus on foreign language curriculum of one particular country – the United Kingdom. The reason that this country is chosen is because traditionally British people are known for their reluctance to learn foreign languages. In a BBC report in July 2004, the low level of foreign language learners in the UK was seen with alarm (BBC News Report, 29 July 2004). The report quoted Linda Parker, the Director of the UK Association for Language Learning, who said that curriculum time in schools for languages had been reduced and students had fewer opportunities to learn a second foreign language in addition to French. In addition, the University Council of Modern Languages (UCML) reported that the numbers of university language students were falling (BBC News Report, 29 July 2004). However, in more recent years, a new enthusiasm in learning Chinese has promoted foreign language teaching in the UK. Some schools have added Chinese to optional foreign language courses, and some have even taken the further step of making Chinese a compulsory subject. On the other hand, Chinese teaching in the UK is still not as common as in some other countries like Australia and the United States.

In this context, UK policy makers and educationalists could look at China's foreign language teaching strategies and outcomes to draw some inspiration, particularly in terms of encouraging more students to learn a foreign language and to draw on the benefits for literacy derived from second language learning, which is addressed in more detail later in this chapter. As Chinese learners of English have gained new perspectives of their first language by learning a very different and distinct foreign language, we can imagine that the same affects might be achieved by native English learners learning Chinese. The secondary affect of learning a foreign language is that it provides a method of learning about the cultures and contemporary contexts of the target language. Hence, the 'English fever' prevalent in China has led to an increased knowledge of and understanding of the West, equipping Chinese people to become more 'internationalised' and able to engage more effectively with the West. If this hypothesis is true, it could provide some theoretical grounds for policy makers and educationalists to promote Chinese as a foreign language in the national curriculum in countries such as the UK, and convince more Westerners to believe that learning Chinese is of value. To be more specific, learning Chinese not only helps learners know more about China and is likely to add to their competitiveness in the job market, it can also help native English speakers to improve their first language literacy. Enhancing one's first language (L1) while acquiring a second language (L2) seems to be an ideal in more globalised contemporary contexts.

Thus, there are multiple benefits to learning a foreign language in terms of individual and national benefits. In the rest of this chapter, I focus on and explore in depth the particular area of the possible effects of Chinese learning on the literacy development of native English speakers, from the perspective of morphological awareness (awareness of word internal structures), and why learning Chinese by native English speakers can provide benefits for literacy development in English.

Morphological awareness of native English speakers learning Chinese: why morphological awareness?

The reason that morphological awareness is a topic of such interest and concern in relation to language learning and development is due to its crucial contribution to literacy development. Good literacy skills are directly linked to a person's academic performance and achievement in life. Hence, policy makers, researchers and practitioners work very hard to develop children's literacy. However, surveys of children's reading abilities in several English speaking countries have raised serious concerns. In the United States, for example, Snow, Burns and Griffin (1998) conducted a study on children with reading difficulties at the request of the U.S. Departments of Education and Health and Human Services and found that a large number of American children could not read well enough to meet the demands of an increasingly competitive economy and a rapidly developing society. In the UK, Seymour (2004) found that British children on average take two and a half years to master the basic elements of literacy, which children speaking other European languages reach within one year. Also native English speaking children are found to be at more risk of dyslexia (British Parliamentary Office of Science and Technology 2004). It is, therefore, of great importance to look into the reading and other literacy development of native English speakers and find ways to improve their skills. Investigating metalinguistic awareness and issues that influence it (such as learning a second language) is one such way of better understanding factors which contribute to improved literacy in the first language (L1).

Within the literature of metalinguistic knowledge, phonological awareness is the one most examined, followed by orthographic awareness. Morphological awareness, on the other hand, is a relatively new area of interest. At present, morphological awareness (awareness of word structures) is attracting more attention as a research interest, and current research has revealed a significant correlation between morphological awareness and reading, writing and vocabulary acquisition. The section maps and examines this trend in research interest, and explores whether the morphological awareness of native English speakers can be changed or even improved by the learning of Chinese, and so, in turn facilitate their reading and other literacy development in their first language (L1).

Definitional and conceptual issues

Morphological awareness literally means the awareness of morphology. Therefore, it is first necessary to introduce the basics of morphology. Then I will discuss some fundamentals of English and Chinese morphology to inform readers who are not familiar with these concepts and also to enable a comparison to be made between these two distinctive languages.

What is morphology?

Morphology, as the name implies, is the study of word internal structures. It is an old sub-discipline of grammar, because traditionally the scope of grammar was almost the same as the study of word structure (Haspelmath 2002: 1) On the other hand, morphology is considered as a new field of study, in the sense that this term did not emerge until the second half of the nineteenth century, centuries after the terms *syntax* and *phonology* were introduced (Haspelmath 2002). According to Matthews (1991), human languages have a dual structure or 'double articulation'. The first one is syntax – rules governing the combination of words to form phrases and sentences; the second articulation refers to phonology – regulation of sound combination and phonemic segmentation of words. However, this is not all. For example, the 's' in 'birds', 'trees', 'cats' expresses the same idea, that is, the plural form of those entities. This is one example of where morphology – the internal structures of the word – plays its role. Haspelmath (2002) also points out that internal structures of words can be analysed in two different ways, phonological segments manifested in the sequence of letters, and forms of words which correlate with semantic change. Morphology deals with the latter form of word structure.

What is a morpheme?

The definition of morpheme was first proposed by Hockett (1958: 123), who stated that 'morphemes are the smallest individually meaningful elements in the utterances of a language'. It is likely that people who are non-linguists tend to consider words as the smallest units in a language, as words in print are clearly defined by the spaces on both sides of the word and thus are easily identified. This concept of a word is what Bauer (1988) calls an 'orthographic' word. For native English speakers, 'word' is an intuitive and clear notion, which the culture makes salient through activities such as the crossword puzzles English people enjoy doing (Packard 2000). Chao (1968) describes this notion of a 'word' as a 'sociological' word (136). However, from the perspective of linguists, a word contains one or more morphemes, in other words, a morpheme is a smaller element than a word.

The above understanding of morphemes and words are generally true in relation to the alphabet linguistic system. Nevertheless, when it comes to non-alphabet language systems such as Chinese, morphemes (or *zi*) rather than words are separated by spaces in written texts. Native speakers of Chinese are more likely to view a morpheme as the smallest unit in this language (Chinese morphology is discussed in more detail later).

In the words 'unhappy', 'unfriendly', 'unchangeable', for example, one can identify the common element of 'un-'. This form 'un-' is a morpheme, which can be found across different words and has the same function – to express the opposite meaning of the adjective to which it is attached. This type of morpheme has a concrete sense and is easy to describe. However, not all morphemes can be analysed in the same way. For instance, the 'ness' in 'greatness', 'shortness', 'loveliness' hardly denotes any meaning, but rather turns those adjectives into nouns. In other words, it only fulfils a grammatical function and is more abstract than the first type of morpheme. A further example of this category is 'ed' for the past tense of regular verbs. As Jensen (1990) notes these abstract morphemes show that morphemes are not necessarily meaningful. Nevertheless, Haspelmath (2002) argues that grammatical constructions ultimately serve the purpose of meaning, so that morphemes still can be said to bear meaning even if they are very abstract. Spencer (1991) proposes two ways of perceiving morphemes as things and rules; a morpheme can be seen either as a smaller and semantically indivisible word or 'the end product of a process or rule or operation'.

English morphology

There are three main areas of morphology in English: inflection, derivation and compounding, which are explained below.

Inflection is the morphological process that fulfils syntactic functions of words in a context. English language has very few inflections compared with other languages such as French, German or Latin (Jensen 1990). Generally speaking, English has only two number variations for nouns, i.e. singular and plural, and one case variation, i.e. possessive (Haspelmath 2002). Derivation is regarded as word formation, or more precisely lexeme[1]-formation (Matthews 1991: 37). From this definition, it is clear that the most salient feature of derivation is that it creates new lexemes out of bases. In other words, derivation basically deals with lexicon. Compounding belongs to lexical morphology, which 'deals with the relations between a complex lexeme[2] and a simple(r) lexeme[3]' (Matthews 1991: 37). To explain this using a compound lexeme such as BASKETBALL for instance; this lexeme is formulated by combining two simple lexemes BASKET and BALL.

Chinese morphology

Chinese morphology is concerned with internal Chinese word structures, thus it is essential to have some basic knowledge of the Chinese writing system. Some distinctive features of Chinese language will be introduced here followed by a discussion of issues related to Chinese morphology.

Distinguished from the majority of modern languages with phonographic writing systems, Chinese language has its unique logographic script. This character script has survived for more than three thousand years and is the oldest script still in existence (Chen 1999). In written languages, speech segments are represented by basic graphic units which either encode sound or both sound and meaning (Chen 1999). DeFrancis (1989) terms those basic graphic units corresponding to the smallest speech segments as *graphemes.* In contrast to phonographic languages whose graphemes are letters, the graphemes of Chinese are characters. An outstanding distinction between different writing systems lies in the grapheme representation – whether it is a phoneme or syllable. The Chinese writing system in the form of characters is syllabic. Also, Chinese characters encode both phonetic value and meaning, distinguished from most other graphemes with only phonetic significance; that is, Chinese characters indicate both a sound and a meaning. As summarised by Chen (1999: 132), 'the writing system of Chinese is characterised as logographic, and its graphemes, i.e. characters, as morpho-syllabic.'

A common belief exists that the Chinese language is a morphologically impoverished language. Such perceptions of Chinese are largely based on the fact that Chinese does not have 'grammatical agreement', or morphophonemic alternation. However, Packard (2000: 1) argues that far from being morphologically impoverished, Chinese is 'a most intriguing and enlightening sort' of language. Similar to English, Chinese also has derivations and inflections, though with distinctive features.

It is interesting to note that Sun (2006: 56) calls Chinese derivational affixes 'derivational-like affixes'. However, in terms of the word-formation function, there is not much difference between Chinese and English derivational affixes, though the Chinese ones have less variation and are smaller in number. Common derivational prefixes often involve morphemes like lao-/xiao- 老/小, di- 第, etc. The first two morphemes literally mean 'old' and 'small'. When attached to a person's surname, they lose their original meanings but function as an indicator of familiarity and status between interlocutors. For example, Chinese people address a senior friend 'lao+ surname', like' lao Wang' 老王, or a junior friend 'xiao+ surname', like 'xiao Wang' 小王. Di- 第 as a bound root literally means social class; as a prefix, it can be combined with numbers to express ordinal sense (Sun 2006: 56–57) so 'di yi' means Number 1 ('yi' meaning 'one'). Nominal suffixes like -xue 学 denote an academic discipline or school; -du 度 relates to different degrees of measure; -hua 化 indicates a change; and -yuan 员 represents a person with a specialised duty, etc. (Sun 2006: 59).

Sun (2006: 64–72) describes four Chinese inflection-like affixes in detail, namely the plural marker -men 们, perfective aspect marker -le 了, experimental marker -guo 过 and the imperfective marker -zhe 着 for verbs. -men 们 is only used for marking plurality of human nouns and pronouns, such as 孩子们 child-plural – 'children'. Apart from that, no other Chinese nominals mark plurality. Second, modern-Chinese does not have a marker for tense, but the morpheme -le 了 fulfils the role as an aspect[4] marker. For instance, 他吃了两碗饭 'He ate two bowls of rice'. In this sentence, -le 了 indicates that the action of eating has been completed. This example might leave the wrong impression that -le 了 marks the past tense. Another example clarifying the situation is 我明天下了课就回家 'Tomorrow I will get out of school and then come home'. This sentence is in future tense but still can use -le 了 as an aspect marker (Sun 2006: 65). One should distinguish -guo 过 from the perfective marker. -guo 过 refers to an event happening in the past at least once (Chao 1968), and such event is repeatable (Ma 1977). In addition, it can not be applied to a sentence with a habitual adverbial (Yeh 1996). For example, 我去过中国. 'I have been to China.' (Sun, 2006: 68) This event happened in the past, and can be repeated in the future without a habitual sense. With regard to imperfective marker -zhe 着, it indicates completion or attainment of action. It cannot be applied to predicates without a temporary nature (Yeh 1996). For example, 他穿着皮鞋 'He wears leather shoes' (Sun 2006: 71).

Now that we have good knowledge of the different aspects of English and Chinese morphology, we can embark on the issues of morphological awareness and literacy development as well as morphological awareness transfer.

Previous studies on morphological awareness and literacy of native English speakers

This chapter examines the possibility of Chinese morphological awareness transfer to native English speakers learning this language, based on the view that morphological awareness can facilitate literacy development. Research has shown that morphological awareness is associated with good readers and a lack of morphological awareness is associated with reading difficulties. It is therefore helpful to look at what previous studies have found in terms of the relationship between morphological awareness and literacy development in native English speakers.

As stated previously, past research has documented the importance of phonological and orthographic awareness in literacy development, but relatively little is known about morphological awareness (see in particular Wang, Cheng and Chen 2006 and McBride-Chang, Cheung, Chow and Choi 2006). However, morphological awareness began to attract more researchers' attention due to some interesting empirical findings (Wang, Yang and Cheng 2009). Prior to this there had been disagreement on the role of word internal structures (morphology) on lexical processing. Some researchers (e.g. Kintsch 1974, Manelis and Tharp 1977, Marslen-Wilson 1984) maintain that morphological complexity does not affect lexical processing, whereas some others (e.g. Bradley 1979, Fowler, Napps and Feldman 1985) suggest that the internal structures of derivational words do play a role. Tyler and Nagy (1990) believed that such different views are derived from examining isolated words, and they propose the examination of learners' use of derivational words to establish meaning and syntax at sentence reading and reading comprehension levels. In their study, Tyler and Nagy (1990) found that good readers rely on both stems and suffixes for establishing meaning for whole words during the reading process, whilst lower-ability readers fail to account for the syntactic information contained in suffixes. This finding suggests that morphological awareness distinguishes good and poor readers.

Fowler and Liberman (1995) described two lines of evidence suggesting that poor readers have difficulty with morphologically complex words. First, as is evident in clinical reports, poor readers have problems with grammatical and derivational morphemes in writing or with reading aloud inflectional suffixes (e.g. Henderson and Shores 1982, cited in Fowler and Liberman, 1995). Second, further studies suggest that letter-sound correspondence alone does not explain those problems; deficits in morphological awareness are above and beyond phonological awareness. This point of view is supported by Carlisle's study (1987) on dyslexic children and Hanson, Shankweiler and Fischer's study (1983) on adolescents with reading disabilities. The results of these two studies show that their subjects could perform as well as normal readers if morphemic structure was not accounted for. In other words, morphological awareness causes difficulties in poor readers above and beyond phonological awareness. This finding suggests that morphological awareness has a unique contribution to reading, independent of phonological awareness.

In fact, the importance of morphological awareness to reading has been documented in previous research. A two-year longitudinal study by Carlisle and Fleming (2003) discovered that early performance on lexical analysis of morphologically complex words (including full forms, base forms and affixes) predicts reading comprehension in later elementary years. Mahony, Singson and Mann's study (2000) lends support to this finding. They examined morphological sensitivity in relation to decoding skills in children in later elementary grades, establishing a significant association between the two after controlling for other variables. Some studies compare morphological awareness of more proficient readers and less proficient readers in relation to reading ability. For example, Ku and Anderson (2003) found that the former had better performance at recognising morphological relationships between words and deriving meanings of low-frequency words from familiar morphemes.

The significant contribution of morphological awareness to reading has been well established in older learners. However, different views have emerged with regard to younger learners. Brittain (1970) found a significant correlation between first and second graders' performance of inflectional morphology and their reading achievement. However, some later studies seem to contradict this finding, suggesting that morphological awareness does not make as significant a contribution as general language knowledge does to reading achievement in early school years. For example, Bowey and Patel (1988) found that syntactic awareness did not add to reading performance in first graders. To interpret such disagreement, Carlisle (1995) suggests that morphological awareness might not have been sufficiently developed so as to influence reading achievement in early years, though she points out that particular tasks employed may affect the outcome. In order to obtain more reliable evidence, Carlisle (1995) conducted a longitudinal study on children from kindergarten through second-grade with better-designed techniques. The results support Brittain's findings, and reveals that the relationship between morphological awareness and reading strengthens as the grade level increases.

Morphological awareness is also found to be strongly associated with vocabulary knowledge. In Nagy and Anderson's investigation (1984) of the distinct words in printed school English, they found that children have one to three additional words associated with every new word learnt, depending on their utilisation of morphology and context. This demonstrated how morphological awareness can facilitate vocabulary acquisition.

Morphological awareness and literacy development of native English speakers learning Chinese

Moving on from this discussion of the role of morphological awareness in literacy development generally, this section explores the specific question of whether the learning of Chinese has any effects on the morphological awareness of native English speakers. This question is broken down into two sub-questions: 1) Can morphological awareness transfer across as typologically distinct languages as English and Chinese in bilingual speakers?; and 2) Can Chinese learning help improve morphological awareness of native English speakers and consequently facilitate their first language literacy growth?

In order to find credible answers to these questions, a systematic review of the literature and existing research was carried out. Initial investigations identified 1,099 papers but only four papers provided specific and credible evidence: Koda 2000, McBride-Chang *et al.* 2006, Wang, Cheng and Chen 2006, and Wang, Yang and Cheng 2009 which are reviewed below.

Can morphological awareness transfer across English and Chinese in bilingual speakers?

Cross-language transfer refers to the tendency of learners to utilise the knowledge and experience gained from one language in dealing with another language (Wang, Yang and Cheng 2009: 5).

Wang, Cheng and Chen's study (2006) investigated the contribution of morphological awareness in Chinese–English bilingual children's literacy development. A battery of tests in English and Chinese were administered to 64 Chinese immigrant children in the United States testing morphological and phonological awareness, oral vocabulary, word reading and reading comprehension. Most of the results were comparable in both languages, but tone awareness and character reading were specific to the Chinese language tests. The hierarchical regression analyses revealed that English compound morphological awareness significantly contributed to Chinese character reading and reading comprehension, after controlling for the Chinese variables. This demonstrates that morphological awareness transfers from one language to the other, even though they are distinctive from each other. Wang *et al.* (2006) further argued that similar functions of compound structures in English and Chinese made such transfer possible although no transfer was observed in the direction of Chinese to English in this study.

In a later study, Wang *et al.* (2009) investigated the respective roles of phonology, morphology and orthography in lexical processing although only the findings concerning cross-language morphological awareness transfer are discussed here. The study used comparable but modified tasks to the study above, using first graders to see if the findings in the previous study held for younger bilingual children. The results showed that English compound awareness explained a significant variance in Chinese character reading, after all other Chinese and English variables were taken into account. One possible explanation is that Chinese character reading involves radical compounding just as morpheme compounding is involved in English compound words. The shared property appears to help bilingual children apply the knowledge and experience with English compounds into Chinese character reading. These studies suggest that morphological awareness transfer from English (L2) to Chinese (L1) is generally true of typical developing Chinese–English bilingual children. However, Chinese morphological awareness failed to account for the variance in English real word reading and pseudo word reading. In other words, morphological awareness transfer did not occur, at least not significantly, from Chinese (L1) to English (L2). This conclusion concurs with the findings of the previous study.

McBride-Chang *et al.* (2006) probed the relationship between metalinguistic skills (phonological awareness and morphological awareness in this research) and vocabulary knowledge in Chinese (L1) and English (L2). Once again, only issues related to morphological awareness will be discussed here. A battery of measures was administrated to 217 Hong Kong kindergarten children. Those related to the examination of morphological awareness included Cantonese receptive vocabulary knowledge, Chinese character reading, English word reading, receptive morphological awareness and morphological construction. It is noteworthy that the two measures of receptive and productive morphological awareness were only conducted in Chinese. As claimed by the researchers, those young children had not attained enough English proficiency to analyse its morphological structure. Results showed that Chinese morphological awareness accounts for 13 per cent of the variance of Chinese vocabulary. Nevertheless, no significant contribution of Chinese morphological awareness was found to predict the variability of English vocabulary. This study found that Chinese morphological awareness only exerts an influence on literacy within a language but not across languages. This finding supports the previous two studies, maintaining that no significant morphological awareness transfer occurs from Chinese (L1) to English (L2). The researchers suggested that the measure of morphological awareness in this study was lexical compounding, which was relatively rare in English. Thus, no significant transfer would occur in this domain.

Koda's study (2000) did not explore the effects of cross-language morphological awareness transfer on literacy development directly, but on lexical processing variation. However, it could be argued that they are fundamentally the same. Although not clearly stated in the previous studies, morphological awareness of one language alters that of the other language to the extent that it exerts influence on its literacy. The most outstanding feature of Koda's (2000) study is that it compared native speakers of two different languages, Chinese and Korean, learning the same language – English. Though both Chinese and Korean are Asian languages, Korean has more in common with English as they are both alphabetic languages, whereas Chinese is a non-alphabetic language. With respect to morphological awareness, Koda (2000) hypothesised that native English and Korean speakers were more sensitive to intra-word structural salience as opposed to native Chinese speakers who were adept at integrating word-internal (morphological) and word-external (context) information. These hypotheses were derived from the properties of their L1 morphological awareness. Measures of intra-word structural sensitivity and analysis efficiency and morphological and contextual information integration were tested on two groups of Chinese and Korean learners of English at two American universities. The results confirmed the hypotheses that Chinese ESL learners were faster and more accurate at integrating morphological and context information, whereas Korean ESL learners were more efficient at analysing intra-word structures.

The findings of Koda's study make two points clear. First, morphological awareness of one's L1 can influence that of one's L2. Second, such influence is specific and predictable. This study provides some evidence that morphological awareness can be transferred from Chinese (L1) to English (L2) in Chinese–English bilingual speakers. Koda's findings contradict the findings of the previous studies, which stated that no significant morphological transfer from Chinese to English appears to occur. I would argue that because this study did not focus on literacy development, we cannot compare the findings of these studies directly.

In summary, there is evidence that morphological awareness transfer does occur across typologically distinct languages such as English and Chinese, however, not all aspects can be transferred. English derivational morphological awareness does not appear to have significant effects on Chinese literacy. Second, English morphological awareness transfer to Chinese has been observed, but there is no strong and reliable evidence that transfer in the opposite direction in relation to literacy development also occurs. These studies do support L2 transfer to L1, adding mainly to the existing literature concerning L1 transfer to L2.

Can Mandarin learning help improve morphological awareness of native English speakers, which consequently facilitates their first language literacy growth?

This question is the central issue under discussion in this chapter. This question can be divided into two parts: 1) Can Mandarin learning help improve morphological awareness of native English speakers?; and 2) Can improved morphological awareness facilitate their English literacy? The validity of the second part of the question is dependent on the first part. Based on the analysis of the research in the section above, this part of the question has already been answered. Morphological awareness is strongly associated with English literacy development, and its contribution is above and beyond that of phonological awareness. To this point, the key to answer this question is to verify the first part.

One limitation of this chapter is that it does not identify studies directly investigating morphological awareness of native English speakers of non-Chinese background learning Chinese. Instead, all four studies included in the in-depth review above recruited Chinese–English bilingual speakers of Chinese origin. Albeit not ideal, these studies are the most relevant that could be found on this question. In Wang *et al.*'s study (2006), 31 per cent of the subjects were simultaneous English–Chinese bilinguals and 35 per cent of the children in Wang *et al.*'s study (2009) acquired English as their L1. Although I concede that these Chinese immigrant children may have different characteristics in terms of English and Chinese acquisition, compared with those of native English speakers of non-Chinese origin, I still believe that some comparable evidence can be drawn.

Wang *et al.* (2006) observed no significant morphological transfer from Chinese to English in their study. However, they found that Chinese character reading and English word reading were strongly associated. As argued by the researchers, the compounding process of Chinese radicals to form characters was parallel with that of English morphemes to form words; in other words, the underlying cognitive processes were similar. This lends significant support for an affirmative answer to the given question. Also, English compound structure was found to be a strong predictor of English reading comprehension in this study. Since most previous studies do not assess the contribution of compound awareness in native English speakers, the researchers suggest that such effects of English compound awareness found might be due to the influence of Chinese. If this is true, we can conclude that Chinese learning can help to facilitate English morphological awareness and hence literacy development. In order to justify this point, however, further research needs to be carried out on compound structure awareness in native English speakers.

A later study carried out by Koda (2006) sheds some light on this research question. This question targets the effects of L2 processing experience on L1 morphological awareness. At first glance, Koda's (2006) study seems to have little relevance, as it basically explores the relationship between L1 processing experience and L2 morphological awareness. However, one crucial thing established by Koda in her study is that a connection can be distinguished between L1 and L2 morphological awareness. Based on this, I would argue that there is a clear possibility of L2 morphological awareness influencing that of L1. However, in order for L2 to have some effects on L1, learners appear to need to have achieved a certain level of L2 proficiency (Wang *et al.* 2006). Although the available research findings do point to this possibility, this can only be determined and measured through empirical studies with native English learners of Chinese.

Conclusion

Some evidence has been found to suggest that learning Chinese may have a positive impact on native English speakers. In order to find more reliable answers to this question, however, it is suggested that empirical studies be conducted on native English speakers of non-Chinese origin learning Chinese. To inquire even more deeply into this topic and to gain a greater understanding of the more complete picture, research could be carried out on morphological awareness of native English speakers learning different languages, including those with similar or distant orthographies, morphologies and phonologies.

There is thus clearly scope and, I would suggest, a pressing need for further research in this area, particularly given the rapid and increasing numbers of Chinese speakers learning English, and English speakers learning Chinese. The possible benefits for literacy development that are explored in this chapter would clearly also have more import for younger language learners, especially in countries such as China and Australia where the learning of a foreign language is a compulsory component of the curriculum.

In conclusion, this chapter began with a description of contemporary foreign language teaching in China, and extended the discussion into foreign language teaching in Western countries, with a particular focus on the benefits of introducing the Chinese language into their curriculum. What has been discussed here does not simply relate to an exchange of ideas in education, or about the learning of foreign languages, but most importantly, it also indicates a trend towards and a means of mutual learning and adaptation between the East and the West.

Notes

1 Those dictionary entries are called lexemes in linguistics, which is rather an abstract concept.
2 Complex lexeme – a lexeme that can be divided into smaller meaningful units or (more) simple lexemes.
3 Simple lexeme – a lexeme that cannot be further divided into smaller morphological elements.
4 Aspect refers to a category of verbs designating primarily the relation of the action to the passage of time, especially in reference to completion, duration or repetition.

References

Bauer, L. (1998) *Introducing Linguistic Morphology*, Edinburgh: Edinburgh University Press.

BBC (2004) 'Why Britons are language barbarians', 29 July 2004. Online. Available HTTP: http://news.bbc.co.uk/1/hi/uk/3930963.stm (accessed 15 January 2010).

BBC (2006) 'Foreigners flock to learn Chinese', 9 January 2006. Online. Available HTTP: <.http://news.bbc.co.uk/1/hi/world/asia-pacific/4594698.stm> (accessed 31 December 2009).

Bowey, J. A., and Patel, R. K. (1988) 'Metalinguistic ability and early reading achievement', *Applied Psycholinguistics*, 9(4), 367–383.

Bradley, D. (1979) 'Lexical representation of derivational relationships', in M. Aronoff and M. L. Kean (eds), *Juncture*, Cambridge, MA: MIT Press.

British (2004) Dyslexia and Dyscalculia, Parliamentary Office of Science and Technology Postnote Number 226, July 2004. Online. Available HTTP: http://www.parliament.uk/documents/upload/POSTpn226.pdf (accessed 15 January 2010).

Brittain, M. (1970) 'Inflectional performance and early reading achievement', *Reading Research Quarterly*, 6(1), 34–48.

Carlisle, J. (1987) 'The use of morphological knowledge in spelling derived forms by learning-disabled and normal students', *Annals of Dyslexia*, 37(1), 90–108.

Carlisle, J. F. (1995) 'Morphological awareness and early reading achievement', in I. Feldman (ed.) *Morphological Aspects of Language Processing*, Hillsdale, NJ: Lawrence Erlbaum.

Carlisle, J. F. and Fleming, J. (2003) 'Lexical processing of morphologically complex words in the elementary years', *Scientific Studies of Reading*, 7(3), 239–253.

Chao, Y. R. (1968) *Language and Symbolic Systems*, London: Cambridge University Press.

Chen, P. (1999) *Modern Chinese: History and Sociolinguistics*, Cambridge: Cambridge University Press.

DeFrancis, J. (1989) *Visible Speech: The Diverse Oneness of Writing Systems*, Honolulu: University of Hawaii Press.

Fowler, A. and Liberman, I. (1995) 'The role of phonology and orthography in morphological awareness', in I. Feldman (ed.) *Morphological Aspects of Language Processing*, Hillsdale, NJ: Lawrence Erlbaum.

Fowler, C., Napps, S., and Feldman, L. (1985) 'Relations among regular and irregular morphologically related words in the lexicon as revealed by repetition priming', *Memory and Cognition*, 13(3), 241–255.

Hanson, V. L., Shankweiler, D. and Fischer, F. W. (1983) 'Determinants of spelling ability in deaf and hearing adults: access to linguistic structure', *Cognition*, 14(3), 323–344.

Haspelmath, M. (2002) *Understanding Morphology*, London: Arnold.

Henderson, A. J. and Shores, R. E. (1982) 'How learning disabled student's failure to attend to suffixes affects their oral reading performance', *Journal of Learning Disabilities*, 15(3), 178–182.

Hockett, C. F. (1958) *A Course in Modern Linguistics*, New York: Macmillan.

Jensen, J. T. (1990) *Morphology: Word Structure in Generative Grammar*, Amsterdam/Philadelphia: John Benjamins.

Kintsch, W. (1974) *The Representation of Meaning in Memory*, Hillsdale, NJ: Lawrence Erlbaum.

Koda, K. (2000) 'Cross-linguistic variations in L2 morphological awareness', *Applied Psycholinguistics*, 21(3), 297–320.

Ku, Y. M. and Anderson, R. C. (2003) 'Development of morphological awareness in Chinese and English', *Reading and Writing*, 16(5), 399–422.

Li, X. (1984) 'In defense of the communicative approach', *ELT Journal*, 38, 2–13.

Ma, J. (1977) 'Some aspects of the teaching of -*guo* and -*le*, *Journal of Chinese*, *Language Teachers Association*, 12(1), 14–26.

Mahony, D., Singson, M. and Mann, V. (2000) 'Reading ability and sensitivity to morphological relations', *Reading and Writing*, 12(3), 191–218.

Manelis, L. and Tharp, D. (1977) 'The processing of affixed words', *Memory and Cognition*, 5(6), 690–695.

Marslen-Wilson, W. D. (1984) 'Function and process in spoken word-recognition', in H. Bouma and D. Bouwhuis (eds), *Attention and Performance X: Control of Language Processes*, Hillsdale, NJ: Lawrence Erlbaum.

Matthews, P. H. (1991) *Morphology*, 2nd edn, Cambridge: Cambridge University Press.

McBride-Chang, C., Cheung, H., Chow, B., Chow, C. and Choi, L. (2006) 'Metalinguistic skills and vocabulary knowledge in Chinese (L1) and English (L2)', *Reading and Writing*, 19(7), 695–716.

Nagy, W. E. and Anderson, R. C. (1984) 'How many words are there in printed school English?', *Reading Research Quarterly*, 19(3), 304–330.

Ng, C. and Tang, E. (1997) 'Teachers needs in the process of EFL reform in China– a report from Shanghai', *Perspectives* [City University of Hong Kong Department of English Working Papers], 9: 63–85.

Packard, J. L. (2000) *The Morphology of Chinese*, Cambridge: Cambridge University Press.

Seymour, P. H. K. (2004) *'Effects of Orthography on Reading Acquisition in European Writing Systems'*, Annual Conference of the British Psychological Society, London, April 2004.

Snow, C. E., Burns, S. and Griffin, P. (eds) (1998) *Preventing Reading Difficulties in Young Children*, Washington, DC: National Academy Press.

Spencer, A. (1991) *Morphological Theory: An Introduction to Word Structure in Generative Grammar*, Oxford: Basil Blackwell.

Sun, C. (2006) *Chinese: A Linguistic Introduction*, Cambridge: Cambridge University Press.

Tyler, A. and Nagy, W. (1990) 'Use of derivational morphology during reading', *Cognition*, 36(1), 17–34.

Wang, M., Cheng, C. and Chen, S. (2006) 'Contribution of morphological awareness to Chinese-English biliteracy acquisition', *Journal of Educational Psychology*, 98(3), 542–553.

Wang, M., Yang, C. and Cheng, C. (2009) 'The contributions of phonology, orthography, and morphology in Chinese-English biliteracy acquisition', *Applied Psycholinguistics*, 30(2), 291–314.

Xinhua News Agency (2008) 'Foreigners studying in China exceeds 200,000 in 2008', 25 March 2008. Online. Available HTTP: http://news.xinhuanet.com/english/ 2009-03/25/content_11072936.htm (accessed 31 December 2009).

Yeh, M. (1996) 'An analysis of the experimental *guo EXP* in Mandarin: a temporal quantifier', *Journal of East Asian Linguistics*, 5(2), 151–182.

Yu, Liming (2001) 'Communicative Language Teaching in China: progress and resistance', *TESOL Quarterly*, 35(1), 194–198.

Zhang, Zheng-dong (2000) *Theories and Schools of Foreign Language Teaching Methodology in China*, Beijing: Science Press (54–57).

11 Bridging the East and West dichotomy: harmonising Eastern learning with Western knowledge

Shijing Xu

This chapter draws on a larger study of Chinese newcomer families in Canada to understand linguistically and culturally diverse school life while studying the cultural tensions and communications in the processes of cultural adaptation by new immigrants. The Chinese family stories show that communication and understanding can be achieved and enhanced through mutual learning and adaptation. Educational researchers and school practitioners can gain insights from the generational family narratives in cultivating 'we-consciousness' in diversity, a vision intended to embrace linguistically and culturally diverse school life in narrative unity through Confucian *continuity of being* and Deweyian *continuity of knowing*.

Introduction

In response to the economic, social and political transformation of China in the twenty-first century, China's education has undergone radical reform of all levels of its educational system, mostly in Western terms. In the meantime, the Western world has been observing the rise of China mostly in economic or political terms, and China's rise is often perceived as a potential threat to the West in the East-and-West dichotomised thinking. What insights may be drawn from the social, cultural and educational values that China can offer to the world? What should China learn from the West for its educational reforms? In what way may we gain mutual understanding, respect and appreciation in the changing world landscape? A study of the increasing number of Chinese immigrant families in Canada may shed a different light on such East-and-West dichotomy and may help create bridges for reciprocal learning with mutual adaptation, respect and appreciation.

This chapter draws on a larger study of Chinese newcomer families in Canada which involved three years of intensive fieldwork and two years follow up at an inner-city school in Toronto. Narrative methodology is used to understand linguistically and culturally diverse school life at the school while studying the cultural tensions and communications in the processes of cultural adaptation by new immigrants. Different as the East and the West appear to be, the Chinese family stories show that communication and understanding can be achieved and enhanced through mutual learning and adaptation. This may be realised when the East, the Chinese families, turn to the West, and the West, in the form of mainstream schools, reach out to the East for mutual learning and adaptation. Generational narratives provide insights for cultivating 'we-consciousness' in diversity, a vision intended to embrace linguistically and culturally diverse school life in narrative unity through Confucian *continuity of being* and Deweyian *continuity of knowing*. In this chapter I focus on the role of grandparents in bridging gaps between Western knowledge and Chinese learning and argue for the importance of reciprocal learning between the newcomer families and the mainstream schools. That is, while the newcomer families are making an effort to adapt to the Canadian school system, it helps improve children's schooling experience if people in the mainstream society, especially educators, understand and appreciate the educational values and insights immigrant families bring into Canadian schools.

Background

The fieldwork for this study reported in this chapter was undertaken during a time when, in Canada, China was ranked by Citizenship and Immigration Canada (CIC 2001, 2004) as the first of the top 10 source countries of immigrants over the previous five years (see Figure 11.1, Census 2006). China

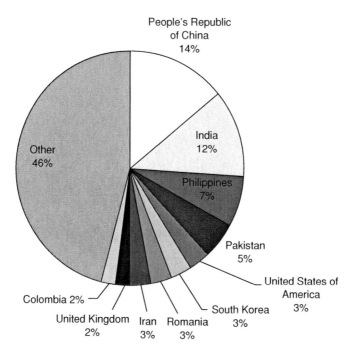

Figure 11.1 Top Ten Source Countries for Canada 2001–2006 (Census 2006, Statistics Canada)

has remained as the top source country over the past 10 years according to statistics provided by CIC 2008. In 1996, Chinese had overtaken Italian as Canada's third most common mother tongue (Carey 2002, CIC 2004). According to the Canadian Census of 2001, 41 per cent of all Canadian residents whose mother tongue was Chinese lived in the Greater Toronto Area. That is, Chinese, Toronto's second most populous language after English, was the first language of 355,270 residents in the Great Toronto area (Carey 2002). I first started my research fieldwork in a Toronto school in May 2002 with the demographic facts that the total number of Chinese immigrants to Canada in 2001 alone was 40,296, with 21,487 of them choosing Toronto as their landing destination (CIC Canada 2001). The influx of newly arrived Chinese immigrants has made Chinese students a visible majority among the student population at some schools in Toronto since then. Figure 11.2 shows that in Bay Street Community School (a pseudonym), an urban Toronto school where my research was located, students who speak Cantonese and Mandarin altogether outnumber those who speak English as their mother tongue.

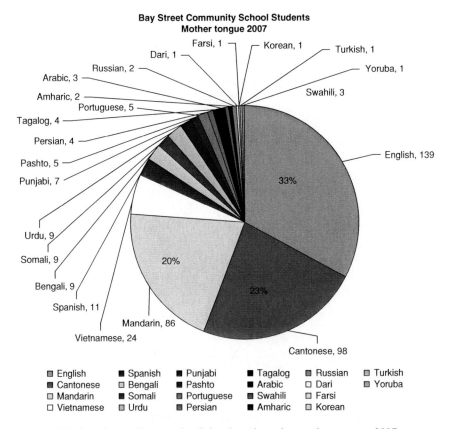

Figure 11.2 Bay Street Community School students by mother tongue 2007

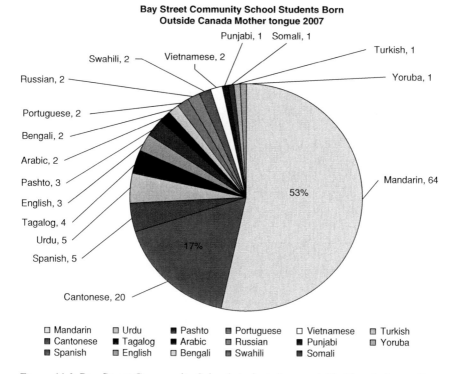

Bay Street Community School Students Born Outside Canada Mother tongue 2007

Punjabi, 1   Somali, 1

Turkish, 1

Swahili, 2   Vietnamese, 2

Yoruba, 1

Russian, 2

Portuguese, 2

Bengali, 2

Arabic, 2

Mandarin, 64

Pashto, 3

53%

English, 3

Tagalog, 4

Urdu, 5

17%

Spanish, 5

Cantonese, 20

☐ Mandarin   ☐ Urdu   ■ Pashto   ■ Portuguese   ☐ Vietnamese   ■ Turkish
■ Cantonese   ■ Tagalog   ■ Arabic   ■ Russian   ■ Punjabi   ☐ Yoruba
■ Spanish   ☐ English   ☐ Bengali   ■ Swahili   ■ Somali

Figure 11.3 Bay Street Community School students born outside Canada by mother tongue 2007

Among the students born outside Canada, 53 per cent speak Mandarin and 17 per cent speak Cantonese at home (see Figure 11.3).

Toronto District School board archives reveal that Bay Street Community School has been home to shifting patterns of immigrant cultural groups and the school was established as a means of addressing the needs of the expanding immigrant population in Canada (Connelly *et al.* 2004). The demographic changes in the school community reflect the shifting patterns of immigration from White European immigrants as the dominant group to the more visible ethnic groups such as Chinese, as the visible majority of the student population. How to meet the needs of this culturally and linguistically diverse community was at that time perceived as quite a challenge to teachers in the school. Many well-intended programmes, events and activities were set up to support newcomer families and their children, such as Newcomer Support Class, LEAP programmes, Curriculum Night, Family Literacy Programme in the Parent Center and Parent Council meetings.

In May 2002 I began my fieldwork as a research assistant for a larger project by volunteering in the Parent Center and the Newcomer Support Class where most of the newcomer families and children came from Mainland China. I was fascinated by the regular programmes as well as the extracurricular programmes in the school that were geared to the needs of newcomer families and children. I started my inquiry into the cross-cultural schooling experience of the Chinese newcomer families to understand how they experienced the Canadian school system in their cross-cultural journey.

A fluid inquiry journey

Purpose of the study

I started my inquiry with a hope of understanding through narrative how Chinese immigrant families and their children experience the Canadian school system. With a special interest in cross-cultural issues between the East and the West, I have been interested in finding ways to bridge cultural and educational values and perspectives and to see newcomers not only as needing to adapt to their new country, but more as active forces for change in their new society.

It was reported by many studies that most newcomer families came to Canada for the sake of their children (see, for example, Anisef, Kilbride, Ochocka and Janzen 2001). A father of a (non-Chinese) newcomer family said, 'What we do not know is that we will be asked to make an even bigger sacrifice: we will be asked to give up our children, as they become not children we know and understand, but Canadian children, and so we lose them' (Anisef *et al.* 2001: 27). Did the Chinese newcomer families also come to Canada for the sake of their children? How have they experienced the school system here in Canada? My three-year intensive fieldwork and two-year follow up at Bay Street Community School helped me to understand the answers to these questions and to develop a narrative understanding of linguistically and culturally diverse school life in Canada.

Family as the unit of study

By using narrative inquiry (Connelly and Clandinin 1990, Clandinin and Connelly 2000, Connelly and Xu 2008, Xu *et al.* 2007), I perceive the family as the unit of analysis in my inquiry. The assumption in my inquiry is that to properly understand Chinese students' educational background, it is necessary to understand something of their families' culture, hopes and ambitions. However, rather than distinguishing newcomer families from the larger Canadian society in terms of an East and West dichotomy, I study each family in the context of family and community on their own terms. I focus on their lived experience to study and understand each family's detailed educational narratives. I see the family as 'fluid and constantly being negotiated and reconstituted both spatially and temporally' (Creese, Dyck and McLaren 1999: 3) on cross-cultural landscapes in transition, not only for newcomer families, but also for the larger Canadian society. My purpose is to explore and understand newcomer families' beliefs and values in their children's education from their lived experience in Canada and to identify what educational values and insights they bring into Canadian schools that may benefit all children.

Hayhoe (1997) points out that Confucian, Taoist and Buddhist views of society, knowledge, and the human person are useful to identify core values that have persisted in modern education in East Asia. But these views have been neglected as a resource useful for the West. The increasing number of Chinese immigrants in the Canadian population may open up various channels whereby they can introduce their values to Canadian and American societies (Hayhoe 1997). By examining family narratives, I hope to gain insights into one of the ways this communication of values occurs through schooling. Hence rather than studying the newcomers as people only in terms of their needs, I perceive them as people who contribute valuable social, cultural, economical and educational resources to an increasingly diverse society.

The fieldwork

On 21 May 2002, I started my negotiation of entry into Bay Street Community School, and was located at the Parent Centre as a research assistant for a larger project sponsored by Social Science and Humanities Research Council of Canada (SSHRC). The Parent Centre is a room set aside in the school where parents, grandparents and other caregivers can drop in, socialise, interact with children and familiarise themselves with schooling. My fieldwork consisted of three to five days a week of school visits from May 2002 to December 2004 and ongoing follow-up visits and continuous participation in school events until September 2006. New projects have been developed from this work between 2006 and 2009.

My school visits involved observing and volunteering in the School's Parent Centre, Newcomer Support Class, LEAP programmes (Literacy Enrichment Academic Programme), International Languages programme (e.g. Mandarin classes), and extra-curricular programmes. Fieldwork also included participant observation of teacher-parent interviews, fieldtrips, and School Council meetings. In addition, I interviewed parents, grandparents, children, the school principal, teachers, and community workers.

I made the following friends in the Parent Centre: Carmen, the staff member at the Parent Centre; Mr Wong, a Chinese grandpa who has been a volunteer at the school for a dozen years and who has also been a School Council member; Julian's grandma with Julian and his baby brother Allen; and 惠兰 Hui Lan, a Chinese mother, whose two little sons were the first two children I talked with at the Parent Centre. I met Hui Lan's eldest son later in the LEAP programme when I followed up with my other student participants in September 2003. I also got to know Grandpa Jiang and other Chinese grandparents and parents when interacting with many families, Chinese or non-Chinese, at the Parent Centre and at various settings in the school. The Parent Centre connected me with the linguistically and culturally diverse school life where I observed the interactions among Chinese families and between themselves and non-Chinese families. It was at the Parent Centre where I first met the Chinese newcomer students such as 志高 Zhi Gao, and 嘉明 Jia Ming, who came to the Parent Centre once a week for a Buddy Reading Programme. With the Parent Centre as my 'home base' at the school, I followed the Chinese newcomer students to their classrooms and on fieldtrips and I also worked with 洋洋 Yang Yang and other Chinese newcomer students who were in Grade 7/8 Newcomer Support Class or LEAP programmes. My inquiry path diverged from the Parent Centre into several classrooms, extra-curricular programmes, school events, School Council meetings, parent–teacher interviews, newcomer students' homes, and the local community centres, where I had direct contact with more Chinese newcomer students and their family members.

While studying the cultural tensions and communications in the processes of cultural adaptation by these new immigrants, I find that what stands out most and has been overlooked in the research field, are the generational narratives from grandparents' perspectives. In this chapter, I highlight the insights gained from the family narratives of Chinese parents, with a focus on grandparents, to discuss the essential roles grandparents play in bridging the gaps between Western *knowing* and Eastern Confucian *being*. I also put an emphasis on the reciprocal learning between newcomer families and the mainstream society in which the educational values and insights brought forward by new immigrant families are valuable and important in improving all children's education.

Educational insights through the lens of generational narratives

Essential roles of grandparents

In Chinese families, grandparents often take a crucial, sometimes central, role in childcare and children's education. At the Parent Centre, in the hallways, and in Bay Street Community School's front yard, and in many other Toronto elementary schools, Chinese grandparents are seen as the major caregivers who care for young children and who bring school-aged children to and from school. Although there are no publicised statistics, my experience with many Chinese families suggests that Chinese grandparents who visited or immigrated to Canada under the category of family reunion do so mostly for the purpose of caring for grandchildren.

Julian's grandma, who was a senior teacher at a high-ranking elementary school in central Guangzhou, took early retirement and came to Toronto with her husband to be the caregiver of her daughter's children. In Canada, she lost her sense of home when the traditional family structure and values, as well as the interdependent family relationship, were challenged by new situations in landscapes in transition.

In one of our conversations Julian's grandma said:

> When in China, everyone in the family came home from work around the same time and we would have dinner together at home or go out together and spend the evening in a restaurant or cinema. Now, one person might come home around 7:00 p.m., another around 8:00 p.m. and another might be still not yet home. There has never been a time for the whole family to be together for dinner since coming to Canada. . . . Money is important but money cannot buy everything; and money cannot buy the heart.
>
> (Fieldnotes, 12 November 2002)

Julian's grandma is not happy with her daughter's new life in Canada, nor is she satisfied with the Canadian school education as a retired elementary school teacher from China.

> We want to go back to China when the boys grow older. I told my daughter that I did not like her laboring like a farm animal. She is not living as a human. She has no time to enjoy life. . . . People came to Canada with their dreams for a better life, but it turns out they cannot enjoy life.
>
> (Fieldnotes, 12 November 2002)

> Children of Julian's age in China have learned a lot in language and math, but Julian plays all day long. There is no homework. . . . Children of Julian's age need spoon-feeding. They do not know the importance of study . . . Canadian schools make it easy for children like Julian.
>
> (Fieldnotes, 12 November 2002)

> Here they do not teach students how to write properly. In China, if a child does not hold the pencil properly, they are corrected and shown good handwriting. But here children do whatever they like. Their handwriting is messy and not in good order.
>
> (Fieldnotes, 19 November 2002)

Julian's grandma tutored her grandsons during their after-school time. She also taught Mandarin to Mr Wong's grandsons on Sundays. In spite of her discomfort, she has remained in Canada. The Chinese family values help explain why Chinese grandparents, such as Julian's grandma, stay in Canada despite their dissonance and disillusion: to help their son or daughter by sharing family difficulties and responsibilities. They take it as the priority in their life to care for their grandsons or granddaughters and help with their education.

This is best expressed by Grandpa Jiang, a grandparent of another Chinese family:

It is a pleasure to take care of my grandsons. It is my happiness to watch them grow up. I do not feel lonely as I have so much to do every day. I do not feel sad about getting old, as I know my grandsons carry on my life. My family grows and moves on even though I will eventually die. The utmost happiness for a grandparent is to watch grandchildren growing up in front of you. My grandsons are my greatest joy. I am old now and cannot work for society. But I can help my son and daughter-in-law care for their children, so they can work. My wife is in Scarborough helping our daughter with her children. It is fair for us to help both our son's and the daughter's families although we have to live separately. We've been old husband and wife for many years. Nothing can change our relationship. But they are young. It is hard for them to bring up the little ones while overloaded with worries of life and pressure from work. Although we two live separately, we are happy to help. Our sacrifices contribute to the harmony of their small families and hence of the big family, so it is worth it.

(Fieldnotes, 5 January 2004)

As expressed in Grandpa Jiang's story, Chinese grandparents find joy and see continuity in their lives in the upbringing of their grandchildren. Wherever they are, Chinese grandparents serve as bridges across the boundaries of age, generation, culture and country.

Freeman Wong and his wife, who were Cantonese Chinese, moved to Canada from Burma. Mrs Wong said she used to take their grandsons to the Parent Centre every day before they attended Grade One at Bay Street Community School. The grandmother said the two boys who were cousins were as close as brothers and never fought or argued with each other. They were together every day at the grandparents' home until two years ago when one boy had to move to the east end of the city with his parents. As the two boys spent most of their pre-school years and after-school time with their grandparents, like their grandparents they could manage several languages: English, Hong Kong Cantonese, Tai-Shan Cantonese, Mandarin, and Burmese. They preferred their grandmother's home-made Chinese meals and Burmese special food. Freeman and his wife celebrated Canadian, Chinese, and Burmese cultural holidays at home with their big family. So, not long after the two boys enjoyed Christmas at the grandparents' home, they celebrated Chinese New Year together. The boys learned many Chinese and Burmese customs and Buddhist values when various Chinese and Burmese traditional holidays were celebrated at the grandparents' home throughout the year.

Grandparents, as revealed in the stories of Julian's grandma, Grandpa Jiang, and Mr and Mrs Wong, contribute greatly to young children's bilingual/bicultural and/or multilingual/multicultural education in Canada. Such grandparents are culture brokers and bridges for the grandchildren on cross-cultural landscapes in transition, as well as role models for the younger generations as to how to be 'human' according to Confucian values. They believe the sacrifices they make are worthwhile because, as Grandpa Jiang pointed out, Chinese grandparents believe they are making a contribution to family harmony, and hence to the harmony and growth of society.

Chinese grandparents and parents' dedication to the family and their sacrifices for the next generations are rooted in Chinese cultural traditions that emphasise family ties. From the Confucian perspective, selflessness as a primary virtue is more self-realisation than self-sacrifice. The grandparents' personal narratives show how Chinese people maintain supportive family connections which benefit family members in difficult times. This value and its practice are rooted in the Confucian tradition in which personal order and social order are mutually entailing (Hall and Ames 1999). As Fei (1947/1972) explains, Chinese society is 'egocentric' in that each person is at the centre of his or her own network. To Confucius, as his follower Mengzi (Mencius) summarised in his works on Confucian thought, self, family and the nation/society are interrelated; hence, one's learning/self-cultivation (修身 *xiu-shen*) contributes to the prosperity of the family (齐家 *qi-jia*) and thus to the harmony of the nation/society (治国平天下 *zhi guo ping tian xia*. In Chinese, speaking of 'nation' is to speak of 'nation family' (国家 *guo-jia*); to speak of 'everyone', is to speak of 'big family' (大家 *da-jia*); to speak of Confucianism or Taoism is to speak of 'the family of Confucian scholars' (儒家 *ru-jia*) or 'the family of Taoist scholars' (道家 *dao-jia*) (see Hall and Ames 1999). Thus, it may be said that Chinese grandparents' sense of home, and sense of family, as revealed in Julian's grandma, Grandpa Jiang and Mr Wong's family stories, are expressed in their help and sacrifice for their children and grandchildren. To help the grandchild is to search for self-value, and to support the family and the society, the *nation family*. Hall and Ames (1999: 33–34) point out that the idea of family is a grounding metaphor in Chinese culture and is based on two Confucian ideas:

> First, the family is that institution in which people give most wholly and unreservedly of themselves . . . Second, the continuity between humanity and the world – between culture and nature – leads to the singular importance of the family metaphor in the definition of relational order within Chinese cosmology. . . . In the Chinese language, 'the world' is *shijie* 世界, literally 'the succeeding generational boundaries' which conjoin one's own generation to those who have come before, and to the generation that will follow this one; the pursuit of wisdom is literally, 'to know the way (*zhidao* 知道).'

Grandpa Jiang summarised everything concisely when, after reflecting on the hardship involved, said, 'so, it is worth it.'

To be human in Confucian values

Some of my participant parents, such as Zhi Gao's mother and Yang Yang's mother, did not finish grade school in China and were marginally literate in Chinese and less so in English, while other participants, such as Mr Wong and Grandpa Jiang, had university qualifications. Yet, while pursuing their children or grandchildren's excellence in learning, the Chinese families in my study, whatever background they are from, all emphasised the importance of being human. To be human is to be a good person with Confucian values; this belief stresses the importance of a person's moral nature. 'To be humane is to be man 仁者人也', Confucius said, in 中庸 *Zhong Yong* (*The Centre of Harmony* or *The Doctrine of The Mean*), one of the four books of Confucianism. To Confucius, humanity, being humane, is the fundamental quality of people, and without this quality a person is not a real human being.

For Chinese families, education includes both school education and family education. Chinese parents and grandparents make special efforts to support their children and grandchildren to pursue academic success, and to adapt to the mainstream culture, which, they believe, is crucial to the children's and hence the family's future. In the meantime, at home, Chinese parents and grandparents emphasise the importance of educating children in how to be human in traditional Chinese values, in the hope that they will bring up their children to be not only a good son or daughter of the family, but also good citizens of the society in a Chinese holistic worldview. In the cases of Zhi Gao and Yang Yang, two boys in my study who had struggled in their school life in transition, both mothers tried their best to keep the boys focused on their schooling and emphasised the importance of their boys *growing up to be a good man even if they might not succeed in school* '不成才要成人'. These values are beautifully and profoundly elaborated in Hayhoe's (2006) portraits of eleven influential Chinese educators. These eleven educators 'have lived lives that expressed many of the same values and concerns – a profound commitment to family and community, a readiness to make sacrifices for the sake of principles they had embraced' in the Chinese educational tradition embedded in Confucianism, Daoism and Buddhism and 'a continuous stream of creative energy that enabled them to adapt to rapidly changing circumstances in their society and nation' (Hayhoe 2006: 35).

In the following section I elaborate further four aspects of Confucian humanity manifested in Chinese family narratives: to help others, return to others in abundance, share with others and care for others and think of others.

To help others

'To help others' is considered the basic moral quality of being human among Chinese people. Mr Wong, who had volunteered at the school's Parent Centre for a dozen years, continues helping Carmen, the staff member of the Parent Centre, and the Chinese families at the Parent Centre even though his family no longer has a child attending Bay Street Community School. This has been a daily practice in the Parent Centre among the Chinese families who help look after others' children or grandchildren while the parents or grandparents have to be away from the Parent Centre, in some cases, away from home.

Grandpa Jiang told me how he helped his younger sister and brother to establish their life and urged his daughter in China to send money to his older sister in-law and another brother in-law who used to help his family when he was in need. He gave money to aged women in the village where the villagers treated him kindly during the Cultural Revolution when he was denounced from the position of a provincial official in 1960s. He returned to his hometown to build a tomb for his older brother and sister in-law, something that, the villagers said, nowadays in China sons may not do for their parents. Grandpa Jiang was concerned over the fact that 'nowadays in China many people do not want to help others'. Grandpa Jiang finds it wrong to discard the old way in which people followed the Confucian principles of how to be human and how to live together with others. He thinks that, 'It is good to do something for others.'

Return to others in abundance

Grandpa Jiang's story also reveals another important human quality cherished in Chinese tradition: 'Return to others in abundance' in return for any help that you receive (滴水之恩当涌泉相报 *Return with a bubbling spring for a drop of water that you received when you were in need*). Grandpa Jiang's older sister in-law came to his family in 1930s as a bride-to-be for his older brother, but the family used the girl more for the purpose of doing housework and looking after Grandpa Jiang who was then a baby boy. Grandpa Jiang left his hometown many years ago, but he has never forgotten what his sister in-law did for him and his younger brothers, and he has paid back generously his sister in-law who is now an aged woman with no source of income.

> I often send money to my big sister in-law, who is my children's eldest aunt. My children cannot understand this either. I asked them to send her 500 yuan. They were unwilling. They said, 'She has her own sons and grandsons. Why should we send her money?' I said, 'When I was little, your big aunt washed my diapers. Even when my brothers and I became big boys, she washed our clothes. I explained how an adopted would-be wife was a family maidservant in 1930s and 1940s. But, the young people, my children, do not understand.

Grandpa Jiang also repaid his gratitude to his wife's brother whose help for Grandpa Jiang and his family during the Cultural Revolution made it possible for the family to survive the difficult times.

Share with others and care for others

Julian's grandma said, 'In China, we always share with others whenever we eat something, or at least we ask if others would like to have some before we eat alone. It would be rude if a person started eating without asking others.' Mr Wong and Mrs Wong, Julian's grandma, and other parents would ask about me and worry when I did not visit the Parent Centre for a few days. They would phone me to find out if everything was all right especially during difficult moments, such as the SARS crisis in 2003, and also during a time when there were a series of robberies in the downtown neighborhood. If Mr Wong saw me in the Parent Centre in the morning, he would phone Mrs Wong to inform her that I was in the school. Around noontime Mr Wong would come back and bring me a lunch box prepared by Mrs Wong. They often invited me to have lunch with them at their home especially at Chinese traditional holidays and insisted that I take Mrs Wong's home-made food with me as they were worried that I would not eat properly by being away from my own family.

Think of others

'Think of others' is the family golden motto at Mr Wong's home. Mrs Wong told me that she and Mr Wong have never argued during their long life together. 'You do not feel so upset if you can think of others from their perspectives.' Mrs Wong said. Her sons, daughters and their spouses follow her example and lead a harmonious family life. She treats her daughter in-law like a daughter and her daughter in-law respects her like her mother. Her big extended family is a family of four generations with a 94-year-old great grandmother, Mrs Wong's mother. Both Mr and Mrs Wong are over 70-years-old, but every Sunday Mr Wong accompanies his wife to visit their great grandmother. They are also close to the families of their brothers and sisters who join in Sunday extended family gatherings. This large extended family wonderfully illustrates a harmonious Chinese 'family of four generations 四世同堂' that respects the old and cares for the young. This example is a dream of elderly Chinese, which can come true when all family members think of others. This may also explain why Mr Wong's grandsons grow up with sunny personalities and academic excellence.

According to Confucian values, to adhere to moral principles is everyone's first and utmost important consideration. For Confucius, humanity is the supreme principle for which one should give up everything else, including one's life if necessary. Confucius said, 'A humane man never gives up humanity to save his life, but he may sacrifice his life to realise humanity 志士仁人，无求生以害仁，有杀生以成仁' (The Analects, 15.9). In connection with humanity, Confucius promoted other virtues, such as righteousness, propriety, wisdom, trustworthiness, loyalty, reciprocity, filial piety, and brotherly love.

Confucian notion of being and Chinese way of learning

The *Canadian National Post* reported on 5 October 2009 that 'An astonishing 88.3 percent of young Chinese immigrants in Canada go to university – more than double the figure for young Canadians as a whole, according to a new study. When community college was added to the mix, 98.3 percent of young Chinese immigrants sought post-secondary education by the time they were 21 years old.' 'These numbers are so high, they don't even seem possible,' said the researcher of the survey, quoted by the *National Post*.

These numbers appear as astonishing or not even possible in the mainstream newspaper because the numbers do not show the educational values and beliefs Chinese immigrant families have adhered to in their children's education nor do the numbers reveal the efforts and sacrifices that parents and grandparents have made. To a great extent, almost all the Chinese families share the Confucian ideal that their children 'learn with pursuit of academic excellence and thus become an official scholar 学而优则仕' by trying to go to the best school and hence the best university.

When talking about their eldest son Yong Chang's education, Hui Lan's husband, who used to be an accountant in China but now works as a chef in a Chinese restaurant in Toronto, said,

> What can you do? If you do not have good English, you have to put up with this. So I urge Yong Chang to study hard so that he won't live the kind of life we live. We do not mind the labour work as long as the boys study hard and do well. My boss asked Yong Chang to come to the restaurant to help in the summer. We agreed. He works 3 or 4 hours a day. Today he works from 6–9 in the evening. It is a learning opportunity for him, to learn how to meet people and talk with people. He can speak Cantonese, Spanish, English and French. So he has an opportunity to speak different languages with different people. It doesn't matter that he is not paid as a regular employee. We just want him to learn that life is not easy so that he understands and can make a choice – whether to do the kind of labour work I am doing or study hard for a better future.
>
> (Summer 2003, at Hui Lan's home)

Jia Ming's father, a professional with a Chinese university degree, has been doing labour work in a Toronto factory.

> We came here for Jia Ming's sake. We wanted him to have a better education and get into a better university. But if he came later by himself, we wouldn't know how he was doing. Therefore, we preferred to come now with Jia Ming although we gave up our life and careers in China.
>
> (17 August 2004, home visit)

Both Yong Chang and Jia Ming who were in Grades 7/8 in 2003 and 2004 are now at university. Their academic success must have been counted in the number reported by the *National Post*; however, the Chinese educational values and insights revealed in immigrant family narratives are yet to be discovered and learned by the mainstream society, which can contribute to the education of all children no matter what ethnic background they are from.

The generational narratives in this study draw attention to the reciprocal educational needs of both newcomers and mainstream people. Immigrant adaptation is not a matter of replacing the old with the new, of exchanging one language for another, one value system for another. It is a process of merging historically founded cultural and personal narratives of experience. The *Canadian National Post* points out that 'the numbers' of Chinese immigrant children who go to post-secondary education 'suggest not just a brain gain for Canada, but the foundation of an entrepreneurial class with schooling in Canada and one foot in another culture.' These numbers reveal the fact that newcomer immigrant families are not only retaining and reshaping their educational values in their cross-cultural schooling experience, but also influencing, modifying and reshaping the recipient society and its cultures in this process. Hence, it is no longer one-way adaptation and/or acculturation but more of a reciprocal learning process for both the newcomer families and the mainstream society.

Thus, Chinese learning, integrated and harmonised with Western learning for the prosperity of the family contributes to the harmony of the society in a changing landscape of increasing diversity.

Bridging the East and West dichotomy: Confucian *continuity of being* and Deweyian *continuity of knowing*

Confucian notion of being

The Chinese family narratives highlight the idea that the focus of Confucian learning is to learn to be human. To learn to become a true person in the Confucian sense is to be honest with oneself and loyal to others. This entails a ceaseless process through which humanity in its all-embracing fullness is concretely realised (Tu 1985). In the concentric circles that define the self in terms of family, community, country and the world, the self is not the generic self as an isolated entity; rather, self is an open and inter-related system and the centre of relationships in which personal identity is realised first and foremost through the cultivation of those roles and relationships that locate one within the family, the community, the country and the world (Hall and Ames 1999).

In the Chinese tradition, self-realisation involves the establishment of an ever-expanding circle of human-relatedness through the structures of the self, the family, the country and the world, where the country and the world are conceived as an enlarged family that emerges out of the process of self-cultivation, and the self is embedded in communal roles and relations (Hall and Ames 1999, Tu 1985, 2002). Therefore, 'self-cultivation', the essential part of Confucian learning, is not only learning for oneself, but is also a societal and communal act.

Deweyian continuity of knowing

In the East–West conversations, Dewey's educational thinking, which emphasises both individual construction and social interaction in the continuity of knowing, offers a conceptual bridge connecting the two apparently different worlds. In contrast to the liberal democratic individualism that tends to dominate modern Western thought, Dewey (1897) believes that the individual is to be educated as a social individual and that society is an organic union of individuals. Dewey (1916) states that society exists through a process of transmission quite as much as biological life. When each individual, each unit who is the carrier of the life-experience passes away in time, the life of the group goes on. Thus, the integrity of the individual is a function of the coherence of a community of shared experiences, and the fullness of the individual's experience can only be guaranteed by that community (Hall and Ames 1999). The individual, as a participant in the community, benefits from the enriching context, and that benefit is shared with the community to the extent that resources for the further enrichment of other individuals are augmented; thus, the end of communal interaction is the enrichment of the individual (Hall and Ames 1999).

Just as Confucius takes self-cultivation as being of utmost importance, Dewey holds the view that education is life and life is growth. Education is a process of living and not a preparation for future living (Dewey 1897). The statement that 'individuals live in a world' means that they live in a series of situations with interaction going on between an individual and objects and other persons, rather than with static adjustment to a fixed environment and rigidity of habit (Dewey 1916, 1938). The conceptions of situation and of interaction are inseparable from each other (Dewey 1938). Thus, in the active union of continuity and interaction, education must be conceived as a continuing reconstruction of experience in which the process and the goal of education are one and the same thing (Dewey 1897). Hence, for Dewey, the fundamental principle of the school is a form of community life (Dewey 1932). Furthermore, the growth of the child entails not only physical, but intellectual and moral growth, in one exemplification of the principle of continuity (Dewey 1932). Dewey's educational thinking further resonates with Eastern wisdom in that the essential feature of Dewey's way of knowing is to maintain the continuity of knowing, a sense of continuity that Dewey believes is at the basis of attention and of all intellectual growth (Dewey 1916: 1932). Accordingly, Dewey sets two conditions for effective education: 'the school must itself be a community life in all which that implies' and 'the learning in school should be continuous with that out of school' (Dewey 1916: 358–359).

As Hall and Ames (1999) point out, the languages of Confucianism and Pragmatism overlap sufficiently to provide more common ground for conversations between the East and the West for the purpose of developing a mutually extended 'we-consciousness' in diversity. To facilitate such 'we-consciousness' for the purpose of cultivating a global democratic community, as Hall and Ames (1999) postulate, self-cultivation in Pragmatism and Confucianism can enable both Chinese and Westerners to include one another in the term 'we', instead of making distinctions in 'othered' terms such as 'they' or 'the others'.

Harmonising Chinese learning and Western knowledge

Different as the East and the West appear to be, the Chinese family stories show that communication and understanding can be achieved and enhanced with mutual learning and adaptation. This may be realised when the East, the Chinese families, turn to the West, and the West, in the form of mainstream schools, reach out to the East for mutual learning and adaptation. Hall and Ames (1999) suggest that traditional Confucianism contains elements that might well be translated into a communitarian form of democratic society with a synthesis of Dewyian Pragmatism and Confucianism. They suggest that both pragmatism and Confucianism promote a rethinking of the dominant Western notion of autonomous individuality, and argue that the tacit assumption that 'modernisation equals Westernisation' must be abandoned (Hall and Ames 1999). In search of a new discourse for East–West dialogues, Hall and Ames' intent is to uncover the resources shared by both Chinese and Western societies and to emphasise what 'we can learn from China' with respect to the revitalisation of the sense of community in America. They hold on to a belief that globalisation should accommodate both Easternisation and Westernisation in the East–West conversations between Western New Pragmatism and Asian New Confucianism. The large numbers of Chinese immigrant families, who travel between the two worlds, are helping to build these bridges.

Accordingly, rather than arguing for self-cultivation as a Confucian way of knowing in contrast with the Western way of knowing rooted in Europian thought, we can seek for the way of knowing with our 'we-consciousness' in a world of increasing diversity. Such 'we-consciousness' is extended and expanded not only in Confucian thought, but also in Dewey's Communitarian Pragmatism and diverse cultural traditions. By bridging the East and West dichotomy and harmonising Eastern learning with Western knowledge, we can find a way that is not defined or categorised in any Eastern or Western terms but *the Way* or *the divine order* as it is, in the *continuity of knowledge* and in the *continuity of being*, which leads to the harmony of societies in diversity and the harmony of the global world community.

Note

1 Citations from Lun Yun (The Analects) are translations modified from the following references:

论语=Analects of Confucius 中文译注 蔡希勤; 英文翻译 赖波, 夏玉和. 北京：华语教学出版社, 1994.

中华文化信息网 Confucius. (1998) *The Analects of Confucius: A philosophical translation* by Roger T. Ames and Henry Rosemont, Jr. New Work: Ballantine Books. Online. Available HTTP: <http://www.ccnt.com/wisdom/rujia/lunyu/lunyu7.htm> (accessed 3 February 2010).

References

Anisef, P., Kilbride, K. M., Ochocka, J. and Janzen, R. (2001) *Study on Parenting Issues of Newcomer Families in Ontario*, Toronto: Joint Center of Excellence for Research on Immigration and Settlement and Center for Research and Education in Human Services.

Carey, E. (2002) Toronto: Canada's linguistic capital, *Toronto Star* (11 December 2001).

CIC Canada (2001) Facts and figures 2001: immigration overview. Online. Available HTTP: <Retrieved from http://www.cic.gc.ca/english/pub/facts2001/3tor-02.html> (accessed 5 January 5 2003).

CIC Canada (2004) Facts and figures 2004: immigration overview, permanent and temporary residents. Online. Available HTTP: http://www.cic.gc.ca/english/pub/facts2004 (accessed 12 March 2005).

CIC Canada (2008) Facts and figures 2008: immigration overview, permanent and temporary residents. Online. Available HTTP: http://www.cic.gc.ca/english/pdf/research-stats/facts2008.pdf (accessed 19 September 2009).

Clandinin, D. J. and Connelly, F. M. (2000) *Narrative Inquiry: Experience and Story in Qualitative Research*, San Francisco: Jossey-Bass.

Connelly, F. M. and Clandinin, D. J. (1990) 'Stories of experience and narrative inquiry', *Educational Researcher*, 19(5), 2–14.

Connelly, F. M., He, M., Phillion, J., Chan, E. and Xu, S. J. (2004) 'Bay Street Community School: where you belong', *Orbit*, 34(3), 39–42.

Connelly, M. and Xu, S. J. (2008) 'The landscape of curriculum and instruction: diversity and continuity', in F. M. Connelly (ed.) with M. F. He and J. Phillion (assoc. eds), *The Sage handbook of curriculum and instruction* (pp. 514–533), Thousand Oaks, CA: Sage Publications.

Creese, Gillian, Dyck, Isabel L. and McLaren, Arlene T. (1999) Reconstituting the family: negotiating immigration and settlement. RIIM (Research on Immigration and Integration in the Metropolis) Working Paper Series #99–10. Online. Available HTTP: <http://Canada.metropolis.net> (accessed 14 December 2002).

Dewey, J. (1897) 'My pedagogic creed', *School Journal*, 54 (January), 77–80.

Dewey, J. (1916/1961) *Democracy and Education*, Old Tappan, NJ: Macmillan.

Dewey, J. (1932) *The School and Society*, Chicago, IL: University of Chicago Press.

Dewey, J. (1938) *Experience and Education*, New York: Kappa Delta Pi.

Fei, X. (1947/1992) *From the Soil: The Foundations of Chinese Society*. A translation of Fei Xiaotong's *Xiangtu Zhongguo* 乡土中国, with an Introduction and Epilogue by Gary G. Hamilton and Wang Zheng, Berkeley and Los Angeles: University of California Press.

Hall, D. L. and Ames, R. T. (1999) *The Democracy of the Dead: Dewey, Confucius, and the Hope for Democracy in China*, USA: Carus.

Hayhoe, R. (1997) 'Education as communication', in John Montgomery (ed.) *Values in Education: Social Capital Formation in Asia and the Pacific* (pp. 92–111), Hollis, New Hampshire: Hollis Publishing.

Hayhoe, R. (2006) *Portraits of Influential Chinese Educators*, Comparative Education Research Centre, The University of Hong Kong.

Tu, W. (1985) *Confucian Thought: Selfhood as Creative Transformation*, Albany: State University of New York Press.

Tu, W. (2002) 杜维明文集 *Tu Wei-Ming Wen Ji* (Collections of Tu Wei-Ming's Works), Vols 1–5, edited by Guo Qi-Yong and Zheng Wen-Long, China: Wu Han Press.

Xu, S. J., Connelly, F. M., He, M. F. and Phillion, J. (2007) 'Immigrant students' experience of schooling: a narrative inquiry theoretical framework', *Journal of Curriculum Studies*, 39(4), 399–422.

Index

academic nationalism 177–8
Ames, R. T.: and Hall, D. L. 239–40; and Rosemont, H. 138
Amnesty International 189
Anderson, R. C.: and Ku, Y. M. 216; and Nagy, W. 216
Appadurai, A. 134
arithmetic 166
arts 39
Australia: citizenship education 185–204; National Centre for History Education (NCHE) 197
Australian Science Education Project (ASEP) 45

Bass, C. 94
Bauer, L. 212
Bauman, Z. 151, 152
Bay Street Community School: Toronto 226–42
Beijing Normal University 22
Beijing Zhongguancun Number 4 Primary School 63–71
Bell, D. 140
Berthrong, E. N.: and Berthrong, J. 138
Berthrong, J.: and Berthrong, E. N. 138
Bishop, A.: Clarkson, P. and Seah, W. T. 172
Blommaert, J. 134
Bowey, J. A.: and Patel, R. K. 216
Brittain, M. 216
Burns, S.: Snow, C. E. and Griffin, P. 210–11

calculators: affordability 174
Canada: Chinese cultural adaptation 224–42
Canadian National Post 237, 238
Canagarajah, S. 151

Carlisle, J. 215, 216; and Fleming, J. 216
Central Education Institute 22
Chao, Y. R. 212
Chen, P. 213
Chen, S.: Wang, M. and Cheng, C. 217
Chen, Y.: and Reid, I. 188, 189, 191
Cheng, C.: Wang, M. and Chen, S. 217
Chinese Communist Party (CCP) 137, 141
Chinese language: exportation 208–10
Chiu, S.: and Wong, V. 141
Citizenship for the 21st Century (Cogan and Derricott) 191–2
citizenship education 15, 185–204; Chinese reform background 187–9; citizenship manual 189; civic education 187; future 200; global reform contexts 185–7; Hong Kong 190, 198–9, 201; ideological and political education 189; ideomoral education 187; ideopolitical education 187; moral dimension 194–6; multidimensional citizenship 186, 187, 191–4; personal dimension 194–6; recent Chinese developments 189–91; Shanghai 190–1, 198–9, 201; social dimension 194–6; spatial dimensions 196–7; temporal dimensions 196–7
Citizenship Education Policy Study (CEPS) 186, 191–2, 197–8
Citizenship and Immigration Canada (CIC) 225–6
civic education 187
civil education: Vietnam 136
Clarkson, P.: Bishop, A. and Seah, W. T. 172

Cogan, J. 201; and Derricott, R. 191–2, 193

Communicative Language Teaching (CLT) 139, 140, 152, 208

Confronting the 21st Century Education Rejuvenation Action Plan (MOE) 23–4

Confucian Heritage Cultures (CHCs) 163

Confucianism 138–41, 146–8, 187, 195–6, 233, 234; caring for others 236; continuity of being 238–9; helping others 234–5; notion of being 237–8; return to others in abundance 235; sharing with others 236; thinking of others 236

continuity of being: Confucianism 238–9

continuity of knowing 239–40

Cope, B.: and Kalantzis, M. 186

Cortazzi, M.: and Jin, L. 113–31, 138, 139, 140

critical thinking 35–6

cultural continuity 133

cultures of learning: educational metaphors 12, 114–15

Dalai Lama 93

D'Ambrosio, U. 171

Dan, Y. 140

DeFrancis, J. 213

Deng, Xiaoping 188

Derricott, R.: and Cogan, J. 191–2, 193

Dewey, J. 239–40

Ding, Y. Q.: and Xue, H. P. 79, 80

Doan, D. H. 135, 136, 137

Dongsheng District of Ordos City: Inner Mongolia 65

Doyle, W.: and Ponder, G. A. 45–6

drill work 39

Duong, T. T. 136

East China Normal University 22, 163

East–West dichotomy: caring for others 236; Chinese way of learning 237–8; Confucian continuity of being 238–9; Confucian humanity 234; continuity of knowing 239–40; family and cultural adaptation 228–9; grandparents 230–3; helping others 234–5; mutual adaptation 224–42; notion of being 237–8; repaying good deeds 235; sharing with others 236; thinking of others 236; Western New Pragmatism 240

education quality and improvement evaluation 11–12, 75–91; emerging themes 84–7; examinations 76–7; high school entrance examinations 77–8, 79; IEEQC project 77, 78, 82–4, 85, 87; school effectiveness research 78–80; value added approaches 77–8, 80–2

educational metaphors 13, 113–31; cultures of learning 114–15; determination 125; devotion and sacrifice 124; direction 125–6; geological features 127–9; guidance 125–6; learning 119–23; learning as journey 123–6; official document teacher metaphors 117–19; sailing 125; teaching 119–23; time dimension 126; traditional Chinese sayings 127

elders: respect 180–1

Elements (Euclid) 166–7

English as an international language (EIL) 13, 133

English language teaching (ELT): College English 116–17; educational metaphors 113–31; external landscape 115–19; gate-keeping role 116; morality 132–57; official document teacher metaphors 117–19; students' learning metaphors 119–23; students' teacher metaphors 119–23; teacher shortage 116; university requirements 116, 117

Entrance Examination for Higher Education (EEHE) 77–8, 79, 80

Erickson, G. 63

ethnomathematics 171–2

examination reform 76–7

Facebook 186

Fairbrother, G. P.: and Zhao, Z. Z. 188

fairness: education 76–7

family: and cultural adaptation 228–9; grandparents 230–3

Fischer, F. W.: Hanson, V. L. and Shankweiler, D. 215

Fleming, J.: and Carlisle, J. 216

Fowler, A.: and Liberman, I. 215

Fullan, M.: and Pomfret, A. 46

Gao, D. S.: and Lu, J. 195

globalisation 133, 134

Goldstein, M. C.: Jiao, B. and Postiglione, G. A. 92–110

grandparents: role 230–3

Griffin, P.: Snow, C. E. and Burns, S. 210–11
Grossman, D. 185, 195, 196, 197
guidelines: reform 23, 43

Haidian District: Beijing 63
Hall, D. L.: and Ames, R. T. 239–40
Han, J.: Wong, N. Y. and Lee, P. Y. 172
Hannum, E.: *et al.* 85, 86–7; and Sargent, T. 45, 47
Hanson, V. L.: Shankweiler, D. and Fischer, F. W. 215
Haspelmath, M. 212
Hayhoe, R. 128–9, 229, 234
high school entrance examinations 31, 32, 36–7, 77–8, 79, 80
high-stakes assessment: mathematics 169–171
Hockett, C. F. 212
Hong Kong: citizenship education 190, 198–9, 201
How Chinese Learn Mathematics (Fan, *et al.*) 162
Hu, Jintao 2, 35
Huang, F. 165
Hulbert, A. 180
Humanities Curriculum Project 45

Improving Educational Evaluation and Quality in China (IEEQC) 77, 78, 82–4, 85, 87
Inner Mongolia: Dongsheng District of Ordos City 65
International Mathematical Olympiad 164, 173, 175
Internet seminars 32

Jacques, M. 3
Jensen, J. T. 212
Jiang, L.: Yang, Z. M. and Yao, S. Q. 79
Jiao, B.: Postiglione, G. A. and Goldstein, M. C. 92–110
Jin, L.: and Cortazzi, M. 113–31, 138, 139, 140

K-12 curriculum reform 1, 9, 21–40; compulsory education national implementation 30–3; compulsory education pilot 27–30; and curriculum culture 34; dissent 33–5; documents design and dissemination 23–7; documents experimental stage 23–7; Expert Team establishment 24;

guidelines development 23, 43; high school entrance examinations 31, 32, 36–7; ideology and planning 22–3; international comparative research 23; Mathematics 24, 31, 33; new elements 33–5; re-reflection and re-interpretation 35–9; secondary curriculum pilot 30–3; secondary school programme 27–30; and teacher development 42–5; teacher research system 28, 29–30
Kalantzis, M.: and Cope, B. 186
Kang, C. 47, 49, 51, 55, 56, 61–71; *et al.* 41–60; and Liu, J. 9, 21–40
Kang, X. 140–1
Kennedy, K. J. 198; and Lee, W. O. 202
Koda, K. 218–19, 220
Kramsch, C. 149
Ku, Y. M.: and Anderson, R. C. 216
Kumaravadivelu, B. 153

language: Tibetan Autonomous Region 105–6
learning as journey metaphor 123–6
Lee, P. Y.: Wong, N. Y. and Han, J. 172
Lee, W. O.: and Kennedy, K. J. 202; and Leung, S. W. 195, 198–9, 200
Leung, S. W.: and Lee, W. O. 195, 198–9, 200
Li Ji (Book of Rites) 128
Li, X. 208
Li, Y. 61–71
Liang, L. L.: and Tang, K. C. 79
Liberman, I.: and Fowler, A. 215
Liu, J.: and Kang, C. 9, 21–40
Liu, K. 61–71
Liu, M. 187
Lu, J.: and Gao, D.S. 195

Ma, Y. P.: *et al.* 44, 47
McBride-Chang, C. *et al* 218
Mahony, D.: Singson, M. and Mann, V. 222
Make Poverty History 192
Man a Course of Study (MACOS) 45
Mann, V.: Mahony, D. and Singson, M. 222
mathematics 5, 14–15, 24, 31, 33; ability training 167; academic nationalism 173; calculators 174; Chinese education history 166–9; Chinese system interest 163–4; comprehensive curriculum reform 167–8; Cultural Revolution 167;

curriculum planning decentralisation 171–2; curriculum reform 161–84; *Elements* (Euclid) 166–7; ethnomathematics 171–2; foundational knowledge 167; heavy teaching loads 176; high-stakes assessment 169–71; ICT integration 174; international comparative studies 163; mathematical well-being 172; and mathematics for all 177, 180, 181; precision 172; professional development 175–7, 179; professional journals 176; reform pedagogy basis concern 172–4; Shanghai curriculum 168; Singaporean textbook importation 165; societal value 166; soft learning role 164–6; Soviet-based curriculum 167; standards/rigour 175, 177; student-centredness 173, 179; teacher research networks 177; tripartite administration model 171–2; two basics 173, 177; values role 177–80; Western 166–7
Matsuura, K. 86
Matthews, P. H. 211
Min, W. F.: and Xue, H. P. 79
Mitchell, I. 63
Mok, K. H. 188
moral citizenship 138
morality and English language teaching (ELT) 13–14, 132–57; China 137–41; Confucianism 138–41, 146–8; criticism 144; English language classrooms 151–2; hybridity 152; local philosophy re-traditionalisation 146–8; love 149; multiple identifications 152; national identity and teacher moral guidance 142–5; *qin he li* concept 149–51; role model resistance/ambivalence 145–6; student-teacher relationship 149; students' local/global worlds 148–51; teacher education 153–4; Vietnam 135–7
Morgan, M.: and Ramanathan, V. 132
Morley, L.: and Rassool, N. 82, 85
morphological awareness 210–11; Chinese learning and native language growth 219–20; Chinese morphology 213–14; cross-language transfer 217–19; definition 211–12; English morphology 213; graphemes 213; morphemes 212; native English

Chinese learners 216–20; native English speakers 215–16
multidimensional citizenship 186, 187, 191–4; key features 194
MySpace 186

Nackchu: basic education 102–3; local perspective 103–6; school access 103–6
Nagy, W.: and Anderson, R. C. 216; and Tyler, A. 215
nation-state: role 134
national identity 134; and teacher moral guidance 142–5
neidi xizang ban policy: Tibetan Autonomous Region 97
nested learning systems 52, 53
Newton, I. 126
Ngari: basic education 103; local perspective 103–6; school access 103–6
Nguyen, T. M. L. 135–6, 137
Nguyen, T. O. 136
Nuffield Science project 45

Oxford University: Chinese educational reform conference (2009) 6–7

Packard, J. L. 214
Patel, R. K.: and Bowey, J. A. 216
Peng, W.-J.: and Thomas, S. M. 75–91
Phan, L. H.: and Phan, V. Q. 132, 134, 137
Phan, V. Q.: and Phan, L. H. 132, 134, 137
physical education 39
Pomfret, A.: and Fullan, M. 46
Ponder, G. A.: and Doyle, W. 45–6
Postiglione, G. A.: Jiao, B. and Goldstein, M. C. 92–110
Programme for International Student Assessment (PISA) 163, 165, 173
Project for the Enhancement of Effective Learning (PEEL) 63

qin he li concept 149–51

Ramanathan, V.: and Morgan, M. 132
Rassool, N.: and Morley, L. 82, 85
Reed, G. G. 138
Reid, I.: and Chen, Y. 188, 189, 191
ren concept 138

respect: elders 180–1
Rosemont, H.: and Ames, R. T. 138
Rudd, K. 196
rural and nomadic communities
92–109; local incentives 100–1;
neidi xizang ban policy 97; parental
support 101; rural areas 99–100;
school access and local perspective
103–6; three guarantees policy 96–7,
101, 102, 104; village households
101–2
Ryan, J. 1–17, 41–60, 63, 69
Rydstrom, H. 136

Sargent, T.: and Hannum, E. 45, 47
school effectiveness research (SER)
77–91
Scollon, S. 138, 139
Seah, W. T. 4, 161–84; Clarkson, P.
and Bishop, A. 172
second language learning: Chinese
exportation 208–10; Chinese foreign
language teaching reform 207–8;
mutual learning and adaptation
207–23
Seventeen Point Agreement: Tibetan
Autonomous Region 93–4
Seymour, P.: H.K. 211
Shanghai: citizenship education 190–1,
198–9, 201; mathematics curriculum
168
Shankweiler, D.: Hanson, V. L. and
Fischer, F. W. 215
Singson, M.: Mahony, D. and Mann, V.
222
Snow, C. E.: Burns, S. and Griffin, P.
210–11
Social Science and Humanities
Research Council of Canada
(SSHRC) 229
Socrates 138, 139
soft knowledge perspective:
Mathematics curriculum reform
14–15, 161–84
Spencer, A. 212
State Education Development
Commission (SEDC) 208
Sun, C. 214

Tang, K. C.: and Liang, L. L. 79
Task-based Language Teaching
(TBLT) 139, 140
teacher professional learning
community development 10–11,
41–60, 61–71, 176–7; academic
collaboration 50–1; aims 63–4;
big curriculum projects era 45–7;
challenges 70–1; character 69;
collaborative group 48–50;
community nature 68–9; community
value 68–9; context 42–5, 63–4;
cross-cultural collaborative success
51–2; developmental project 56–7;
discussion forums 66; focused
observation 68; foreign colleagues
role 69–70; future directions 57–8;
Internet research 65–6; nested
learning systems 52, 53; nurture 69;
on-site communication 66; open-door
teaching 67; operation 64–8; project
recruitment 67; responsibility 54–6;
shared leadership 54–6; small
strategies 67–8; structure 69; teacher
knowledge 47–8; teacher research 66;
teacher research role 47–8; Western
perspective 45–51
Thomas, S. M.: and Peng, W.-J. 75–91
three guarantees policy 96–7, 101, 102,
104
Tibet Commission of Science and
Technology (CST) 103
Tibet Poverty Alleviation Fund 98
Tibetan Autonomous Region 12,
92–109; boarding schools 99; class
warfare 93; continuing education
challenges 98–9; education 93–5;
geography 92–3; illiteracy 94; labour
demands 104; language 105–6; local
incentives 100–1; Nackchu basic
education 102–3; *neidi xizang ban*
policy 97; Ngari basic education 103;
parental support 101; population
92–3; rural areas 99–100; and
rural/nomadic education 96; school
construction 95–6; school enrolment
rates 95; school facilities 95–6;
Seventeen Point Agreement 93–4;
society 93; tertiary education 98–9;
three guarantees policy 96–7; village
households 101–2
Toronto: Chinese immigration 226–42
Trends in International Mathematics
and Science Study (TIMSS) 163,
173
Tu, W. M. 187
Tudball, L. 185–204
Twitter 186
Tyler, A.: and Nagy, W. 215

United Kingdom (UK): foreign language curriculum 209–10; native morphological awareness 210–11, 215–16
United Nations Children's Fund (UNICEF) 86, 87
United Nations Educational Scientific and Cultural Organization (UNESCO) 85, 86, 87
University of British Columbia 63
University Council of Modern Languages (UCML) 209
university entrance examinations 37, 76

value added approaches: education quality evaluation 11, 77–8, 80–2, 84
values: and mathematics curriculum reform 177–80
Vietnam: civil education 136; English teachers and morality 13–14, 132–57; moral education 135–7; national identity and teacher moral guidance 142–5; *qin he li* concept 149–51
Villa, A. 169
vocational education 76

Wang, M.: Cheng, C. and Chen, S. 217; *et al.* 217, 220

Watson-Gegeo, K. 153
Wen, Jiabao 2, 3, 36, 75, 76
When China rules the world (Jacques) 3
White Deer Grotto Academy 128
Wong, N. Y.: Han, J. and Lee, P. Y. 172
Wong, V.: and Chiu, S. 141
Wu, X. W.: and Zhou, H. 79

Xu, S. 17, 224–42
Xue, H. P.: and Ding, Y. Q. 79, 80; and Min, W. F. 79

Yang, Z. M.: Yao, S. Q. and Jiang, L. 79
Yao, S. Q.: Yang, Z. M. and Jiang, L. 79
Yu, T. L. 195–6

Zhan, W. C. 195
Zhang, L. 167
Zhao, L. 181
Zhao, Z. Z.: and Fairbrother, G. P. 188
Zhong, J. 16, 207–23
Zhong Yong (The Mean) 127, 128, 129
Zhou, H.: and Wu, X. W. 79
Zhu, Xi 128